# Stabilization and Renegotiation Clauses in State Contracts, National Law and Investment Treaties

# Nijhoff International Investment Law Series



VOLUME 25

The titles published in this series are listed at *brill.com/iils*

# Stabilization and Renegotiation Clauses in State Contracts, National Law and Investment Treaties

*By*

Abdallah Abuelfutuh Ali

BRILL | NIJHOFF

LEIDEN | BOSTON

Library of Congress Cataloging-in-Publication Data

Names: Ali, Abdallah Abuelfutuh, author.
Title: Stabilization and renegotiation clauses in state contracts, national law and investment treaties / by Abdallah Abuelfutuh Ali.
Description: Leiden; Boston: Brill/ Nijhoff, 2024. | Series: Nijhoff international investment law series; volume 25 | Includes bibliographical references and index. | Summary: "As global investment flows continue to grow, the role of stability guarantees in protecting the interests of both host states and foreign investors has become increasingly important. In this book, we undertake a critical assessment of stabilization and renegotiation clauses in international investment law"– Provided by publisher.
Identifiers: LCCN 2023054241 (print) | LCCN 2023054242 (ebook) | ISBN 9789004692749 (hardback) | ISBN 9789004692756 (ebook)
Subjects: LCSH: Investments, Foreign (International law) | Guaranteed investment contracts. | Clauses (Law) | Investments, Foreign–Law and legislation. | Treaties.
Classification: LCC K3830 .A4235 2024 (print) | LCC K3830 (ebook) | DDC 346/.092–dc23/eng/20231201
LC record available at https://lccn.loc.gov/2023054241
LC ebook record available at https://lccn.loc.gov/2023054242

Typeface for the Latin, Greek, and Cyrillic scripts: "Brill". See and download: brill.com/brill-typeface.

ISSN 2351-9542
ISBN 978-90-04-69274-9 (hardback)
ISBN 978-90-04-69275-6 (e-book)
DOI 10.1163/9789004692756



This book is printed on acid-free paper and produced in a sustainable manner.

*This book is dedicated to*
*My beloved Father and Mother,*
*my wife and my daughters,*
*Farida & Maryam & Noureen*

# Contents

# Preface

As global investment flows continue to grow, the role of stability guarantees in protecting the interests of both host states and foreign investors has become increasingly important. In this book, we undertake a critical assessment of stabilization and renegotiation clauses in international investment law.

Through a comprehensive review of existing literature, analyses of arbitral awards and court decisions, and case studies from the UNCTAD, OECD, and World Bank, we aim to provide a nuanced understanding of the different forms of stability guarantees available to foreign investors. Our goal is to offer recommendations that balance the competing interests of states and investors and to shed light on the most effective mechanisms for achieving regulatory stability in the complex world of international investment.

Firstly, Traditional Contractual Stabilization Clauses (CSCs) are widely used by investors to achieve regulatory stability, but their legal validity and effectiveness have been challenged in recent years. We examine the different types of CSCs, their legal status, and their value in practice and compare them with other stability guarantees available to foreign investors. Secondly, Renegotiation Clauses offer a potential alternative to CSCs, allowing parties to renegotiate investment terms in case of unforeseeable events or changes in circumstances. We analyze the legal framework and practical implications of renegotiation clauses and explore whether they can offer a more flexible and adaptive approach to regulatory stability. Thirdly, Legislative Stabilization Clauses (LSCs) are increasingly used by host states to increase the appetite of foreign investors to invest in their territoies. We propose a new taxonomy of LSCs and analyze their legal status and effectiveness, drawing on national investment case studies. Finally, Stability provisions in International Investment Agreements (IIAs), such as express stabilization clauses and the Fair and Equitable Treatment (FET) clause, offer additional protections for foreign investors but may also limit the host state's regulatory space. We examine the relationship between these provisions and CSCs/LSCs and their implications for regulatory stability.

The book is structured into six chapters:

Chapter 1 provides a background to the study and explains the aims and objectives of the research. Chapter 2 offers an overview of traditional contractual stabilization clauses, examining their types, significance, validity, legal effect, and value within doctrinal discussions, national and international practice, and empirical work. Chapter 3 provides a comprehensive analysis of renegotiation clauses as a potential alternative mechanism to traditional CSCs, addressing the issue of renegotiation from the perspective of law and practice. Chapter 4 proposes a new taxonomy of Legislative Stabilization Clauses (LSCs) and analyzes their legal status of effectiveness, drawing on national investment case studies. Chapter 5 examines the stability provisions in International Investment Agreements (IIAs), such as express stabilization clauses and Fair and Equitable Treatment (FET) clause, and their implications for regulatory stability. Finally, Chapter 6 summarizes the key findings of this study and presents the recommendations flowing from the previous chapters.

The book is intended for a diverse audience of legal practitioners, scholars, policymakers, investors, and students. The content is presented in a manner that balances technicality with accessibility, making it suitable for readers with varying levels of familiarity with international investment law. Legal practitioners and scholars will find the book to be a valuable resource for understanding the legal framework and practical implications of stabilization and renegotiation clauses. Policymakers will gain insights into the competing interests of states and investors and the most effective mechanisms for achieving regulatory stability. Investors will benefit from the comprehensive review of stability guarantees available to them, including traditional contractual stabilization clauses, renegotiation clauses, legislative stabilization clauses, and stability provisions in international investment agreements. Finally, students will find the book to be a useful resource for understanding the complex world of international investment law and the role of stability guarantees in protecting the interests of host states and foreign investors. By doing so, we hope to contribute to the ongoing discussions on how to strike a balance between the competing rights and interests of states and investors in the context of international investment.

# Acknowledgments

This book is derived from my J.S.D thesis written at the University of the Pacific, McGeorge School of Law. I feel privileged to take this opportunity to express my gratitude to Professor Jarrod Wong, my supervisor, for his intellectual guidance, encouragement, and cooperation throughout my study. His invaluable comments and suggestions on the draft chapters helped improve the quality of my thesis. This book would not have been realized without his academic support and guidance through complex and disputed legal issues.

I am most grateful to my thesis committee examiners, Professor Omar Dajani, Professor Stephen McCaffery at McGeorge School of Law, and Professor Jason Yackee at the University of Wisconsin Law School, who generously provided knowledge and expertise and made strong recommendations in favor of publication. Also, a special thank you goes to the staff members of the McGeorge School of Law, Law Library, who impacted and inspired me.

I would also like to thank the Republic of Egypt, the Egyptian State Lawsuits Authority, for awarding me a scholarship that made it possible for me to pursue a Master of Laws (LL.M.) degree. It was during this program that I developed the idea for the book I have written. I am truly appreciative of this opportunity and the support I received that enabled me to bring this work to fruition. Also, I want to express my deepest appreciation to Mr. Kais Menoufy, the president of Delegata Corporation, for his unlimited support and unconditional guidance during my Ph.D. journey. His steadfast dedication to my growth has made a significant impact on my life, and I cannot thank him enough for his invaluable support.

Finally, a big special thanks to my wonderful wife, Hanaa Moustafa, who encouraged me through some stressful times. My greatest gratitude should also go to my lovely daughters, Farida, Maryam, and Noureen Ali, for "disturbing" me during study time. I dedicate this work to my family. I am proud of the work that has been accomplished and appreciate any feedback for improvement.

*Dr. Abdallah Abuelfutuh Ali*
September 2023

# Figures and Tables

## Figures



## Tables

# Abbreviations

| | |
|---|---|
| AAA | American Arbitration Association |
| AMINOIL | American Independent Oil Company |
| BITS | Bilateral Investment Treaties |
| CSCS | Contractual Stabilization Clauses |
| DAS | Development Agreements |
| ECSOC | United Nations Economic and Social Council |
| ECT | Energy Charter Treaty |
| EIU | Economist Intelligence Unit |
| EECS | Economic Equilibrium Clauses |
| EMG | Est Mediterranean Gas |
| FDI | Foreign Direct Investment |
| FET | Fair and Equitable Treatment |
| FPS | Full Protection and Security |
| FIL | Foreign Investment Law |
| FTAS | Free Trade Agreements |
| GDP | Gross Domestic Product |
| IIA SCS | International Investment Agreements' Stabilization Clauses |
| ICSID | International Convention for the Settlement of Investment Disputes |
| IFC | International Finance Corporation |
| IIAS | International Investment Treaties |
| ILM | International Law Materials |
| ISDS | Investor-State Dispute Settlement |
| KRG | Kurdistan Regional Government |
| LETCO | Liberian Eastern Timer Corporation |
| LSAS | Legal Stability Agreements |
| LSCS | Legislative Stabilization Clauses |
| MIGA | Multilateral Investment Guarantee Agency |
| MINE | Maritime International Nominees Establishment |
| MITS | Multilateral Investment Treaties |
| OECD | Organization for Economic Co-operation and Development |
| PSA | Production Sharing Agreement |
| PSC | Production Sharing Contract |
| RD | Royal Decree |
| SCS | Stabilization Clauses |
| U.N. | United Nations |
| UNCITRAL | United Nations Commission on International Trade Law |
| UNCTAD | United Nations Conference on Trade and Development |

| | |
|---|---|
| UNCTC | United Nations Center on Transnational Corporations |
| U.S.-PPI | United States Producer Price Index |
| VAT | Value-Added Tax |
| WTO | World Trade Organization |

CHAPTER 1

# Introduction

## 1.1 Background

At the heart of every stabilization clause is a simple concept: To stop time. Stabilization clauses (SCs) are provisions in a contract, treaty, or legislation pursuant to which the host state undertakes not to unilaterally apply any subsequent changes of the law to the state contract. The fundamental purpose of such a clause is to impose restraints on the host state during the life of an investment contract so that the host state cannot interfere with the foreign project.[1] Not surprisingly then, SCs are often found in state contracts,[2] including petroleum development contracts, which are often prone to changes of circumstances that may occur from "unforeseen political, economic, regulatory and technical circumstances."[3] This is especially true in developing countries.[4] Naturally then, before investing in a host state, a potential foreign investor will necessarily make a risk and reward assessment of the investment project's

---

1 *See* A.F.M. Maniruzzaman, *Drafting Stabilisation Clauses in International Energy Contracts: Some Pitfalls for the Unwary*, 5 Oil Gas & Energy. L. 23 (2007) [hereinafter Maniruzzaman, Drafting Stabilisation Clauses].

2 Note that the term "state contract" can be used to refer to several interlinked concepts, such as international contract, international development contract, investment contract, quasi-international contract, transnational agreement, economic development agreement, foreign investment contract, etc. *See* Thomas W. Waelde & George Ndi, *Stabilizing International Investment Commitments: International Law Versus Contract Interpretation*, 31 Tex. Int'l L. J. 215, 234 (1996); R. Y. Jennings, State Contracts in International Law, 37 Brit. Y. B. Int'l L. 156 et seq (1961); Jola Gjuzi, Stabilization Clauses in International Investment Law: A Sustainable Development Approach 33 (2018). State contracts are often long-term multi-year contracts that involve multiple parties, large sums of money, and complex technical and financial issues.

3 *See* Jeswald W. Salacuse, *Renegotiating International Project Agreements*, 24 fordham int Fordham Int'l L.J. 1319, 1327 (2001) [hereinafter Salacuse, *Renegotiating International Project* (2001)].

4 *Id*, at 1327; *See also*, Abdullah Al Faruque, *Renegotiation and Adaptation of Petroleum Contracts: The Quest for Equilibrium and Stability*, 9 J. World Investment & Trade 113, 113 (2008) (noting that the "[p]etroleum contracts need to survive the change of circumstances that may occur from external factors due to their long-term nature and the uncertainty associated with exploitation of petroleum resources, and which are often beyond the control of the parties.").

 | DOI:10.1163/9789004692756_002

fiscal and regulatory framework.[5] If the foreign investor decides to invest in that state, it conceivably anticipates the stability of the host state's fiscal and regulatory framework that governs the investment project.[6] In response, various stabilization mechanisms have been developed and adopted in various legal instruments such as long-term investment contracts, host state's national laws, and international investment treaties to address foreign investors' concerns.[7] Among the most familiar of these instruments is the contractual stabilization clause (CSC).

CSCs are frequently used in investment contracts in developing countries vulnerable to political and economic crises.[8] Such potential instability leads foreign investors to seek the protection of their investments, not only against overt expropriatory actions of the host state but also against a variety of more nuanced government measures that may affect the viability of their projects.[9] The balancing form of SCs may serve to correct any resulting instability by requiring an automatic restoration of the status quo. However, if an automatic adaptation is absent, the contract may require some form of revision that

5 Zeyad A. Al Qurashi, *Renegotiation of International Petroleum Agreements*, 22 J. Int'l Arb. 261,261 (2005).

6 *Id.*

7 A.F.M. Maniruzzaman, *The pursuit of stability in international energy investment contracts: A critical appraisal of the emerging trends*, 1 J. WORLD. ENERGY. L& BUS, 121, 121 (2008) [hereinafter Maniruzzaman, *The pursuit of stability* (2008)].

8 RUDOLPH DOLZER, PETROLEUM CONTRACTS AND INTERNATIONAL LAW 192 (2018) (noting in the context of petroleum contracts that "stability provisions are still widely provided in developing countries, and here to stay for the foreseeable future").

9 *See* PETER D CAMERON, INTERNATIONAL ENERGY INVESTMENT LAW: THE PURSUIT OF STABILITY 69 (2010)[hereinafter CAMERON 2010] (noting that "[p]rotection may be sought both against unilateral modifications to the contract and against taking the rights of the investor"); *See also* Andrey V. Kuznetsov, *The Limits of Contractual Stabilization Clauses for Protecting International Oil and Gas Investments Examined through the Prism of the Sakhalin-2 PSA: Mandatory Law, the Umbrella Clause, and the Fair and Equitable Treatment Standard*, 22 WILLAMETTE J. INT'L L. & DIS. RES. 223, 224 (2014) (noting that "[g]iven the capital intensive, long-term, and risky nature of oil and gas development projects in emerging markets, international oil and gas companies (IOCs) and their lenders wish to protect themselves not only against the most egregious forms of State conduct, but against a variety of government measures that fall short of impairing the viability of the investment project but still adversely affect it."); *See* MUSTAFA ERKAN, International Energy Investment Law, Stability through Contractual Clauses 141–42 (2011) (noting that, stabilization clauses are crucial for parties of state contract to achieve their aims. Foreign investor may be hesitated in deciding to invest in developing countries without inclusion such stability provisions in the state contract. In petroleum contracts, a stabilization clause can be inserted to preclude "arbitrary and discriminatory regulations in areas like human rights and environmental protection").

involves a process like renegotiation.[10] Renegotiation clauses are increasingly seen as a way to provide stability and flexibility in long-term investment contracts, particularly for petroleum development. Unlike traditional CSCs, which mainly benefit foreign investors by limiting the host state's ability to enact new legislation, renegotiation clauses offer a broader scope by allowing parties to renegotiate terms that have become onerous. However, it is unclear whether renegotiation clauses effectively achieve contractual stability and predictability, and the lack of data on their success raises questions about their value compared to traditional CSCs.

More recently, to increase the appetite of investors to invest in their territories, various countries have gone further and provided stability provisions in their domestic laws, such as constitutions, statutes, regulations, and administrative issuances like governmental permits and licenses.[11] Like their prototype CSCs, legislative stabilization clauses (LSCs) are seen by developing countries as essential instruments for attracting foreign direct investment (FDI), which, in turn, would promote sustainable economic development. However, what scant commentary there is focuses on whether LSCs, given their unilateral nature, are enforceable to aid investors. Further, there has been little scholarly attention on whether LSCs, in fact, influence FDI inflows in host states. States are potentially liable for any subsequent regulations that violate legislative stability guarantees, and LSCs are as such a singularly poor bargain for host states should they not induce investments.

Developing countries and emerging market economies are often vulnerable to political risks[12] that hamper FDI in-flows.[13] To attract FDI and promote

10 *See* CAMERON (2010), *supra* note 9, at 83.

11 GJUZI (2018), *supra* note 2, at 34; *see also* Joseph E Neuhaus, *The enforceability of Legislative Stabilization Clauses, in* PRACTICING VIRTUE: INSIDE INTERNATIONAL ARBITRATION 318. n 4 (David D. Caron et al. eds., 2015) (explaining that "[w]e have found legislative stabilization clauses in the investment laws of Armenia, Georgia "repealed", Kuwait, Tajikistan, Turkmenistan, Ukraine, Uzbekistan, and Vietnam".); *Protection of Foreign Direct Investment in a New World Order: Vietnam--A Case Study,* 107 Harv. L. Rev. 1995, 2001 n. 50 (1994) (explaining that "stabilization clauses are guarantees by the host state that in the event of a detrimental change in laws, such as in tax rates or in export duties, the old law will be grandfathered and will continue to apply to investor's enterprise. For example, the investment laws of Ukraine, Uzbekistan, Turkmenistan, and Russia all provide that if a change in law adversely affects a foreign investment, the old law as it stood at the time of the enterprise's initial registration will remain valid for 10 years from the registration date.").

12 Today's political risks include unstable governance, changes of regulatory framework, adverse contract changes imposed unilaterally by a host state, environmental and human rights measures, and efficiency of the host state's judiciary system. *See* CAMERON (2010), *supra* note 9, at 146; *See also* ERKAN (2010), *supra* note 9, at 57.

13 CAMERON (2010), *supra* note 9, at 146.

economic growth, these countries may conclude International Investment Agreements (IIAs)[14] that offer legal stability guarantees to foreign investors. IIAs can provide stability guarantees explicitly through express Stability Clauses (IIA SCs) or implicitly through Fair and Equitable Treatment (FET) provisions. Stability Clauses typically aim to protect investors against adverse changes in the legal and regulatory environment, while FET provisions provide investors with a right to fair and equitable treatment in accordance with international law. However, while these provisions can offer important protections to foreign investors, there is ongoing debate over their scope and application. For example, some argue that FET provisions are too vague and open to interpretation, which can lead to uncertainty and disputes between investors and host states.

## 1.2 Aims and Objectives

Stabilization clauses are a significant tool employed by multinational corporations in mitigating a host state's political risks. However, the validity and legal impact of such clauses are debatable. Even with the internationalization of state contracts, there are no guarantees that the host state will not assert sovereignty over natural resources to exclude investors previously granted access to such resources. As a result, traditional contractual stabilization clauses cannot provide absolute protection against the host state's intervention. This does not mean that traditional CSCs have no effect. These clauses might nevertheless render nationalization or expropriation an unlawful act and thereby affect the amount of compensation that the arbitral tribunal might grant or lead more readily to a determination that the state has violated an applicable IIA.

Certainly, inserting traditional SCs in the state contracts creates an inescapable tension between the competing rights of states and foreign investors. While the host state needs the flexibility of the contract to exercise its regulatory and sovereign powers over its natural resources, the investor seeks firmer stability guarantees. The conflict of interest between a foreign investor and the host state often makes it difficult for traditional SCs in state contracts to work.

---

14 *Id; See also* DUDOLF DOLZER & CHRISTOPH SCHREUER, PRINCIPLES OF INTERNATIONAL INVESTMENT LAW 22 (2nd. ed. 2012) [hereinafter DOLZER & SCHREUER 2012] (noting that "[t]hus, the purpose of investment treaties is to address the typical risks of a long-term investment project, and thereby to provide stability and predictability in the sense of an investment-friendly climate").

The pitfalls of traditional CSCs in state contracts have led some scholars to suggest that using adequate renegotiation clauses would be much better for providing contractual stability and predictability than traditional CSCs. Essentially, in the event of any unilateral measure taken by the host state in the future, the parties may agree to negotiate their contract to return to the same rights and obligations as before. The present study examines the value and legal effect of renegotiation clauses in state contracts to provide a perspective on how these clauses are perceived and how they operate in practice, a matter rendered difficult by the dearth of data on whether such clauses have led to successfully renegotiated agreements and whether parties have avoided arbitration. The argument advanced in this study is that inserting a renegotiation clause in the state contract would, theoretically, provide the parties with stability and flexibility by bringing the parties together where the terms are onerous to establish a new balance. However, the veracity of this premise is uncertain at best. First, the ability of the renegotiation clause to achieve stability and flexibility is greatly limited and constrained. For example, one limitation of renegotiation clauses is that they may be difficult to enforce or may not be sufficient to address all potential changes in the regulatory environment.

Second, the lack of data makes it difficult to determine whether renegotiation clauses have led to successfully renegotiated agreements and whether parties have avoided arbitration.

Critics of renegotiation clauses have also raised concerns that renegotiation clauses could add unnecessary expenses by dragging out disputes needlessly. Do renegotiation clauses add value given that parties always have the incentive to settle their disputes amicably in any event, and there is nothing to stop them, even in a traditional CSCs setting, from renegotiating and coming to a different agreement?

In its attempt at comprehensiveness, this study attempts to fill gaps in the published literature, but its main objective is more ambitious: to find a well-developed mechanism that would be more effective in achieving stability and flexibility of the contractual regime. To this end, the present study pays special attention to legislative stabilization clauses (LSCs) and proposes a new taxonomy of LSCs that divides them into three fundamental categories: Aspirational LSCs, Standard LSCs, and Contractual LSCs. The study argues that Contractual LSCs grant investors stability guarantees through contracts approved by the government, often conditional on meeting particular investment profile criteria. These clauses signal to investors a more transparent and reliable process to access enhanced stability guarantees by way of stabilization contracts generated under the legislation. They also enable host states to better target investment projects and manage their stability obligations. From this perspective, the contractual LSCs would be more effective than traditional CSCs and renegotiation clauses. But a caveat must be made here: The Contractual LSC, in most cases, is limited to certain sectors, and in the occasional high-value contract outside the prescribed sectors for the LSC, it could possibly work in tandem with a traditional CSC or renegotiation clauses.

Finally, international investment agreements (IIAs) offer enforceable protections to foreign investors based on the premise that these protections will promote FDI, which, in turn, promotes sustainable economic development. The key feature of such IIAs is that they contain provisions that aim to create stability in the investment legal framework by imposing restrictions on the host state's regulatory power and restraining the host state's interference with the rights of foreign investors.[15] These stability guarantees can be provided explicitly through the express stabilization clause (IIA SC) or implicitly through the fair and equitable treatment standard (FET). While a significant number of the old generation IIAs particularly Italy's BITs, contained the express SCs, these clauses have attracted limited scholarly scrutiny. The present study attempts to fill gaps in the published literature. It seeks to appraise and investigate the issue of the IIA SC and its effectiveness in achieving stability and predictability of the contractual regime. The study also aims to tackle the sensitive issue relates to the question of whether the FET clause does indeed provide foreign investors legal stability equal to SCs in state contracts. In this vein, the argument advanced by this study is that unless there is an express SC in the IIA, which is rare and no longer found in the new generation IIAs, the FET clause is a poorer substitute as it does not provide legal stability equal to CSCs, but merely provides that any changes will be fair, reasonable, and equitable. Therefore the purpose of the FET clause should not be understood to extend to strict stability. Otherwise, the existence of SCs in state contracts—which takes us nicely back to where our discussion started—would be redundant.

## 1.3 Overview of Methodology

This book adopts a comprehensive approach to analyzing stability and flexibility provisions within international investment law. The methodology used involves both doctrinal analysis and practical considerations.

---

15 *See* PRABHASH RANJAN, INDIA AND BILATERAL INVESTMENT TREATIES: REFUSAL, ACCEPTANCE, BACKLASH 1 (2019).

In the doctrinal analysis, the book examines the legal concepts and issues underlying stability and flexibility provisions in investment contracts, national laws, and international investment agreements. This involves a detailed analysis of the legal language and the interpretation of relevant provisions, as well as an examination of case law and arbitral decisions related to these issues. In addition to the doctrinal analysis, the book also considers practical considerations related to stability and flexibility provisions. This involves an examination of the functional context in which these provisions operate, including their impact on investment decisions, national sovereignty, and public policy objectives. The practical considerations also involve an analysis of the economic and social implications of stability and flexibility provisions, as well as their relationship with other legal and policy frameworks, such as human rights, environmental protection, and sustainable development.

To support the analysis, the book relies on both primary and secondary sources. Primary sources include national legislation, investment contracts, international investment agreements, and arbitral decisions. Secondary sources include authoritative books, journal articles, reports from international organizations, and other relevant publications. Overall, the methodology adopted in this book provides a comprehensive and nuanced approach to analyzing stability and flexibility provisions within international investment law, taking into account both legal and practical considerations.

CHAPTER 2

# Traditional Contractual Stabilization Clauses

## 2.1 Introduction

Contractual Stabilization Clauses (CSCs), in the traditional sense, are contractual provisions that aim to isolate the state contract from any subsequent adverse changes by the host state in the regulatory framework or fiscal regime.[1] Accordingly, the host state is precluded from applying a new law inconsistent with the original contract under traditional CSCs.[2] This means that a host state may not apply with impunity subsequent negative changes in its domestic law to the investor and the investment and agrees to leave the investment project unaffected by these changes.[3] However, the host country is not prohibited from exercising its legislative power and changing its laws. The state merely promises to spare the investment from any later and adverse regulatory changes or reimburse the investor for any damages incurred as a result.[4] In its contractual form, the stabilization clause is ubiquitous in foreign investment.[5] The future government of a host state, especially in developing countries, may or may not follow the same policy that the former government adopted when that contract was signed.[6] Such concerns mean that both parties will seek safeguards to

1 CAMERON (2010), at 68; *See also* Stefan Michael Kroll, *The Renegotiation and Adaptation of Investment Contracts, in* ARBITRATING FOREIGN INVESTMENT DISPUTES: PROCEDURAL AND SUBSTANTIVE LEGAL ASPECTS 425, 437 (2004).

2 ERKAN (2010), at 141.

3 Aguaytia Energy, LLC v Republic of Peru, ICSID Case No ARB/06/13, Award, 89 (Dec. 11, 2008) [hereinafter Aguatiya Energy Award]; ERKAN (2010), at 105.

4 *See* CHRISTOPH H. SCHREUER ET AL., THE ICSID CONVENTION: A COMMENTARY 588, paras. 117 (2d ed. 2009); CAMERON (2010), at 70.

5 *See* Sam Foster Halabi, *Efficient Contracting Between Foreign Investors and Host States: Evidence from Stabilization Clauses*, 31 NW. J. INT'L L. & BUS. 261, 290 (2011) (stating that "not all investment contracts include stabilization clauses, but they are common in contracts for a wide range of industries in most regions of the world") (citations omitted); Erin O'Hara O'Connor & Susan D. Franck, *Foreign Investments and the Market for Law*, 2014 U. Ill. L. Rev. 1617, 1631 (2014) (noting "the common inclusion of stabilization clauses in investment contracts"). Commentators have traced the origin of stabilization clauses all the way back to the period between World War 1 and World War 2 when US companies began to include them in concessionary agreements because of nationalizations in Latin America. *See* ERKEN (2010), at 103; GJUZI (2018), at14; DOAK R. BISHOP, INTERNATIONAL ARBITRATION OF PETROLEUM DISPUTES: THE DEVELOPMENT OF A LEX PETROLEA 23 (2002).

6 *Id.*

 | DOI:10.1163/9789004692756_003

protect their respective interests. Foreign investors, on the one hand, will seek to protect their investment abroad through stabilizing the legal framework of their investment to avoid any unilateral changes by the host government and reducing any market volatility. The host developing country, on the other hand, gains an economic advantage in attracting foreign investors to invest in its territory, attracts foreign portfolio investment funds, and achieves the goals of sustainable development.[7] The inclusion of SCs in state contracts has long been a response to such interconnected issues. However, the validity and legal effect of SCs have been subject to much debate as an SC, when considered under domestic law, is frequently seen as a fetter to the host state's power to regulate.[8]

Notably, in order to avoid the subsequent application of the applicable domestic law and to prevent the national courts of the host state from possibly interpreting SCs as invalid clauses, foreign investors usually seek to internationalize the state contract through stabilization clauses.[9] Under international

---

7 The history and background of SCs has been aptly summarized by arbitrator Sir G. Fitzmaurice in his separate opinion in Aminoil v. Kuwait, as he noted that "[b]y what historical process did provisions such as Article 17 come to be inserted in agreements between States and foreign commercial or industrial entities? In contracts between private parties, they would have been thought quite superfluous. If the contract provided that it was made for a certain period, then it would follow automatically that it could not be terminated unilaterally by either party during, or before the end of, that period, except for reasons specifically provided for elsewhere in the contract. To 'spell-out' all this at length would have been thought exaggerated and really somewhat invidious. Again, even in contracts between States and foreign corporate entities, the same view would normally have been taken at any time up to about the date of the first world war. But between the two wars things began to change. Particularly in Latin-America, there were increasing cases in which the local government, having granted a concession to a foreign corporate entity for the construction and running of railways, tramways etc., or to extract and process mineral products, would wait until the undertaking had got past its 'teething' troubles and had become a 'going concern,' and would then step in and take it over. The appellation of 'nationalisation' was not then much in vogue, but the effect was the same, namely that the State compulsorily acquired the undertaking, either itself to operate it, or to hand it over to a corporation of local nationality. It was specifically in the light of those occurrences that stabilization clauses began to be introduced into concessionary contracts, particularly by American Companies in view of their Latin-American experiences, and for the express purpose of ensuring that Concessions would run their full term, except where the case was one for which the Concession itself gave a right of earlier termination." Kuwait v. American Indep. Oil Co. (Aminoil), 21 I.L.M. 976 (1982), Separate Opinion, at 64–65.

8 Rachel Frid de Vries, *Stability Shaken? Israeli High Court of Justice Strikes Down the Stabilization Clause in the Israeli Government's Gas Plan*, 18 J. WORLD INV. & TRADE 332, 339 (2017).

9 Abdullah Faruque, *Validity and Efficacy of Stabilization Clauses, Legal Protective v. Functional Value*, 23 J. INT'L. ARB. 317, 326 (2006) [hereinafter, Faruque 2006 a].

law, particularly the law of treaties, the discussion of the legal validity of SCs focuses on two potentially conflicting principles: the principle of *pacta sunt servanda* and the concept of the state's sovereignty, in particular, the country's permanent sovereignty over natural resources.[10]

Doctrinal opinion has espoused divergent approaches over the question of the precise status and impact of SCs.[11] There are three approaches adopted by the scholars: the acceptance of SCs as being absolutely valid, the denial of SCs as being invalid, and the "middle ground" approach, which accepts the validity of SCs, but denies them full effect.[12] Arbitral jurisprudence and arbitral awards have generally supported this middle-ground view.[13] The traditional CSCs will not prevent a determined government from expropriating a foreign project if the host government has a mind to do so. International law has recognized a host state's right to nationalize or expropriate a foreign investment in the public interest with appropriate compensation, even if the state contract contains contractual commitments (i.e., SCs).[14] Therefore, SCs do not invalidate a nationalization act concerning the investment project.

However, SCs can render nationalization an unlawful act and thereby affect the amount of compensation that the arbitral tribunal might grant.[15] Based thereon, the current trend in stabilization practice is that SCs cannot prevent a

---

10 ERKAN (2010), at 110. *See also* Waelde & Ndi (1996), at 242.

11 *See infra* part 2.7.2.1.

12 Among the scholars to discuss and examine this, *see e.g.* Prosper Weil, *Les clauses de stabilisation ou d'intangibilité insérées dans les accords de développement économique, in* MÉLANGES OFFERTS A CHARLES ROUSSEAU, LA COMMUNAUTÉ INTERNATIONALE, 301–328 (Charles Rousseau ed., 1974); Waelde &Ndi (1996), at 243-245; Samuel K.B. Asante, *Stability of Contractual Relations in the Transnational Investment Process,* 28 INT'L & COMP. L.Q. 401, 409 (1979); CAMERON (2010), at 89–102; Faruque (2006 a), *supra* note 9, at 323–329.

13 *See, e.g.,* Kuwait v. American Indep. Oil Co. (Aminoil), 21 I.L.M. 976 (1982); Libyan Am. Oil Co. (LIAMCO) v. Libyan Arab Republic, 20 I.L.M. 1 (1981).

14 GA Resolution 1803 (XVII), para 4 (Dec. 14, 1962) (The declaration provides that, "[n]ationalization, expropriation or requisitioning shall be based on grounds or reasons of public utility, security or the national interest which are recognized as overriding purely individual or private interests, both domestic and foreign. In such cases the owner shall be paid appropriate compensation, in accordance with the rules in force in the State taking such measures in the exercise of its sovereignty and in accordance with international law"), *available at* https://www.un.org/ga/search/view_doc.asp?symbol=A/RES/1803%28XVII%29.

15 Peter D Cameron, *Stabilization in Investment Contracts and Changes of Rules in Host Countries: Tools for Oil& Gas Investors,* AIPN Research Paper Final Report, at 15(2006), *available at* https://www.international-arbitration-attorney.com/wp-content/uploads/arbitrationlaw4-Stabilisation-Paper.pdf. [hereinafter, Cameron 2006].

host government from altering the law applicable to the investment contract,[16] because arbitral tribunals have often seen pecuniary compensation as "the appropriate remedy" for the breach of an SC.[17] In this vein, it is worth noting that an arbitral tribunal is unlikely to award a specific performance or "*restitutio in integrum*" against the host state that breached its contract contained a stabilization clause. To do so, the order would involve a direct challenge to the host state's sovereignty and prove impossible to enforce.[18] The decision in *TOPCO v. Libya* was remarkable. The sole arbitrator Dupuy ordered Libya to reinstate its contract with the foreign investor but the Libyian government ignored the order, and the parties later reached a settlement.[19]

The value of SCs, therefore, operates as a "financial value," just like the function of penalty clauses in private contracts. Such controversy between scholars and arbitral tribunals regarding the validity and legal effect of SCs raises a logical question regarding the viability of such provisions for developing countries and calls into question why some developing countries still agree to the traditional SCs in investment contracts, as including SCs in the state contracts undermine the rule of law, negatively impact state's willingness and ability to regulate in the public interest, and may grant better compensation to foreign investors. The traditional CSCs have some functions; they might reduce the host state's political risk, or at least they can render nationalization or expropriation an unlawful act and thereby affect the amount of compensation that the arbitral tribunal might grant. However, these clauses, to some extent, have been seen as an ineffective tool for protecting the foreign investor against unilateral changes in the host state's regulatory framework and imposing undue restrictions on the regulatory powers of the host governments. Therefore, reconsidering traditional CSCs and seeking an alternative mechanism to recalibrate the balance of interests and rights between the host state and foreign investors becomes essential. Such legal safeguard clauses might include, Legislative Stabilization Clauses (LSCs) and renegotiation clauses, or a combination thereof.

16 Faruque (2006 a), *supra* note 9, at 329.

17 CAMERON (2010), at 93.

18 *Id.*

19 Libyan Am. Oil Co. (LIAMCO) v. Libyan Arab Republic, 20 I.L.M. 1 (1981).

## 2.2 Definition of Stabilization Clauses

SC, in a traditional sense, refers to any clause contained in a contract between a host government and a foreign investor whereby a host government undertakes neither to modify, derogate, nor annul the contract, either by legislative power or administrative measures.[20] A traditional example of a SC can be found in the concession agreement of 1933 between Iran and the Anglo-Iranian Oil Company. Article 21 of the agreement states that the "concession shall not be annulled by the Government, and the terms therein contained shall not be altered either by general or special legislation in the future or by administrative measures or any other acts whatever of the executive authorities."[21] In exceptional cases, an SC is contained in the international investment treaty concluded between the host state and the home state of an investor.[22] Accordingly, the fundamental purpose of SCs is to "tie the hands of the host state" during the life of the investment contract to prevent interference with such a contract.[23] In other words, the legislation adopted after the date of the host government agreement does not apply automatically to the foreign investor or the investment project unless the foreign investor agrees. Hence, SCs are tools for foreign investors to mitigate or manage several sovereign risks associated with their investment projects. However, the practice of using SCs has evolved and led to new stability provisions, which are often called "economic stabilization clauses." These new versions of SCs aim to keep the economic equilibrium of the state contract established between the parties upon its conclusion by including contract provisions that allow for the renegotiation of the

---

20 ERKAN (2010), at 103; Weil, *supra* note 12, at 301–328; Asante, *supra* note 12, at 401, 409 (1979) (explaining that stability clauses are "designed to stabili[z]e or freeze the essential provisions of the agreement by strictly prohibiting any legislative or administrative act which derogates from or is otherwise inconsistent with the provisions of the agreement or the legal environment of the transaction."). Similarly, the ICSID tribunal in Total S.A. v. Argentina, defined SCs as " Stabilization clauses are clauses, which are inserted in state contracts concluded between foreign investors and host states with the intended effect of freezing a specific host State's legal framework at a certain date, such that the adoption of any changes in the legal regulatory framework of the investment concerned (even by law of general application and without any discriminatory intent by the host State) would be illegal." Total S.A. v. Argentina, ICSID Case No. ARB/04/01, Decision on Liability, 101 (Dec. 27, 2010).

21 Esa Paasivirta, *Internationalization and Stabilization of Contracts Versus State Sovereignty*, 60 BRIT. Y.B. INT'L. L. 315, 324 (1989).

22 For instance, the Argentina-Panama BIT 1996, and Italy-Mozambique BIT 1998. *See infra* p 18.

23 Maniruzzaman, *Drafting Stabilisation Clauses* (2007), at 23.

rights and obligations of the parties. "[T]hus, upon disruption of the *status quo*, the parties are obligated to negotiate in good faith to restore the original balance."[24] Although some authors do not agree that these latter clauses are SCs, others have adopted a broader definition of stabilization clauses and described them as: "all of the mechanisms contractual or otherwise, which aim to preserve over the life of the contract the benefit of specific economic and legal conditions which the parties considered to be appropriate at the time they entered into the contract."[25]

The broad meaning of SCs reflects two interrelated dimensions of stability: the first is the temporal dimension and the second is the economic dimension. The temporal dimension is the "continuity of the relationship until the successful completion of the project and accomplishment of the objectives agreed upon by the parties in the contract" and the economic dimension refers to "preserving the original economic equilibrium" of the contract that was already established between the parties upon its conclusion over the life of the contract.[26] Indeed, "any clause, which, according to the parties, is aimed at stabilizing an investment, may be called a stabilization clause."[27] In *CMS v. Argentina*, the tribunal concluded that "[g]old standards or reference currencies embodied in financial transactions, stabilization clauses built into contracts and more recently the vast network of bilateral investment treaties are all expressions of the search for stability and legal certainty."[28] A SC can, therefore, exist under a different name, such as a "stability clause," "non-aggravation clause," "clause of non-interference," "clause-of-legislative stability," "binding agreement," "applicable law clause," "choice-of-law clause," "change-of-aw clause," etc.[29] Given the rich diversity of the SC and its different names, the two aforementioned dimensions can assist the arbitral tribunal in identifying such clauses and their key features.

24 J. Nna Emeka, *Anchoring Stabilizing Clauses in International Petroleum Contracts*, 42 INT'L LAW. 1317, 1321 (2008).

25 GJUZI (2018), at 12–13 (quoting CAMERON (2010), at 69).

26 *Id*, at 12–13.

27 Syamal Kumar Chatterjee, *The Stabilisation Clause Myth in Investment Agreements*, 5 J. INT'L ARB. 97, 98 (1988).

28 CMS Gas Transmission Co. v. Republic of Argentina, ICSID Case No. ARB/01/8, Decision of the Tribunal on Objections to Jurisdiction, 28 (July 17, 2003), 7 ICSID Rep. 492 (2004).

29 GJUZI (2018), at 13–14.

## 2.3 Origins of Stabilization Clauses

Ultimately, SCs as defined above have three main sources, namely, investment contracts, domestic laws, and international treaties.

### 2.3.1 *Stabilization through Investment Contracts*

State contracts are the traditional tools in the legal system of the host state for establishing legal stability and predictability.[30] Undoubtedly, contractual commitments such as SCs are the most robust basis for a foreign investor's legitimate expectations.[31] The host state, through such contractual obligations, undertakes not to apply any subsequent changes to the investment contract during the life of the investment project. The most striking feature of the contractual arrangements is that they reflect the parties' negotiations in the investment contract and provide the highest level of legal protection to the foreign investor.[32] In *Continental Casualty v. Argentina*, the ICSID tribunal concluded that "contractual undertakings by governments ... generate as a rule legal rights and therefore expectations of compliance."[33]

CSCs are ubiquitous in state contracts,[34] particularly in developing countries.[35] Despite criticism that SCs restrict developing countries' sovereign power

30 *See* Michele Podestà, *Legitimate Expectations in Investment Treaty Laws: Understanding the Roots and Limits of controversial Concept*, 28 ICSID REV. – FOREIGN INVESTMENT L. J. 88, 101 (2013); *See also* Waelde &Ndi (1996), at 234 (An investment agreement [also referred to as a "state contract" or economic development agreement] is therefore the preferred legal instrument of setting and firmly anchoring the rules of the game for large-scale and high-risk projects. It is, however, not because of the contract per se, but by reason of the presence of specific provisions in the agreement, that defenses can be raised against any subsequent government intervention. Such specific provisions will often include arbitration clauses, applicable law provisions, and stabilization provisions).

31 El Paso Energy International Co v. Argentina, ICSID Case No. Arb/03/15, Award, 376–377 (Oct. 31, 2011) [hereinafter El Paso Energy Award].

32 *Id*, at 103.

33 Continental Casualty v. Argentina, ICSID Case No. ARB/07/27, Award, 261 (Sep. 5, 2008) [hereinafter Continental Award].

34 Halabi, *supra* note 5, at 290; O'Connor & Franck, *supra* note 5, at 1631; ERKAN (2010), at 103; GJUZI (2018), at 14; BISHOP, *supra* note 20, at 23 (2002).

35 Andrea Shemberg, *Stabilization Clauses and Human Rights*, INT'L FIN. CORP. at 14–18 (2009), *available at* https://www.ifc.org/wps/wcm/connect/0883d81a-e00a-4551-b2b9-46641e5a9bba/Stabilization%2BPaper.pdf?MOD=AJPERES&CACHEID=ROOTWORKSPACE-0883d81a-e00a-4551-b2b9-46641e5a9bba-jqeww2e. [hereafter U.N. IFC report]; Halabi, *supra* note 5, at 290; O'Connor & Franck, *supra* note 5, at 1631 (stating that "[f]rom a public policy perspective, the state might prefer to grant some rights only in return for investor commitments. Consider, for example, the common inclusion of stabilization clauses in investment contracts.").

to regulate as well as their permanent sovereignty over natural resources,[36] SCs are "still widely provided in developing countries, and are here to stay for the foreseeable future."[37] According to a study undertaken by Andrea Shemberg on stabilization clauses in international investment contracts, only three investment contracts out of a total of 76 did not include some form of SCs.[38]

### 2.3.2 *Stabilization through Domestic Laws*[39]

Host states often see SCs as instruments to encourage inland investment and create a favorable investment climate.[40] FDI has been considered a crucial factor in achieving economic and sustainable development for developing countries. consequently it becomes fundamentally important for these nations to guarantee stable regulatory frameworks, which, in turn, encourage multinational corporations to invest within their territories. Governments in developing countries use SCs as a tool to attract FDI, particularly to their extractive sectors,[41] and they often include such provisions in their domestic law such as in constitutions, investment codes, regulations approved by the government, and individual administrative acts such as permits and licenses.[42]

### 2.3.3 *Stabilization through IIAs*[43]

Other mechanisms for stability can be found expressly or implicitly in international investment treaties, such as BITs. Generally, all BITs contain provisions

---

36 *See* Dennis Kakembo, *Stabilisation Clauses in International Petroleum Contracts: Illusion or Safeguard?* DELOITTE & TOUCHE 2 (April 2014). https://www2.deloitte.com/content/dam/Deloitte/ug/Documents/tax/tax_StabilisationClauses_2014.pdf.

37 DOLZER (2018), *supra* note 8, at 192 (quoting Mario Mansour& Carole Nakhle, *Fiscal Stabilization in Oil and Gas Contracts: Evidence and Implications,* THE OXFORD INSTITUTE FOR ENERGY STUDIES 22 (Jan. 2016)).

38 U.N. IFC report, *supra* note 35, at 18 tbl.6.1 (2009). The sample contains 24 contracts from the 1990s, 49 contracts from the 2000s, and 3 contracts that are undated but were indicated to be from one of those two periods. The duration of the contracts generally ranges from 10 years to 25 or more years, which means that most of the contracts in the study are likely still in force today. The sample also contains 12 model contracts10 from the 2000s, 1 from 1990s, and 1 undated. The contracts and models analyzed include 11 from Sub-Saharan Africa; 14 from East Asia and Pacific; 16 from the Middle East and North Africa; 10 from Eastern Europe, Southern Europe and Central Asia; 5 from South Asia; 19 from Latin America and the Caribbean; and 13 from OECD countries. *See id,* at 14; *See also infra*-p 38.

39 *See infra* Chapter 4.

40 Faruque (2006 a), *supra* note 9, at 335.

41 *Id; see also infra*-part 2.4.3.1.

42 CAMERON (2010), at 62–63; Waelde &Ndi (1996), at 240; GJUZI (2018), at 34. *See infra* Chpater 4.

43 *See infra* Chapter 5.

whereby the investment is protected during the lifetime of the BITs and even for a specific period after the BIT has expired or been canceled. As put by Professor Cameron,[44]

> A BIT will typically include substantive protection for the treatment of foreign investment through the application of standards such as "fair and equitable treatment," non-discriminatory and most favored nation treatment, full protection and security, free transfer of currency and limitation on the sovereign right to expropriate, such as prohibition to do so without due process, a public purpose goal and the payment of prompt, adequate and effective compensation to the investor. A BIT's duration may be in the range of ten years or more but will often contain provisions whereby an investment made while it is in force will continue to be given protection for a specific period after the BIT has expired or been canceled. In a sense, they create artificial light in the form of continuing obligations after the sun has set on the state's relationship to the treaty instrument itself.[45]

In exceptional cases, a SC is expressly contained in the international investment treaty concluded between the host state and the home state of the foreign investor.[46] For example, the Italy-Mozambique BIT of 1998 and the Argentina-Panama BIT of 1996 contain such stability provisions:

The Italy-Mozambique BIT, 1998 provides that

> Whenever, after the date when the investment has been made, a modification should take place in law, regulations, acts or measures of economic policies governing directly or indirectly the investment, the same treatment shall apply upon request of the investor that was applicable to it at the moment when the investment was agreed upon to be carried out.[47]

---

44 Cameron is a director of the center and professor of International Energy Law and Policy. He is also the Associate Dean for Research in the Graduate School of Natural Resources Law, Policy and Management. He is a Professorial Fellow of the Law School at the University of Edinburgh, Fellow of the Chartered Institute of Arbitrators, and a member of the London Court of International Arbitration. He is the author or editor of more than a dozen book-length publications. Professor Peter D. Cameron, OIL, GAS & ENERGY LAW, https://www.ogel.org/about-author-a-z-profile.asp?key=599.

45 CAMERON (2010), at 150.

46 GJUZI (2018), at 36.

47 Agreement on the Promotion and Reciprocal Protection of Investments, It.-Mozam., art 12.3, Dec. 14, 1998, https://investmentpolicy.unctad.org/international-investment-agreements/treaty-files/3388/download.

Argentina-Panama BIT 1996 provides that

> neither contracting party will engage in direct or indirect expropriation nor any other similar measures, including the modification or derogation from the laws, which has the same effect.[48]

It is worth mentioning that if the investment treaty contains explicit SCs, it provides a strong incentive for a host state to respect its commitments under international law and its agreement with the foreign investor. Therefore, "[w]hen a host state violates the rights guaranteed to the investor by the treaty, that state has not only violated norms of customary international law … but has also breached a treaty with the investor's home state."[49] (see Chapter 5).

### 2.3.4 *Stability through a Multi-tiered Approach*

To establish a conducive investment climate, several developing countries may provide a multi-tiered approach in their legal regimes, combining a wide range of stability mechanisms such as state contracts, national laws, and IIAs.[50] Although this approach is evident in some Latin American countries, it is also evident in the case of Kazakhstan, where the legal regime contains a wide range of stability mechanisms such as state contracts, legislation (as in the constitution, civil code, investment law, law on subsoil, petroleum law, the tax code, presidential edicts, and government decrees), court decisions, letters from state authorities (such as the Ministry of Finance, and various committees of the Ministry of State Revenues), and international treaties, including the Energy Charter Treaty (ECT) and many IIAs.[51]

## 2.4 Justification and Purpose of Stabilization Clauses

Based on the different forms of SCs elaborated above, this section analyzes the rationale and justifications of such clauses as a commitment of a host state to a foreign investor. This analysis takes into account the perspective of all parties

48 Agreement for the Promotion and Reciprocal Protection of Investments, Arg.-Pan., art. 3.1, Oct. 5, 1996, 2033 U.N.T.S. 205.

49 Paul E. Comeaux & N. Stephen Kinsella, *Reducing Political Risk in Developing Countries: Bilateral Investment Treaties, Stabilization Clauses, and MIGA & (and) OPIC Investment Insurance*, 15 N.Y.L. Sch. J. Int'l & Comp. L. 1, 6 (1994).

50 Cameron (2010), at 329.

51 For discussion, *see id.*, at 328–330.

concerned in the state contract, including foreign companies, the host state, and overseas project lenders, as is described more fully below.

### 2.4.1 *From the Perspective of a Foreign Investor*

A foreign investor uses SC as "a risk-mitigation tool drafted to help protect investments from a range of 'sovereign' risks in the context of foreign investment."[52] The foreign investor, being risk-averse, seeks to secure the stability of the contractual provisions based on the applicable law in effect at the time the project was made.[53] Given the legal nature of state contracts as drafted between two legally unequal parties, the foreign investor seeks to rebalance the power of the parties through SCs. The host state, on the one hand, enjoys extraordinary sovereign advantages and powers which are not available to individuals. Additionally, the host enjoys a specific status under public international law. The foreign investor, on the other hand, is not subject to the rules of public international law and generally does not get protection under these rules. This inequality between the parties of state contracts has prompted foreign investors to seek protection of their investments through the stability of the legal regime of the host state that applies to the investment agreement. A SC is a contractual tool developed in response to such concerns; it aims to insulate the state contract from any changes in the applicable law of the contract.[54] In addition to the financial concerns above, which may constitute the core of SCs, other matters gain further relevance in the current international investment contract. For instance, environmental regulations of host states have become financially prohibitive for foreign investors, leading some of them to seek protection for their investment against such changes in the host state's law. The inclusion of SCs in state contracts has long been a response to such interconnected issues. As some experts have concluded, SCs are necessary to ensure that the host state bears the cost of implementing the environmental and social legislation. For example, a host state might issue a new

---

52 U.N. IFC report, *supra* note 35, at 4. *See also* Waelde & Ndi (1996), at 232 ("Stabilization clauses can be appreciated as one of a substantial number of methods to deal with the political risk of foreign investment in proto-states. To properly understand how these clauses function as one of many methods of political risk management, it is useful to briefly review both the concept and the various methods of managing this form of risk. Political risk can be understood as the occurrence of events in the political sphere (governmental actions, politically motivated insecurity in the country, and international conflict) which impede the normal operations of a business venture and detrimentally impact the commercial viability of the venture.").

53 Faruque (2006 a), *supra* note 9, at 317.

54 *Id.* at 318.

ecological regulation mandating an advanced pollution control technology that introduces financial difficulties for existing foreign companies which use old technology.[55] SCs are a life raft for foreign investors and foreign investment without these clauses would not be possible in many regions in the world.[56]

Given the fact that state contracts are often long-term contracts, the SC is a unique approach to deal with the effect of the time element in the contractual relationship. Considering its legal nature, the SC is substantive in nature, as it deals with the rights and obligations of both parties: the host state, and foreign investors. Thus, the breach of these clauses may result in significant changes in the rights and obligations of the contracting parties.[57] For example, concession agreements in the extractive industry are long-term contracts that require a relatively long time to become economically viable. These projects are prone to several significant risks, "in which the host state forces renegotiation, and the foreign investor often has a hard time refusing, due to significant sunk costs."[58] Consequently, the foreign investor needs to be assured that once his project begins, all obligations under the agreement with the host state will not unilaterally change to the detriment of the investment.[59] SCs in such cases become inevitable results.

### 2.4.2 *From the Perspective of Foreign Project Financiers*

Foreign investors usually turn to external loans financing to fund their investment projects.[60] Indeed, the core concern of the financing institution (*e.g.*, banks, expert financing institutions, and long-term purchasers of production) is to ensure the ability of a foreign project to recoup costs and repay its debt[61] given the fact that a state contract is a long-term contract that requires a long period of operation to become profitable, and such contracts are prone to the intervention of the host state by enactment of new laws that eliminate or derogate the economic efficiency of the foreign project.[62] Therefore, the stability and predictability of the host state's legal framework are fundamentally important for the lenders to finance the foreign project. Foreign project lenders have considered the inclusion of SCs as a response to these interconnected

---

55 U.N. IFC report, *supra* note 35, at 4–5.
56 *Id.* at 5.
57 Faruque (2006 a), *supra* note 9, at 318.
58 U.N. IFC report, *supra* note 35, at 5.
59 *Id.*
60 Waelde & Ndi (1996), at 228.
61 *Id.*
62 U.N. IFC report, *supra* note 35, at 5.

issues and therefore essential to the bankability of an investment project.[63] Therefore, SCs, from the foreign project lenders' view, are a requirement to secure repayment of their loans, especially if the host state has a volatile legal and institutional system which the foreign project lenders do not trust.[64]

In sum, international bankers and financiers view SCs as a legal safeguard against any unilateral alteration by the host state, which could impair their returns. Consequently, international project lenders often, before providing any financing to the investment project, add their thoughts and concerns to the negotiation and enforcement of stable regimes on the investment contract.[65]

### 2.4.3 *From the Host State's Perspective*

From the host state's point of view, SCs are a way to encourage foreign direct investment and create a favorable investment climate to entice multinational corporations to invest within the territory of the state. Using a SC as a tool of "'controlling the future' by means of stabilization clauses would then depend on a combination of different variables in each host country, including the richness in natural resources, the level of economic development, the interest in attracting foreign investment, the general investment climate, the rule of law and institutional capacities, etc."[66] The rationales for SCs differ among countries and depend entirely on the classification status of the state itself. In other words, perspectives of SCs differ among less developed countries, developing countries, developed countries, and countries with precious natural resources as described below.

#### 2.4.3.1 Developing and Less Developed Countries

Developing and Less Developed Countries, in their effort to develop their economies, might see the SCs as essential instruments for attracting FDI Several factors urge some of these countries to be eager to attract foreign investment.[67] These factors might include: lacking technological expertise; experiencing financial crises; participating in a competitive international market; suffering from unstable regimes; suffering from weak rule of law; and having a record of hostility to foreign investors, as in the case of resource nationalism.[68]

63 *Id.*
64 Waelde & Ndi (1996), at 229.
65 *Id.*
66 GJUZI (2018), at 29.
67 *Id.*
68 *Id.*

All these factors, as well as some others, can adversely affect the host state's negotiation power. As a result, when the host state negotiates with foreign investors, the factors mentioned above can decrease these countries' bargaining power and force them to accept less favorable conditions, including any obligations to keep the stability of the applicable law governing the international project by waiving their sovereign rights and legislative power to regulate. Accordingly, the rationale of the SC from the perspective of less developed countries, developing countries, and economies in transition is to entice foreign direct investment to achieve sustainable development goals.[69] So, it is fundamentally crucial that these countries are able to guarantee legal protection for foreign investors. Contracting parties of state contracts seek to provide such protection by including specific provisions in such agreements[70] (*e.g.*, SCs). The government in developing countries use SCs as a tool of encouragement for foreign investment and they often include them in domestic legislation.[71]

#### 2.4.3.2 Developed Countries

Conversely, previous empirical studies indicate that it is rare to find stabilization provisions in state contracts concluded between a developed country and a foreign investor because foreign investors are unlikely to insist on SCs from developed countries. Even if foreign investors insisted on including SCs in a contract with developed countries, they would not succeed because developed countries rarely contract with multinational companies under a specific investment regime detracting from the host state domestic law, which governs the contract.[72] There are several features of developed countries that explain why SCs are not common in the contracts concluded with these countries:

69 Faruque (2006 a), *supra* note 9, at 336 (argued that the critical feature of stabilization clauses is its instrument value to enticing foreign direct investment. Therefore, he added that developing states agree to insert stabilization clauses in the petroleum sector to gain an economic advantage in encouraging foreign investment "by making their investment climate more competitive and favorable to the foreign investor."); *See* Paasivirta, *supra* note 21, at 330 (argued that SCs have a significant "market function" as a means of encouraging foreign investment); *But cf.* Sotonye Frank, *Stabilisation Clauses and Foreign Direct Investment: Presumptions versus Realities*, 16 J. WORLD INVESTMENT & TRADE 88 (2015) (Argued that "contrary to popular belief, stabilization clauses do not play an essential role in attracting FDI into developing countries").

70 Christopher T. Curtis, *The Legal Security of Economic Development Agreements*, 29 HARV. INT'L. L. J. 317, 319 (1988).

71 GJUZI (2018), at 31.

72 Waelde & Ndi (1996), at 221.

- A former government of a developed country cannot, constitutionally, conclude agreements with a private party that bind the next government;[73]
- A manifestation of stable liberal democracy is a distinctive aspect of developed countries;[74]
- The political risks from unreasonable or unjustifiable regulatory changes are presumably lower;[75]
- Developed countries have a stronger rule of law which can prove that the domestic legal system can efficiently and independently address the government's legal violations;[76]
- SCs would limit their sovereign power to regulate; and
- Developed countries, as capital-exporting countries, enjoy a high bargaining power when negotiating with a foreign investor, which means that there is no reason to accept such clauses.[77]

In sum, where the risk is seen as low (i.e., generally in developed states), using SCs as a mechanism to mitigate that risk is "less frequent, less relevant, and rarely invoked."[78] Similarly, countries abundant with natural resources sometimes abstain from providing SCs in state contracts when these countries enjoy a strong bargaining advantage at the time of contract negotiation.[79] For example, when the oil price is high, foreign investors, faced with the host government at the bargaining table, might be less able to persuade the host government to agree to include a SC in the petroleum contract. Moreover, some countries (*e.g.*, Saudi Arabia, Brazil) could pose certain political risks, but their geological risk is low with promising oil discoveries. Hence, foreign investors are likely to accept the petroleum contract without SCs if the investment project looks sufficiently profitable due to low geological risk.[80]

---

73 Alisher Umirdinov, *The End of Hibernation of Stabilization Clause in Investment Arbitration: Reassessing Its Contribution to Sustainable Development*, 43 DENV. J. INT'L L. & POL'Y 455, 459 (2015).

74 Gjuzi (2018), at 31.

75 *Id.*

76 *Id.*

77 Waelde & Ndi (1996), at 221–23.

78 Thomas W. Wälde, *Renegotiating acquired rights in the oil and gas industries: Industry and political cycles meet the rule of law*, 1 J. WORLD ENERGY L. & BUS. 55, 59 (2008).

79 ERKAN (2010), (noted that "one respondent commented that, it is true that stabilization clauses are given by government in a weak bargaining position, but they are also sometimes given by governments in a much stronger position but wanting something out of the ordinary from investors.") Emphasized added.

80 Cameron (2006), *supra* note 15, at 13.

## 2.5 Types of Stabilization Clauses

From a practical point of view, the foreign investor has several strategies to mitigate the risk to their investments from the measures of the host state. Structurally speaking, SCs may be divided into two categories based on how these clauses are drafted to protect the investment: traditional stabilization clauses (*stricto sensu* and intangibility clauses) and modern stabilization clauses (economic equilibrium and allocation of burden clauses). The technique for achieving the stability of the investment project regime is the basis for differentiating between classical and modern stabilization clauses.

### 2.5.1 *Traditional Stabilization Clauses*

Traditional stability provisions contain two types of stabilization clauses: stabilization clause *stricto sensu* and intangibility clause.

#### 2.5.1.1 Stabilization Clause *stricto sensu*

The stabilization clause *stricto sensu* (in its strictest form) is the more traditional approach which ties the hands of the host state during the life of the foreign investment. Such a clause may take two forms: the freezing and the non-application clause.

##### 2.5.1.1.1 *Freezing Clause*

A freezing clause is the most obvious and familiar traditional SC.[81] Such a traditional clause aims to freeze the host state's law governing the state contract, "the fiscal regime, or other necessary investment conditions" over the course of its lifespan.[82] According to this clause, the host government, contractually, promises the foreign investor that any subsequent legislation will not apply to the contract.[83] Importantly, with this type of freezing clause, the state does not waive its legislative sovereignty to enact new laws; rather it excludes the application of subsequent changes in the law to the state contract.[84] For example, the Petroleum Concession agreement between the government of Libya and the Libyan American Oil Company laid down that:

> (1) The Government of Libya will take all steps necessary to ensure that the Company enjoys all the rights conferred by this Concession. The

81 CAMERON (2010), at 70; Gjuzi (2018), at 38.
82 Waelde & Ndi (1996), at 260.
83 Faruque (2006 a), *supra* note 9, at 319.
84 *Id.*

> contractual rights expressly created by this concession shall not be altered except by the mutual consent of the parties.
>
> (2) This Concession shall throughout the period of its validity be construed in accordance with the Petroleum Law and the Regulations in force on the date of execution of the Agreement of Amendment by which this paragraph (2) was incorporated into this Concession Agreement. Any amendment to or repeal of such Regulations shall not affect the contractual rights of the Company without its consent.[85]

Another example of a freezing stabilization clause can be found in Mauritania's model production sharing contract 1994. Article 27.3 provides that:

> The Contractor shall not be subject to any legislative provision which would give rise to an aggravation, whether directly or indirectly, in the charges and obligations arising from this Contract and from the legislation and regulations in force on the date of signing this Contract, unless as mutually agreed upon by the Parties.[86]

As seen in these examples, the aim of freezing stabilization clauses is to protect the investor against the subsequent changes of the law. This clause cannot preclude the host state from exercising its sovereign right to regulate. Instead, it bans the application of the new law to the state contract with the foreign investor.

#### 2.5.1.1.2 *Non-application Clause*

The non-application clauses achieve the same legal impact as freezing clauses. Yet, in terms of their language technique, these clauses fall under a "more moderate version".[87] The non-application clause stipulates that in case of conflict between the new law and the law governing the investment contract or any provisions of the contract, the latter will prevail.[88] With the non-application clause, the host state explicitly precludes the application of subsequent

85 Libyan Am. Oil Co. (LIAMCO) v. Libyan Arab Republic, 20 I.L.M. 1 at 31 (1981).

86 ISLAMIC REPUBLIC OF MAURITANIA, PRODUCTION SHARING CONTRACT, art. 27.3 (1994) (Unofficial English Translation), https://resourcegovernance.org/sites/default/files/MauritaniaContracttypeAngl.pdf.

87 GJUZI (2018), at 40.

88 Faruque (2006 a), at 319.

non-favorable changes in the law to the state contract.[89] For example, in an Albanian mining contract, the state authority undertakes:

> [t]o guarantee the Concessionaire, also in its capacity of representative of the State as owner in the mining industry, that the legislation pursuant to which this Agreement has been concluded, shall apply during the whole concession period. The amendments to this legislation, including the entry into force of new laws, shall not be applicable, except where such amendments or new laws that enter into force, are favorable to the concessionaire.[90]

Under the non-application clause, foreign investors purport again to limit the host state's legislative power in connection with the state contract. This clause doesn't waive the host state's legislative sovereignty *per se*; rather, it excludes the applicability of subsequent legislation to the specific investment contract. From the perspective of the legal effect, while the host state's obligation under the freezing clause is implied, here, the non-application clause explicitly states that the host state undertakes not to apply inconsistent changes of its legislation to the state contract. In terms of their enforceability, any interference with non-application clauses using subsequent conflicting changes in law establishes a breach of the contract, thereby triggering the host state's compensatory duties.[91] The stabilization clause *stricto sensu,* as elaborated above, is compatible with the principle of non-retroactivity of laws.[92] As the arbitral tribunal in *LIAMCO v. Libya* held, the SC contained in clause 16 of Liamco's Concession Agreement is consistent with the principle of non-retroactivity of laws. The non-retroactivity principle denies retrospective effect to new law

---

89 GJUZI (2018), at 40–41.

90 Ber-Oner Mining Contract, Art. 7(j), approved by Law No 8761(2001) *available at* http://80.78.70.231/pls/kuv/f?p=201:Ligj:8761:02.04.2001. The Ber-Oner Mining Contract was amended by the parties in 2017 and approved by Law no. 73, dated 27 April 2017, *available at* http://www.ikub.al/LIGJE_CATEGORY2/18/03/06/PeR-MIRATIMIN-E-SHTE SeS-Se-MARReVESHJES-Se-KONCESIONIT-NDeRMJET-MINISTRISe-Se-EN-0151.aspx. (Interestingly, in the amended contract the parties kept the same original structure of the stabilization clause, while also added further stipulations, namely that "the legislation in force pursuant to which this Agreement has been concluded" shall include "not only the mining legislation", and that the state guarantees a special stabilization of the VAT, profit tax and tax on dividend as per an annex enclosed to the Contract). Gjuzi (2018), at 41.

91 Gjuzi (2018), at 42.

92 Faruque (2006 a), at 319.

and asserts the respect of vested rights (*droits acquis*) that acquired under previous statute.[93]

#### 2.5.1.2 Intangibility Clauses (Prohibition on Unilateral Changes Clauses)

An intangibility clause provides that the contractual relationship between the foreign investor and the host state cannot be amended, modified, or abrogated except with the mutual consent of the parties.[94] Although the intangibility clause might be seen as similar to the freezing clause, it freezes the investment agreement rather than the law.[95] However Professor Prosper Weil proposed a distinction between traditional SCs (freezing clause) and intangibility clause (clauses d'intangibilite) as follows:

> Stabilization clauses purport to protect the investor against the legislative risk (alea legislative), i.e., the modification of the contractual situation by a legislative act, whereas the 'clauses d'intangibilite' seeks to avert the effect of the exercise by the State of its public authority in contractual matters.[96]

An example of such a clause can be found in Article 33 of the 1967 contract between the Ruler of Abu Dhabi and three Japanese companies which provided that "[t]he mutual consent of the Ruler and the Companies shall be required to annul, or modify, the provisions of this Agreement."[97]

Another example can be found in the 1992 agreement between Yemen and a foreign investor, which provides that "Contractor shall be solely governed by the provisions of this Agreement and [the contract] may be altered or amended only by the agreement of the parties."[98]

Unlike freezing clauses and non-application clauses, an intangibility clause expressly allows the host government to change the law and regulations and

---

93 Libyan Am. Oil Co. (LIAMCO) v. Libyan Arab Republic, 20 I.L.M. 1 (1981), at 19.

94 Paasivirta, *supra* note 21, at 323.

95 CAMERON (2010), at 74.

96 Weil, *supra* note 12; Ahmed Z. El Chiati, *Protection of Investment in the Context of Petroleum Agreement, in* 204 COLLECTED COURSES OF THE HAGUE ACADEMY OF INTERNATIONAL LAW 9, 115 (1987).

97 The Concession Agreement between the Ruler of Abu Dhabi and Maruzen Oil Co. Ltd., Daikyo Oil Co. Ltd. and Nippon Mining Co. Ltd., Art. 33 (Dec. 6, 1967), ARABIAN GULF DIGITAL ARCHIVES, https://www.agda.ae/en/catalogue/tna/fco/8/899/n/1.

98 Mayfair production sharing agreement between the Ministry of Oil and Natural Resources and Yamen Mayfair Petroleum Corporation (Al Zaydiah, Block 22, Tihama Area), Art.18.2 (July. 29, 1992) (as cited in CAMERON 2010, *supra* note 9, at 74).

apply them to the investment contract, provided that mutual consent of the parties is obtained. This mutual consent feature in intangibility clauses reflects more flexibility of such clauses compared to the earlier ones. Therefore, the intangibility clause opens the door to potential negotiation and modifications of the contract, which are excluded by freezing and non-application clauses.[99]

Regarding its legal effect, the intangibility clause doesn't differ from the earlier forms. Although technically, the intangibility clause offers a moderate formulation, it aims to neutralize sovereignty by imposing upon the host state a duty to obtain the foreign investor's consent before applying any changes of law to the investment contract. If the host state fails to secure such consent, it must include an exemption in the subsequent law or otherwise ensure that such changes are not implemented by the foreign investor. Finally, breaching an intangibility clause by the host state considers a breach of contract triggering the host state's compensatory duties, the same consequences as in the case of SCs *stricto sensu*.[100]

Importantly, the intangibility clause has a distinctive feature. By requiring mutual consent, it establishes a procedural mechanism for discussion between the parties about the future of the state contract.[101]

### 2.5.2 *Modern Stabilization Clauses*

Modern stabilization clauses, as tools to protect a foreign investment, address stability in a different manner concerned neither with changes of the law *per se* nor with the "quest for mutual consent as such," but with the economic impacts that the foreign investor may suffer as a consequence of these changes.[102] The two primary forms of modern stabilization clauses are …

#### 2.5.2.1 Economic Equilibrium Clauses (Rebalancing of Benefits)

Economic equilibrium clauses or balancing clauses stipulate that if the host state enacts new legislation or takes new measures subsequent to the conclusion of the investment contract that adversely affect the rights of foreign investors, a re-balancing shall take place. Accordingly, the provisions of the agreement will be readjusted by itself or through re-negotiation so that the host state will restore the economic loss of the foreign investor. Unlike the freezing stabilization clause, the economic equilibrium clause does not impose a prohibition on alterations to the legal and fiscal regimes governing a project.

99 GJUZI (2018), at 43.
100 *Id*, at 44.
101 CAMERON (2010), at 74.
102 GJUZI (2018), at 45.

Instead, it contemplates that in the event of such modifications, the contracting parties shall be reinstated to the position they held prior to the occurrence of said changes.[103] The foreign investor, therefore, will enjoy the same financial position that it was in at the time of the contract.[104] An example of a balancing provision can be found in article 17.1 of the Vietnamese Model Production Sharing Contract of 2004, which provides that

> If after the effective date, existing laws and regulations are amended or annulled, or new laws and regulations are introduced in Vietnam ... in any case adversely affecting the economic rights or benefits expected by the contractor from this contract ... the parties shall meet and consult promptly with each other and make such changes to this contract as are necessary both to maintain the Contractor's rights, benefits, and interests hereunder and to ensure that any revenues or incomes or profits ... derived or to be derived under this contract ... shall not in any way be diminished as a result of such changes.[105]

Similarly, the Model Production Sharing Contract issued by the autonomous Kurdistan Region of Iraq stipulates that:

> The obligations of the CONTRACTOR in respect of this Contract shall not be changed by the GOVERNMENT and the general and overall equilibrium between the Parties under this Contract shall not be affected in a substantial and lasting manner.
>
> The GOVERNMENT guarantees to the CONTRACTOR, for the entire duration of this Contract, that it will maintain the stability of the legal, fiscal and economic conditions of this Contract, as they result from this Contract and as they result from the laws and regulations in force on the date of signatureof this Contract. The CONTRACTOR has entered into this Contract on the basis of the legal, fiscal and economic framework prevailing at the Effective date. If, at any time after the Effective Date, there is any change in the legal, fiscal and/oreconomic framework under

---

103 *See* Evaristus Oshionebo, *Stabilization Clauses in Natural Resource Extraction Contracts: Legal, Economic and Social Implications for Developing Countries*, 10 ASPER REV. INT'L BUS. & TRADE L. 1, 4 (2010).

104 *Id.* at 46; CAMERON (2010), at 74–75; Faruque (2006 a), at 320.

105 Vietnam Model Production Sharing Contract 2004 Art. 17.1, Basic Oil Law and Concession Contracts, Barrows Supplement (Asia and Australasia) Supp. No 164, at 130 (as cited in Faruque (2006 a), *supra* note 9, at 320–321.).

> the Kurdistan Region Law or other Law applicable in or to the Kurdistan Region which detrimentally affects the CONTRACTOR, the CONTRACTOR Entities or any other Person entitled to benefits under this Contract, the terms and conditions of the Contract shall be altered so as to restore the CONTRACTOR, the CONTRACTOR Entities and any other Person entitled to benefits under this Contract to the same overall economic position (taking into account home country taxes) as that which such Person would have been in, had no such change in the legal, fiscal and/or economic framework occurred.[106]

The economic stabilization clause constitutes a remedial measure aimed at the indemnification of the economic repercussions arising from legislative actions, rather than preempting their enactment. This form of economic stabilization clause pursues the re-establishment of the contractual relationship by providing compensation to the affected private party to cover incurred losses adequately.[107] Economic stabilization clauses are increasingly favored due to their restrictive nature and their endeavor to strike a balance between the state's legislative autonomy and the legitimate expectations of private investors. These clauses do not outrightly preclude the introduction of new regulations that modify the governing laws of a contract but rather aim to mitigate the adverse consequences of such regulatory changes. The primary aim of an economic stabilization clause is to uphold the financial balance of the contract as originally envisioned at the time of its formation. This equilibrium takes into account multiple elements, such as the contractual term's definition, the surrounding context, and any voluntary adjustments made by the parties during the contractual association.[108]

In the event of subsequent legislation impacting the contract's economic balance, mitigation can be achieved through compensation payment to the affected party. However, economic equilibrium may not necessarily involve a direct payment of monetary sums to the affected party. Instead, economic equilibrium could be reached by offsetting the expenses incurred in adhering to the modifications brought about by alterations in the legal and/or fiscal frameworks, or by making adjustments to the tariffs payable by the company. Another approach to achieve economic equilibrium could be through an

106 The Kurdistan Regional Government of Iraq, Model Production Sharing Contract, arts. 43.2, 43.3 (2007), *available at* https://www.resourcecontracts.org/contract/ocds-591adf-6005604716/download/pdf.

107 Faruque (2006 a), at 331.

108 *Id.* at 332.

extension of the concession's duration or by reducing the taxes and royalties owed by the company to the host country.[109]

> Additionally, economic equilibrium may be attained by compelling the involved parties to engage in good faith negotiations to amend the contract in a manner that restores the intended economic equilibrium as envisioned in the resource concession contract. For example, Article XIX (Stabilization) of the model Concession Agreement for gas and crude oil exploration and exploitation in Egypt Provides that:In case of changes in existing legislation or regulations applicable to the conduct of Exploration, Development and production of Petroleum, which take place after the Effective Date, and which significantly affect the economic interest of this Agreement to the detriment of CONTRACTOR or which imposes on CONTRACTOR an obligation to remit to the A.R.E. the proceeds from sales of CONTRACTOR's Petroleum, CONTRACTOR shall notify EGPC of the subject legislative or regulatory measure and also the consequent effects upon issuing legislation or regulation which impact on the stabilization. In such case, the Parties shall negotiate possible modifications to this Agreement designed to restore the economic balance thereof which existed on the Effective Date. The Parties shall use their best efforts to agree on amendments to this Agreement within ninety (90) days from aforesaid notice.[110]

In case the parties could not agree on the measures that required to restore the economic equilibrium, the matter may be submitted to the arbitrator as stipulated in the terms and conditions outlined within the concession contract.[111]

#### 2.5.2.2 Allocation of Burden Clauses

Allocation of burden clauses provide that in case of any unilateral changes in the legal or regulatory framework applicable to the state contract, the clause shifts the burden, that the investor might bear, as a result of the contract's unilateral intervention, to the state or state-entity.[112] Interestingly, the allocation of burden clause may look like the economic balancing clauses that "specify

---

109 Oshionebo, *supra* note 103, at 6.

110 Egypt, Model Concession Agreement for Petroleum Exploration and Exploitation (2017). *Available at* https://s3.amazonaws.com/rgi-documents/18826eb7d13cfd736e24f7da74756 98150218b07.pdf.

111 Oshionebo, *supra* note 103, at 6.

112 CAMERON (2010), at 80.

the means of offset."[113] As one commentator stated, the allocation of burden clauses are "close cousins of economic balancing provisions."[114] However, there are two main differences that distinguish the allocation of burden clause and equilibrium form of balancing. First, while the economic equilibrium clause is intended to maintain the economic benefits of the original bargain among the parties,[115] in the allocation of burden clause, no rebalancing or amendment of the state contract is implied. Instead, these clauses transfer the economic effect of the subsequent change of law to the other contracting party (the state or state-entity).[116] Second, in the economic equilibrium clause, the contract may be rebalancing automatically or through negotiation of the parties without actual amendment of the original contract. In contrast, the allocation of burden clause requires the state or state-entity to take a specific action upon the occurrence of the triggering event.[117] This remedial action often involves payment of any additional tax or royalty from the state's oil company's (in petroleum contract) share of oil on behalf of the foreign corporation.[118] An example of allocation of burden clauses can be found in the Production Sharing Agreement (PSA) of the Kurdistan Regional Government (KRG). It reads: "The government shall indemnify each contractor entity upon demand against any liability to pay any taxes, duties, levies, changes impositions or withholdings assessed or imposed upon such entity which relate to any of the exemptions granted by the government under this Article 31.1."[119] Article 31.1, as elaborated hereinabove, exempts the foreign project from all the taxes listed, except the income tax which the state pays on its behalf.[120] Another example of this can be found in the Egyptian model concession agreement, in which Article XVIII (c) reads that: Except as provided in Article III (g) for Income Taxes, EGPC, Contractor and Operating Company shall be exempted from all taxes and duties, whether imposed by the government or municipalities including among others, sales tax, value-added tax and taxes on the

113 *Id.*

114 Frank Alexander, *Comment on Articles on Stabilization by Piero Bernardini, Lorenzo Cotula and AFM Maniruzzaman.* 2 J. World Energy L & Bus, 243 (Nov. 1, 2009), *available at* https://doi-org.eres.qnl.qa/10.1093/jwelb/jwp015.

115 CAMERON (2010), at 74; ERKAN (2010), at 107.

116 CAMERON (2010), at 80; Gjuzi (2018), at 52.

117 *Id.*

118 *Id.*

119 CONSTANTINE PARTASIDES QC & LUCY MARTINEZ, *Of Taxes and Stabilisation, in* THE GUIDE TO ENERGY ARBITRATIONS 60 (J William Rowley QC 2d ed. 2019). For other examples involving Algeria and Azerbaijan, *see* CAMERON (2010), at 80–81.

120 CAMERON (2010), at 80.

exploration, development, extracting, producing, exporting or transporting of Petroleum and LPG as well as any and all withholding taxes that might otherwise be imposed on dividends, interest, technical service fees, patent, and trademark royalties, and similar items. Contractor shall also be exempted from any tax on the liquidation of the contractor, or distributions of any income to the shareholders of the contractor, and from any tax on capital.[121]

### 2.5.3 *Hybrid Stabilization Clauses*

The methods employed by these different stabilization clauses, as elaborated above, can be combined in one clause, or provided separately in one contract. An example of a combination clause can be found in Azerbaijan's Shah Deniz contract. Article 23.2:

> The rights and interests accruing to contractor (or its assignees) under this Agreement … shall not be amended, modified, or reduced without the prior consent of the contractor [*intangibility clause*]. In the event that any governmental authority invokes any present or future law, treaty, intergovernmental agreement, decree or administrative order which contravenes the provisions of this Agreement or adversely or positively affects the rights or interests of Contractor hereunder, including, but not limited to, any changes in tax legislation, regulations, or administrative practice, or jurisdictional changes pertaining to the contract area, the terms of this Agreement shall be adjusted to re-establish the economic equilibrium of the parties[*balancing clause*], and if the rights or interests of Contractor have been adversely affected, then SOCAR (Azeri state oil company) shall indemnify contractor (and its assignees) for any disbenefit, deterioration in economic circumstances, loss or damages that ensue therefrom[*allocation burden clause*].[122]

In sum, despite the great diversity of SCs, they all share the same purpose: to prohibit the application of the subsequent statutory or regulatory acts of the host state that change the legal situation of the foreign investor.[123]

---

121 Natural Resource Governance Institute, CONCESSION AGREEMENT FOR PETROLEUM EXPLORATION AND EXPLOITATION BETWEEN THE ARAB REPUBLIC OF EGYPT AND THE EGYPTIAN GENERAL PETROLEUM CORPORATION XVIII, https://www.resourcedata.org/document/rgi-concession-agreement-model-for-petroleum-exploration-and-exploitation.

122 CAMERON (2010), at 81.

123 WOLFGANG PETER, ARBITRATION AND RENEGOTIATION OF INTERNATIONAL INVESTMENT AGREEMENTS 214 (2d ed. 1995).

## 2.6 At What Point Are Stabilization Clauses Typically Included in State Contracts? (an Analysis Using Statistical Methods)

A critical empirical study, "Stabilization Clauses and Human Rights," was conducted in 2008 by Andrea Shemberg for the International Finance Corporation (IFC) and U.N. Special Representative to Secretary General on Business and Human Rights, Professor John Ruggie.[124] This study found that freezing clauses continue to be used in the state contracts in Sub-Saharan Africa, Eastern Europe, Southern Europe, Central Asia, the Middle East and North Africa.[125] 12 of 76 contracts in these countries covering the 1990s and 2000s had some form of freezing clauses, meaning that almost 16% of state contracts concluded at the time in the sample contained some form of freezing stabilization clauses.[126] In contrast, no contract from OECD countries (Organization for Economic Co-operation and Development) contained either full or limited freezing clauses. SCs in the OECD contracts and models take the forms of finite economic equilibrium clauses, which are relatively rare in the contracts from Sub-Saharan Africa, the Middle East, North Africa, Eastern Europe, Southern Europe, and Central Asia.[127] The manifestation of this is elaborated in Table 1, which provides a listing of investment contracts used in the study by region, and Figure 1 shows the types of SCs contained in contracts used in the study.

The preceding study emphasizes that only 16% of state contracts concluded at the time in the sample contained some form of freezing stabilization clauses. In comparison, almost 72% of the contracts contained some form of modern SCs. This result, therefore, indicates that the role of traditional SCs lost ground in favor of modern SCs, which have been seen as an essential tool to strike a fair balance between stability and flexibility of long-term investment contracts.

## 2.7 Validity and Legal Effect of Traditional Stabilization Clauses

A choice of law clause contained in the investment contracts plays a vital role in determining the validity and legal effect of SCs. In other words, the validity and legal effect of the SCs rely heavily upon the law applicable to the state contract. There are three possible scenarios with regards to the applicable law in a contract. The first is where the contract is subject to the national law of the

124 U.N. IFC report *supra* note 35.
125 *Id*, at 17.
126 *Id*, at 19.
127 *Id*, at 17.

TABLE 1 Stabilization clauses in modern state contracts, by region[a]

| Region | Full freezing | Partial freezing | Full econ. equilibrium | Partial econ. equilibrium | Full hybrid | Partial hybrid | None | Total |
|---|---|---|---|---|---|---|---|---|
| East Asia & Pacific | 1 | 0 | 5 | 5 | 0 | 0 | 1 | 12 |
| Eastern, Southern Europe & Central Asia | 0 | 1 | 2 | 1 | 2 | 3 | 1 | 10 |
| Latin America & Caribbean | 0 | 1 | 7 | 9 | 0 | 0 | 0 | 17 |
| The Middle East & N. Africa | 1 | 2 | 6 | 2 | 0 | 1 | 1 | 13 |
| OECD | 0 | 0 | 2 | 6 | 0 | 0 | 0 | 8 |
| South Asia | 0 | 1 | 2 | 2 | 0 | 0 | 0 | 5 |
| Sub-Saharan Africa | 4 | 1 | 3 | 3 | 0 | 0 | 0 | 10 |
| Total Contracts | 6 | 6 | 27 | 28 | 2 | 4 | 3 | 76 |

a *Id,* at 18, tbl6.1.

SOURCE: ANDREA SHEMBERG, *ID.*

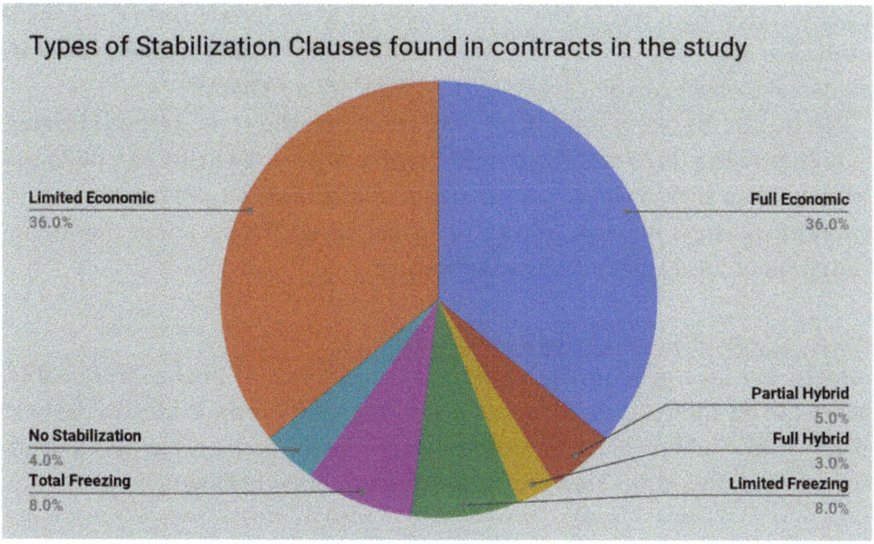


FIGURE 1 Shows the type of stabilization clauses
*Id.* at 20, Figure 6.1.
SOURCE: ANDREA SHEMBERG, *ID.*

host state. The second is where the contract is exclusively governed by international law, general principles of law, or principles of law common to multiple countries. The third scenario involves the contract being governed by domestic law, with the possibility of resorting to international law if necessary, or a combination of both domestic law and international law, as well as decisions made by international tribunals.[128]

Notably, before embarking upon a detailed consideration of the validity and legal impact of SCs, a caveat is made here. This section focuses mainly on the traditional SCs and does not intend to address the validity or legal effect of other types of SCs.

### 2.7.1 *Validity and Legal Effect of Stabilization Clauses under Domestic Law*

If the domestic law of the host state governs the contract, then the SC should be consistent with the constitutional and legal requirements of the local law. In other words, the legal validity and effect of the SC under national law depend on the constitutional and statutory constraints on the contractual capacity of

128 Faruque (2006 a), *supra* note 9, at 333.

the host state. As a result, the SC cannot modify or detract from the constitutional or statutory powers of government and legislature to make commitments not to exercise their sovereign and legislation rights.[129]

Practically, the host government may argue that the SC is an invalid clause under *ultra vires* doctrine. The manifestations of such doctrine can be found in many ways such as unconstitutionality of stabilization provisions, lack of power of the state officials, and institutional disagreement about the implementation of local laws, as elaborated below.

#### 2.7.1.1 Unconstitutionality of Stabilization Provisions

Notably, the host government could, on the grounds of unconstitutionality, invoke the invalidity of the SC contained in the state contract. Ideally, the host government could invoke two long-standing constitutional principles to challenge the validity of SC. These principles are elaborated below.

##### 2.7.1.1.1 *Principle of Separation of Power (Legislative, Executive, and Judicial)*

The violation of this constitutional principle can occur when the government (the executive branch) enters into an investment contract with a foreign investor which contains a SC. When this occurs, the legislative branch is prohibited from enacting subsequent laws or exempting the contract from the applicability of new laws where such laws adversely affect the investment contract. Thus, this contractual commitment would result in conflict between two separate powers of the host state, thereby putting the validity of the SC in doubt as a result of a violation of the constitutional principle of separation of powers.[130] An example of this issue can be found in the ICC case between an African state and a foreign investor.[131] In this case, the government had entered into a concession agreement with a foreign investor that contained a SC whereby the government would create specific legislation for the investment project that would last for ten years. A new government was formed later and argued for the nullity of the concession agreement that the former government concluded with a foreign investor. The new government based its argument on three specific principals, *inter alia*, the former government which had concluded this concession was acting *ultra vires*. The government argued that the grant of such commitments was a matter for Parliament, not executive authority. The tribunal, however, rejected the government's arguments and upheld the concession agreement, including the SC. The arbitral tribunal found that

---

129 Wadele & Ndi (1996), at 238–239.
130 GJUZI (2018), at 191.
131 This unpublished case is discussed in CAMERON (2010), at 91–92.

the tribunal should apply to the contract the principle of international law that a state cannot rely upon its own domestic law to avoid its international obligations.[132]

#### 2.7.1.1.2 *Principle of Public Interest*

Furthermore, a state, as a matter of constitutional theory, must act for the benefit of the public. Thus, it may not be possible, theoretically, for the state to bind itself by a contract with a foreign party to "fetter its legislative power."[133] It is argued that the host state authorities carry out their programs and policies under the auspices of the public interest. Thus, any contractual provisions that may detract the power of host state authorities which are aimed at the public interest, could be void based on unconstitutionality.[134]

This argument seems to be one of the reasons behind the decision of the Federal High Court of Nigeria, in *Niger Delta Development v. Nigeria Liquefied Natural Gas Company Ltd*,[135] when addressing the issue of the validity of legislative stability provisions.[136] The court found that the SC is unconstitutional

132 *See* CAMERON (2010), at 91–92.

133 M. SORNARAJAH, THE INTERNATIONAL LAW ON FOREIGN INVESTMENT 282–283 (3rd.ed. 2010).

134 GJUZI (2018), at 194 (noting that "[t]he origins of this principle are found in the doctrine of executive necessity in which the court relied on in its decision of *Amphitrite v. The King* (1921)." In this case, the court concluded that: "it is not competent for the government to fetter its future executive action, which must necessarily be determined by the needs of the community when the question arises. It cannot by contract hamper its freedom of action in matters which concern the welfare of the State."). *See also Amphitrite v. The King* (1921) 3 KB 500. All ER Rep 542, p. 503. At a time of war, a British government contract with a Swedish steamship company contained an undertaking that the ship would not be detained in a British port. Yet the government withdrew the undertaking, and the Amphitrite ship was detained by the British government causing losses to the Swedish company. The High Court that addressed the Company's petition for damages, held that such a government contract was not enforceable because it was not within the competence of the Crown to make a contract which would have the effect of limiting its power of action in the future; GJUZI (2018), at 194.

135 Niger Delta Development Commission v. Nigeria Liquefied Natural Gas Company Limited, Suit Number FHC/PH/CS/313/2005, unreported Judgment, 11 July 2007 [Niger Delta Case (Judgment 2007)]. For the fact and analysis of the case, *see* Bayo Adaralegbe, *Stabilizing Fiscal Regime in Long Term Contracts: Recent Development in Nigeria*, 3 J. World Energy L & Bus. 239(2008); GJUZI (2018), at 195.

136 The Schedule II. Section 9 of Nigeria Liquefied Natural Gas (LNG) (Fiscal Incentives, Guarantees and Assurances) Act 39/1990 (as amended), provides that [T]he guarantees, and assurances are as follows… ("2. The venture shall be subject to the fiscal regime contained in the provisions of this Act. Such fiscal regime shall not be amended in any way, except with the prior written agreement of the Government, the Company and each of the Company's shareholders."); ("3 … neither the Company nor its shareholders in their

and contrary to the principle of the rule of law because it restricted the legislature's power to regulate, which is inconsistent with the Nigerian constitution that empowers the legislature to enact laws for the good of all Nigerian citizens.[137] In the words of the court:

> [h]owever, the provision on New Laws under Schedule II paragraph 3, I find, and hold is against the tenets of the Rule of Law .... This particular provision is very wide and not consistent with the tenets of the constitutional provision which allows the National Assembly to make laws for the good of all people of this country .... I sincerely hope that the legislation per National Assembly will look at that paragraph of the Second Schedule of Nigeria LNG to ensure conformity as this Court can only interpret/expound, not change the law.[138]

In *the Movement for Quality Government in Israel v. Prime Minister*,[139] the Israeli High Court of Justice addressed the legal validity of a stabilization clause. The court provides significant insights on the relationship between foreign investors' rights and host state's freedom to regulate; the court also raised the question of whether the government (the executive power) had the authority to commit to such a clause, where there is a basic administrative law rule prohibiting the restriction of an authority's discretion. The court concluded that the stabilization clause was invalid because it unduly restricted present and future governments' freedom to regulate the gas market, thus being undemocratic

---

capacity as shareholders in the Company, shall in any way be subject to new laws, regulations, taxes, duties, imposts or charges of whatever nature which are not applicable generally to companies incorporated in Nigeria."); ("6. .... the Government further agrees to ensure that the said guarantees, assurances and undertakings shall not be suspended, modified, or revoked during the life of the venture except with the mutual agreement of the Government and the shareholders of the Company.") *See* Nigeria Liquefied Natural Gas (LNG) (Fiscal Incentives, Guarantees and Assurances) Act 39/1990(as amended), *available at* https://www.nigerialng.com/the-company/Shared%20Documents/NLNG%20ACT.pdf.

137 Oshionebo, *supra* note 103, at 12. However, the current arbitral practice shows a different picture of upholding validity of stabilization provisions as a matter of national law. *See* discussion *infra* pp. 49–66.

138 Niger Delta Case (Judgment 2007), *at* 32; *See also* Adaralegbe, *supra* note 139 at 240. The Nigerian Appeals Court dismissed appealed claim. *See*, Niger Delta Development Commission v. Nigeria Liquefied Natural Gas Company Limited, Suit Number CA/PH/520/2007, 2 Dec 2010. https://lawcarenigeria.com/niger-delta-development-commission-v-nigeria-liquified-natural-gas-limited-2010/.

139 The Movement for Quality Government v. Israeli Prime Minister (2016) (Isr.) HCJ 4374/15. [hereinafter, Movement for Quality Government v. Israeli Prime Minister, 2016].

and unconstitutional.[140] The court examined: The stabilization clause in this chapter of the framework, in which the government undertakes for a decade to not only not legislate but to also fight any legislation against the framework's provisions, was decided without authority—and as such is rejected. It was made in contrast to the general principle of administrative law regarding the prohibition of shackling the authority's ability to govern. The government does not have the power to decide not to decide and not to act. [This is especially where the government seeks to limit the discretion of the subsequent government] … whose composition and ideology will be different than this one's.[141]

#### 2.7.1.2 Unconstitutionality of the National Law

If the municipal law that authorized the stabilization clause was judicially unconstitutional and void because it fettered the legislature power to make laws, it therefore follows that the SC signed by the host government under the unconstitutional law is itself void and ineffective under national law.[142] However, it has been argued that, once an agreement is made, a host state is precluded from relying on its municipal laws to invalidate the SC contains thereof. In the *Sapphire v. NIOC* arbitration case, Judge Cavin, a sole arbitrator, concluded that a foreign investor cannot be expected to aware of all the laws of the host state.[143]

#### 2.7.1.3 Lack of Power of State Officials

An argument can be advanced by the host government that their officials who signed the contract with foreign investors had no authority to undertake stability commitments under an investment contract. In *Egypt v. SPP*,[144] the court of appeals of Paris held that Egypt does not become a party to a contract

---

140 *See* Rachel Frid de Vries, *supra* note 8; *See also* GJUZI (2018), at 196.

141 Movement for Quality Government v. Israeli Prime Minister, 2016, *supra* note 143. (As cited in Gjuzi, *supra* note 2, at 196); *See also*, Arie Reich, *Israel's Foreign Investment Protection Regime in View of Developments in Its Energy Sector*. EUI Working Papers 2017/02, at 14, *available at* httpc://cadmus.eui.eu/handle/1814/45005.

142 *Id.*

143 SORNARAJAH (2010), *supra* note 137, at 283–284. (Sornarajah, further, indicated that the origin of such rule is derived particularly from the ICC arbitrations practice, accordingly the state cannot make an ultra-vires defense based on its own laws). *See also* GJUZI (2018), at 205 n. 94.

144 Court of Appeals of Paris Decision in Arab Republic of Egypt v. Southern Pacific Properties, Ltd. et al. (Appellate Review of Arbitral Awards between States and Private Parties), 23 I.L.M. 1048 (1984).

concluded between Southern Pacific Properties (Middle East) and EGOTH, which is an Egyptian government entity, merely because the minister of tourism signed the contract in his capacity as EGOTH's supervisory. Accordingly, the state officials do not have the power to commit their state as such, to obligations under the contract with a private party.[145]

#### 2.7.1.4 Institutional Disagreement

In some countries that are suffering from a weak rule of law and significant domestic political issues, disagreement between state institutions about the interpretation and implementation of local laws often occur. In that case, a host state may challenge the validity of stabilization commitments under the ground of institutional disagreement about the interpretation of domestic laws and procedural requirements for the approval of state contracts. A notable example here can be found in the 2008 agreement between the Iraqi Oil Ministry and Royal Dutch Shell in which the institutional contravention occurred between the Iraqi Parliament (legislative authority) and the government (executive authority) regarding the validity of such a contract. In 2009, the Parliamentary committee on oil and gas held that this agreement was illegal because the parliament had not approved it.[146] Another example can be found in the 2005 agreement that was concluded by Est Mediterranean Gas (EMG), a joint Egyptian Israeli venture, to supply Israel with Egyptian natural gas over a period of fifteen years. The Egyptian oil minister made the decree No. 100 of 2004, whereby the Egyptian government would supply 1.7bcm of gas to Israel through the EMG. In 2008, the gas exports began amidst sharp criticism, because the price was underpriced, and the agreement was not approved by the Egyptian parliament. The government argued before the Egyptian administrative court that the transaction was a private business matter and therefore, not subject to the parliament's approval.[147] The administrative court did not agree with the government's arguments. The court held that the agreement was void and null, as it was inconsistent with the constitution, which requires such state contracts to be approved by the parliament.[148] However, the supreme administrative court reversed this judgment and held that the

---

145 SORNARAJAH (2010), *supra* note 137, at 283–284; *see also* GJUZI (2018), at 192 n. 31.

146 For a comprehensive analysis of institutional disagreement as ground to challenge stabilization clauses, *see* CAMERON (2010), at 64–65.

147 *Id.*

148 Mahkama al-Qada al-Idari [Administrative Court], Case No 33418, Session of 18 Nov. 2008, year 62 (Egypt).

agreement was valid and constitutional as the government acted in its role as a sovereign power.[149]

From the preceding discussion, it can be asserted that the host government's undertakings must be given in a form that is consistent with constitutional and legislative requirements.[150] Therefore, when the host government enters into a state contract with a foreign investor without sufficient authority, such contract is *ultra vires* and void.[151] As a result, a SC contained therein might be found null and void. Importantly, foreign investors, to avoid the nullity of stabilization commitments, have a due diligence obligation to ascertain the inconsistency of SC under host state's legal framework.[152] If a foreign investor failed to do that, then their argument that they had a legitimate expectation in the validity of such provisions might be unacceptable. As put by Professors Waelde and Ndi, "[c]lauses negotiated under the shadow of *ultra vires* and constitutional invalidity cannot generate valid rights simply by appearance or legitimate reliance on the state agency's contracting powers."[153] Based thereon, if a host state's national law authorizes the government agency to enter into a state contract with a SC, then arguments about the validity of such clause can hardly be raised, at least *ex ante*.[154] In this vein, Professors El-Kosheri and Riad noted that "[i]n fact, the legality of the stabilization clauses can only be established on the basis of a public law rule which authorizes the contracting governmental party to include such clauses in the development agreement and to be bound thereby."[155]

In sum, the validity and legal effect of the SC under host state's national law relies heavily on the legal system of each country.[156] No arguments can be advanced by the host state about validity of the SC, if its national law clearly

149 Al-Mahkama al-Idariyah al-Ulya [Supreme Administrative Court], Case No 5546, Session of 27 Feb. 2010, year 55 (Egypt).

150 Cameron (2006), *supra* note 15, at 13. (noting that "any undertakings given by the host country government must be given in a form that is consistent with the country's legal and constitutional framework. In most countries (including the UK, for example), the executive cannot give binding commitments about taxes or rates of taxation in the future.").

151 Waelde & Ndi (1996), at 235.

152 In this regard, a foreign investor is strongly recommended to carefully review the constitution and other applicable laws of the host state to confirm that the stability provisions valid under host state national law.

153 Waelde & Ndi (1996), at 239.

154 *Id.*

155 Ahmed S El-Kosheri & Tarek F. Riad, *The Law Governing a New Generation of Petroleum Agreements: Changes in the Arbitration Process*. 1 ICSID Rev. Foreign Inv.L.J, 257, 266(1986).

156 GJUZI (2018), at 204.

admits SC in contracts.[157] However, even if the SC is found to be valid under a host state's national law, the future effect of such clause is in the hand of the host state's legislative power.[158] Given the above discussion, Professors Waelde and Ndi aptly summarized some significant conclusions:

(a) The provisions of stability under municipal law may often be invalid *ab initio*. In this case, no remedies can be granted for the injured foreign investor. The foreign investor cannot claim indemnification for the damage suffered based on a legitimate expectation in the validity of the SC. The clauses agreed under *ultra vires* (beyond the scope of the power) cannot grant valid rights merely by legitimate reliance on the contracting powers of the state-entity.[159]

(b) If stabilization clauses are found valid *ab initio,* their continuing legal effect remains in the hands of the national legislature of the host state. The legislature may revoke the governing law by subsequent legislation in which the foreign investor may claim compensation based on their legitimate expectations arising from the existence of stabilization clauses.[160]

(c) There may be one effect of SCs under national law, and that is a guide to interpretation. An explicit SC can be understood by its wording and meaning that the unilateral action of the host state needs to be exercised through sovereign action "the legislature." This formal action of the intervention of a state contract would establish significant protection for the investment project.[161]

### 2.7.2 *Validity and Legal Effect of Stabilization Clauses under International Law*

If international law is the applicable law to the state contract,[162] then the most critical question concerns the validity and impact of such clauses under international law. While arbitral tribunals have upheld the validity and legal effects

157 ERKAN (2010), at 111.

158 Waelde & Ndi (1996), at 239.

159 Waelde & Ndi (1996), at 239.

160 *Id.*

161 *Id.* at 239–240.

162 Indeed, international law is not itself applicable to investor-state agreement. The foreign investor, to avoid national law of the host state to govern the investment contract, will try to seek to internationalize the contract by choosing international law as the applicable law to the investment agreement. *Id.* at 241.

of CSCs, there is a considerable divergence of views on this question among international legal scholars and jurists, summarized below.

#### 2.7.2.1 Stabilization Clauses within Doctrinal Discussions

Scholarly opinion has remained sharply divided over the question of the precise status and impact of such clauses. There are three approaches adopted by scholars: the acceptance of SCs as being valid clauses, the dismissal of SCs as being invalid clauses, and the 'middle ground' view, which accepts the validity of SCs, but denies them full effect. The arbitral jurisprudence and arbitral awards have supported this middle-ground view.

##### 2.7.2.1.1 *Trends in Favor of the Validity of Stabilization Clauses Approach*

According to this first approach, SCs are valid under international law for many reasons. First, the SC is a manifestation of the parties' autonomy of will because the parties agreed on the SC by their mutual consent; then, the parties shall intend such provisions to be valid undertakings.[163] Second, when the host state enters into a state contract, which includes a SC, it must be legal under the law of the host state, and hereby the host state can renounce the exercise of other public law prerogatives. Therefore, by undertaking the obligation of stability, the host is granting certain legislative immunity to the foreign investor.[164] Third, in subscribing to the SC, the host state has established to the benefit of the foreign investor a legitimate expectation. Thus, based on the principle of estoppel, a host state should not violate its promises, which the foreign investor has relied on.[165] Fourth, the SC is valid under the principle of sanctity of contract: *pacta sunt servanda*,[166] and accordingly, if the state can bind itself by a treaty with another state, then it may also bind itself by a contract with a private party. Finally, according to this school of thought, when the investment contract contains a SC, this means that the contract has an international character. The overseas investor, when contracting with the state, acquires a quasi-international legal personality. Such personality entails that all rights and obligations of the parties under that contract are to be governed by international law;[167] accordingly, any violation of such agreement by

163 Faruque (2006 a), *supra* note 9, at 323.

164 *Id*; El-Kosheri &Riad, *supra* note 159.

165 PETER, *supra* note 123, at 225; Faruque (2006 a), *supra* note 9, at 323.

166 *Pacta Sunt Servanda*, BLACK'S LAW DICTIONARY 1133 (7th ed. 1999) (Latin "agreement must be kept". The rule that agreements and stipulations, esp. those contained in treaties, must be observed.).

167 Texaco Overseas Petroleum Co./California Asiatic Oil Co. v. Libyan Arab Republic, 17 I.L.M. 3, 49 (1977); GJUZI (2018), at 216.

the host state constitutes an internationally wrongful act, which applies evenly to the investment agreement itself and the SC contained therein.[168]

If the SC, according to the foregoing approach, is valid under international law, then one should now ask the very pertinent question concerning the legal effect of the existence of stabilization provisions in the state contract. If international law were applicable, could the host state unilaterally mandate or terminate the investment agreement that contains such stabilization promise?

No clear answer has been given in this regard, although two opinions emerged among jurists and arbitrators. The first opinion asserts that SC have no additional value in state contracts; these clauses are just a drafting technique to make the agreement "doubly safe."[169] Therefore, SCs, according to those who subscribe to this school of thought, are a corollary of *pacta sunt servanda* that would be subjected to the same constraints as those in *pacta sunt servanda* such as considerations of public interest or change of circumstances.[170] Accordingly, the presence of a SC in the state contract does not necessarily prevent the host state from unilaterally amending or terminating the investment contract for the purpose of public interest. The second opinion argues that SCs have been deemed as an exception to the principle of public interest as a justification for intervention of the host state in the investment project. Thus, the presence of the SC in a state contract means that the state voluntarily binds itself to exercise its right to act in the public interest.[171] According to this latter opinion, when the host state breaches the state contract and stabilization guarantee contained therein, then such action would be considered illegal by its very nature, regardless of whether the act of the host state relates to the public interest. As a result, the arbitral tribunal should order comprehensive compensation to the injured party.

##### 2.7.2.1.1.1 Analyzing the Validity Approach

Indeed, there are several difficulties in accepting the principle of sanctity of contract (*pacta sunt servanda*) as a general principle of law applicable to the contractual relationship between the host state and foreign investors. The notion of the sanctity of contract is taken from laws applicable to private contracts, whereas state contracts are public contracts because the state or state-entity is a party of such agreements. The concepts of "administrative" and "public" contracts reflect the necessary accommodation of public interests

---

168 Wadele & Ndi (1996), at 243.

169 *Id.*

170 *Id.* at 244; GJUZI (2018), at 234.

171 Wadele & Ndi (1996), at 244.

and the interests of individuals of the host state. Given the fact that the state or state agency is a contractor party, such contracts have different characteristics compared to ordinary private contracts. The manifestations of this distinguishability are the right of the administration to terminate its contract unilaterally in the public interest. Thus, the protection that the foreign investors enjoy against the host state cannot be granted to them, *de facto* and *de jure*, by their home state.[172] Moreover, the principle of sanctity of contract deprives the state, once it entered into the contract with the foreign investor, of its status as a legal person in public law along with all its other power as a result of such status. Furthermore, the state contract is often a long-term contract governing a foreign project that takes several years to complete. Therefore, saying that the host state is absolutely prohibited from applying any subsequent legislation over the state contract containing a SC could lead to a freeze of its own legal system. Indeed, the freezing of the host state's legal system is not commensurate with the role it is to play in the development of the rule of law to suit the change of circumstances.[173]

Also, saying that the state's sovereignty and its contractual rights are incompatible means that when the state enters into a contract with the foreign investor, such agreement accordingly restricts the sovereignty of the state and prevents it from interfering with the contract unilaterally. Practically, however, such an assumption is fundamentally mistaken because the state, even if the state contract contains a SC, has the right to mandate it unilaterally for a public purpose.[174] The state also can apply the new law to the contract containing the stability provisions in response to the public interest. Furthermore, the principle of sanctity of contract (*pacta sunt servanda*) has never been treated as an absolute and unqualified principle in any of the major legal systems. The French doctrine of *imprevision*,[175] the corresponding doctrine of *Wegfall der*

172 HAFEZA EL-HADDAD, ALA'KOUD ALMBRMAH BIN ALDOUL WALA'SHKHAS ALA'JNBIAH, [THE CONTRACTS BETWEEN THE STATES AND FOREIGN INDIVIDUALS] 391 (2007).

173 *Id.* at 347.

174 *Id.* at 351.

175 Article 1195 of French Civil Code provides that "[i]f a change of circumstances that was unforeseeable at the time of the conclusion of the contract renders performance excessively onerous for a party who had not accepted the risk of such a change, that party may ask the other contracting party to renegotiate the contract. The first party must continue to perform his obligations during renegotiation Ordonnance n° 2016–131 du 10 février 2016 portant réforme du droit des contrats, du régime général et de la preuve des obligations." [Law 2016–131 of Feb 10,2016 on the Law of Contract, The General Regime of Obligations, and Proof of Obligations], Art. 1195, Journal Officiel De La Republique Francaise [Official

*Geschäftsgrundlage* in German law,[176] and the concept of good faith in other civilian systems, all provide for limitations on such principle.[177]

#### 2.7.2.1.2 *Trends in Favor of the Invalidity of the Stabilization Clauses Approach*

A group of commentators has adopted the second view—foremost among them, Samuel Asante, who expressed doubts about the validity of SCs.[178] This group of scholars generally rely on the principle of permanent sovereignty over natural resources, which would prevent governments from signing away their sovereignty. According to this school of thought, an SC is an invalid clause because it would impede the host state's permanent sovereignty over its natural resources. The principle of the state's sovereignty over its natural resources constitutes *jus cogens,* the waiving of which is not permissible.[179]

According to Samuel Asante, the state contracts (*e.g.,* concessions, economic development agreements, management agreements, joint ventures, service contracts, sales or purchasing contracts, etc.) should not be treated as private contracts, and therefore, cannot be subjected to all traditional rules on this subject including the principle of sanctity of contract (*pacta sunt servanda*).

---

Gazette of France] *translation at* http://www.textes.justice.gouv.fr/art_pix/THE-LAW-OF-CONTRACT-2-5-16.pdf.

176 Section 313 of German Civil Code provides that "(1) If circumstances which became the basis of a contract have significantly changed since the contract was entered into and if the parties would not have entered into the contract or would have entered into it with different contents if they had foreseen this change, adaptation of the contract may be demanded to the extent that, taking account of all the circumstances of the specific case, in particular the contractual or statutory distribution of risk, one of the parties cannot reasonably be expected to uphold the contract without alteration. (2) It is equivalent to a change of circumstances if material conceptions that have become the basis of the contract are found to be incorrect. (3) If adaptation of the contract is not possible or one party cannot reasonably be expected to accept it, the disadvantaged party may revoke the contract. In the case of continuing obligations, the right to terminate takes the place of the right to revoke." *See* Bürgerliches Gesetzbuch[BGB] [Civil Code],§ 313, *translation at* https://www.gesetze-im-internet.de/englisch_bgb/englisch_bgb.pdf.

177 *See* for a discussion of these doctrines and their differences under various national laws, Hans van Houtte, Changed Circumstances and Pacta Sunt Servanda. In Transnational Rules in International Commercial Arbitration, ed. Emmanuel Gaillard, 105. Paris: ICC Publication, at 113–115 (1993), *available at* https://www.trans-lex.org/117300/_/van-houtte-hans-changed-circumstances-and-pacta-sunt-servanda-in:-gaillard-transnational-rules-in-international-commercial-arbitration-paris-1993-at-105-et-seq/.

178 Samuel Asante is a former Solicitor-General of Ghana; Visiting Fellow of Clare Hall, Cambridge University, 1978–1979; Senior Adviser on Legal Matters, United Nations Centre on Transnational Corporations, New York, since 1977.

179 Wadele & Ndi (1996), at 244.

The practical effect of applying the theory of sanctity of contract to the state contract is that the state is prohibited unilaterally to modify or abrogate their contracts with foreign investors.[180] To avoid such negative impact of the contract's sanctity, Asante suggested that the state contract should be governed by the national law of the contractor host state, and therefore subject to all review or modification per the applicable rules of national law in which the host state is entitled unilaterally to modify or abrogate.[181] According to the preceding view, subjecting a contract to the host state's national law lead to saying the invalidity of SCs due to the nature of state contracts, being long-term contracts are not immutable.

2.7.2.1.2.1 Analyzing the Invalidity Approach

The revolutionary ideas that characterized the above approach are not unknown to Western scholars.[182] Some of the Western jurists, such as the great French jurists Cohen-Jonathan and Bruno Oppetit, stated that the contract concluded between the state and a private party is not immutable, and it may be reviewed or modified by the state in response to change of circumstances.[183] Moreover, the Anglo-American theory of contract has been changed over the years. Professor Morton J. Horwitz of Harvard Law School has illustrated that the modern will theory of contract did not appear until the eighteenth and early nineteenth centuries when the spread of markets forced jurists to attack concepts of an equitable exchange.[184] Previously, the courts were enabled to intervene actively to amend the provision of contract on the ground of equity

180 Asante, *supra* note 12, at 405.

181 *Id.* at 406.

182 El-Haddad (2007), *supra* note 176, at 360.

183 COHEN-JONATHAN, *LES CONCESSIONS EN DROIT INTERNATIONAL PUBLIC*, These dactyl., (Paris 1966); Bruno Oppetit, *L'adaptation des contrats internationaux aux changements de circonstances: La Clause de (Hardship)*, 101 Clunet,794 (1974), *available at* https://www.trans-lex.org/127600. Professor Oppetit noted that " [i]ndeed, the new figures that international contractual practice offers for consideration by jurists significantly invalidate the classic contractual scheme of civil law, which is based on the idea that the contract reflects the reconciliation of the opposing interests of two people and therefore finds itself endowed with stability over time and binding force on the parties: here, on the contrary, nothing is final, everything can be called into question, and the parties themselves integrate the change into the process ... We are very far now general rules of contractual civil law the refiles applicable to international contracts. Perhaps we are rather witnessing the formation of an international custom in which the principle of the binding force of the contract would be replaced by the principle of adaptation to new situations [Unofficial English translation]. *Id,* at 798–799.

184 *See* Morton J. Horwitz, *The Historical Foundations of Modern Contract Law*, 87 HARV. L. REV. 917 (1974); *see also* Asante, *supra* note 12, at 402.

by applying an objective standard of contract. Recent years witnessed a legislative intervention to repair the excesses of the standard on the same theory.[185] Also, Professor Kessler, a Yale Law School Professor, ably demonstrated that such intervention makes nonsense of the will theory of freedom of contract.[186] It follows that there is no immutable doctrine of contract, and the developing countries are entitled to invoke ideas of fairness and equity in reviewing contracts in response to their public interests.[187] On the other hand, the analogous arguments regarding sovereignty over natural resources have been implicitly abandoned by the UN resolution.[188] Many arbitral awards have concluded that the UN resolution regarding state sovereignty over its natural resources does not stop the state from binding itself with a SC.[189]

In sum, despite the principle of permanent sovereignty over natural resources, the prevailing view argues that SCs are valid because the state's freedom of contract remains pristine. Conversely, the right of the state to unilaterally amend or derogate the contract with the foreign investors,, if it is based on grounds of the public interest, has become accepted and recognized even if the agreement contains a SC.[190]

#### 2.7.2.1.3 *The Middle-Ground Approach*

Professor Prosper Weil, a French jurist, established a middle-ground approach to conciliate the conflicting views. According to this middle-ground approach, the basis for determining the validity and legal effect of SCs depends upon the legal framework of the state contract itself. Such a legal system could be the national law of the contractor host state or international law.[191]

If the domestic law of the host state governs the contract, then the SC, as elaborated earlier, should be consistent with the constitutional and legal requirements of the local law. In other words, under a host state's national law,

---

185 *Id.*

186 *See* Friedrich Kessler, *Contracts of Adhesion--Some Thoughts about Freedom of Contract*, 43 COLUM. L. REV. 629, 630–631 (1943).

187 Asante, *supra* note 12, at 401–403.

188 Faruque (2006 a), *supra* note 9, at 330.

189 Texaco Overseas Petroleum Co./California Asiatic Oil Co. v. Libyan Arab Republic, 17 I.L.M. 3, at 29–31 (1977); Kuwait v. American Indep. Oil Co. (Aminoil), 21 I.L.M. 976, at 1021–1022(1982); *See also* Timothy B. Hansen, *The Legal Effect Given Stabilization Clauses in Economic Development Agreements*, 28 Va. J. Int'l L. 1015, 1029 (1988).

190 A great example can be found in the AMINOIL v. Kuwait case (1982). The tribunal, in this case, had sought aptly to reconcile the conflicting interests of the parties. *See* Kuwait v. American Indep. Oil Co. (Aminoil), 21 I.L.M. 976 (1982).

191 Weil, *supra* note 12.

the legal validity and effect of the SC depend on the extent to which constitutional and statutory requirements are respected by the state when it enters into a contract with a foreign investor that contains a SC.[192] As a result, the SC cannot modify or derogate the constitutional or statutory powers of government and legislature to make commitments not to exercise their sovereign and legislation rights.[193] If international law is the applicable law[194] to the state contract, then the most critically raised questions surround the validity and impact of such clauses under international law. According to this school of thought, the SC is valid under international law because the parties of the state contracts freely agreed to not apply any subsequent changes in legal provisions applicable to the contract as of the date of its conclusion. However, the stability provisions, as a part of the legitimate expectation of foreign investors, offer only limited protection under international law. The freezing function which SCs are intended to perform constitutes just part of the larger picture; the political, economic, and social factors of the relationship will develop over time, affecting the balance of the contract. Moreover, other factors, including the principle of *rebus sic stantibus,*[195] can balance stabilization clauses.[196] According to this school of thought, when a host state breaches a SC contained in the state contract, the investor will have a right to due compensation.[197] The value of SCs, therefore, has become a *"financial value"* in which they strengthen the bargaining position of the foreign investor as a private contractor with a host state. As aptly summarized by Gaetan Verhoosel,

> [The SCs] strengthen the private contractor's bargaining position. When a government knows that it will be publicly embarrassed by an arbitral ruling upholding the stabilization clause and giving it its full effect, it will be willing to compromise. When a government is found to have breached a stabilization clause, the investor will not be entitled to *restitutio in integrum,* but it will have a right to due compensation.[198]

---

192 PETER, *supra* note 123, at 221–222.
193 Waelde & Ndi (1996), at 239.
194 *See supra* note 166.
195 *Rebus sic stantibus,* BLACK'S LAW DICTIONARY 11th ed. 2019 ["Law Latin: matters so standing"](The principle that all agreements are concluded with the implied condition that they are binding only as long as there are no major changes in the circumstances.).
196 Waelde & Ndi (1996), at 245.
197 *See* Gaetan Verhoosel, *Foreign Direct Investment and Legal Constraints on Domestic Environmental Policies: Striking a Reasonable Balance between Stability and Change,* 29 LAW & POL'Y INT'L BUS. 451, 456 (1998).
198 *Id.*

Similarly, Professor Cameron espoused the same view and confirmed the functional role of SCs; as he put it:

> The presence of stabilization clause (and the threat of its use in arbitral proceedings) may encourage the host state to reach a settlement with the investor and to do so on terms that are more favourable to the investor than would be the case if no stabilization clause were present in the contract. As a number of arbitral awards have shown, the presence or absence of a stabilization clause (whatever its form) in an investment contract can have an important effect on the outcome of an arbitral proceeding.[199]

It is worth noting that, according to the middle ground view, arbitral tribunals should avoid deciding in a legal void and instead follow a case-by-case approach when they analyze SCs. The tribunal should consider all relevant circumstances and changes that happen in real practice out of the disputed documents.[200]

###### 2.7.2.1.3.1 Analyzing the Middle Ground Approach

The prominent feature of the above approach is that it has tried to link the validity and legal effect of SCs to the legal framework, which governs the contract itself. A significant number of jurists followed this approach. One of the manifestations of this trend was the arbitral award in *Texaco v. Libya* in which Professor Dupuy, as a sole arbitrator, espoused this approach when deciding in that case.[201]

#### 2.7.2.2 Stabilization Clauses within the Arbitral Practice

The validity of stabilization clauses (SCs) in state contracts has been the subject of debate in international law. However, numerous international arbitral tribunals have consistently recognized the validity of SCs, as evidenced in several landmark cases. In the case of *Texaco v. Libya*,[202] the sole arbitrator acknowledged the potentially negative impact of SCs,[203] which can exclude a contract from administrative contracts and give it the characteristic of

199 CAMERON (2010), at 61.
200 Waelde & Ndi (1996), at 245.
201 Texaco Overseas Petroleum Co./California Asiatic Oil Co. v. Libyan Arab Republic, 17 I.L.M. 3, 55 (1977).
202 *Id.*
203 *Id.* 56.

internationalization.[204] However, the arbitrator applied the significant principle of *pacta sunt servanda* in relation to the SC, and concluded that while the effect of a SC is to stabilize the position of the contracting party, it does not impair the sovereignty of the state.[205]

Similarly, in *LIAMCO v. Libya*,[206] the tribunal held that SCs were legally binding under international law,[207] justified by the Libyan Petroleum legislation and the general principle of the sanctity of contracts.[208] However, most contemporary legal scholars uphold the sovereign right of a state to nationalize foreign property.[209] Accordingly, nationalization was not contrary to the SCs but was unlawful due to the state's failure to pay compensation.[210] Furthermore, in the *AMINOIL v. Kuwait* case,[211] the tribunal recognized the validity of SCs but refused to interpret the SC as an absolute prohibition of nationalization.[212] Instead, the tribunal determined that the interpretation of the SC must be restricted and provide protection only against measures that have a confiscatory character.[213]

---

204 *Id.* 54–57. The arbitrator concluded that [it is true that, in a certain way, the view could be held that the 'stabilization clauses' [in the instant case Clause 16 of the Deeds of Concession] appear as clauses going beyond the ambit of ordinary law in the sense that they are not usually found in contracts entered into between private parties].

205 *Id.* 71.

206 Libyan Am. Oil Co. (LIAMCO) v. Libyan Arab Republic, 20 I.L.M. 1 (1981).

207 *Id.* at 19.

208 *Id.*

209 *Id.* at 35.

210 *Id. at* 18.

211 Kuwait v. American Indep. Oil Co. (Aminoil), 21 I.L.M. 976 (1982).

212 The stabilization clauses in the 1948 Concession Agreement and the 1961 Supplemental Agreement were placed in Article 17 and Article 7 (g) respectively as follows: Art 17 of the 1948 Agreement states that "[T]he Shaikh shall not by general or special legislation or by administrative measures or by any other act whatever annul this Agreement except as provided in Article 11. No alteration shall be made in the terms of this Agreement by either the Shaikh or the Company except in the event of the Shaikh and the Company jointly agreeing that it is desirable in the interest of both parties to make certain alterations, deletions or additions to this Agreement."; Article 7(g) of the 1961 Supplemental Agreement reads as follows: "Save as aforesaid this Agreement shall not be terminated before the expiration of the period specified in Article 1 hereof except by surrender as provided in Article 12 or if the Company shall be in default under the arbitration provisions of Article 18." *Id*, at 17–18.

213 *Id.* at 44, 102. *But see* Separate Opinion *id.* at 64–66 (The arbitrator Sir G. Fitzmaurice again disagreed, finding that the stabilization clauses were concerned with a termination of the concession by "special legislation or by administrative measures or by any other act whatever," and not at all with confiscation; as a result, he concluded that "the nationalization [...] was irreconcilable with the stabilization clauses."); *see also* Pierre-Yves Tschanz,

#### 2.7.2.2.1 *Analyzing Arbitral Practice of Stabilization Clauses*

The preceding survey of the validity and legal effect of SCs from the view of arbitral jurisprudence leads to several conclusions. First, the language of SCs and their scope of application play a significant role in practice; arbitral tribunals have to understand and apply the SC in accordance with its particular terms and give effect to such a clause based on its language and scope.[214] Second, the arbitral tribunals, in deciding on the validity of SCs, seem to rely heavily on the principle of sanctity of contract: *pacta sunt servanda.* Third, no arbitral tribunal has considered that SCs would be invalid due to the lack of a host state's competence to agree upon such stability provisions.[215] Fourth, according to the arbitral tribunals, SCs have legal effects regardless of the applicable law. In this vein, no arbitral award has ruled that national law or international law should be considered to derogate the efficiency of SCs. In this regard, the arbitral tribunals have not fully explained why the application of international law results in the effect of SCs. The tribunals also never explained why the application of the national law of the host state would not preclude the impact of SCs.[216] Fifth, the validity and legal effect of SCs are affected by the length and scope of the use of such provisions. SCs may be valid if they are limited to a relatively short period as a temporary limitation upon the sovereignty of the host state. Conversely, an unconscionably long period, such as sixty years of a state contract, make a modification or cancellation act by the host state of such agreement is justifiable when the social and economic interests of this state are at stake.[217] Sixth, no arbitral tribunal has denied the right of the host state to nationalize or expropriate the foreign investment project, as an inherent right of the state under international law. The tribunals ruled that a SC cannot ban such a right regardless of the form

---

*The Contributions of the Aminoil Award to the Law of State Contracts*, 18 INT'L L. 245, 276 (1984).

214 DOLZER (2018), at 207.

215 *Id.*

216 *Id.*

217 Faruque (2006 a), *supra* note 9, at 326, n 28. (noted that according to Report of the UN on permanent sovereignty over natural resources states that "A current provision, even in very recent contracts, is the freezing of the tax regime applicable at the time of the negotiation. Some of the freezing clauses negotiated at present tie the hands of the Government for a very long period. Long and comprehensive 'freezing' clauses seems to run counter to the principle of permanent sovereignty over natural resources, although it may be conceivable that provisions to stabilize the fiscal regime for a reasonable period, so as to assure loan repayment, for example, can be found acceptable under specific conditions".) *See* Report of the Secretary General of the United Nations on Permanent Sovereignty over Natural Resources, at 24, para 68, U.N. Doc E/C/119 (1981).

or language of such a clause. Accordingly, stability provisions did not invalidate a nationalization act. However, they made it an unlawful act and thereby affected the amount of compensation that might be awarded by the arbitral tribunal.[218] Finally, in all these arbitral awards that addressed the issue of SCs, compensation was issued for breach of the SC. Such compensation was sometimes higher when the contract contained stability provisions.[219]

## 2.8 Stabilization Clauses in Empirical Work

An important and interesting study, International Energy Investment Law: Stability through Contractual Clauses, was conducted in 2010 by Mustafa Erkan.[220] In this study, the author surveyed business community on the debate of validity and legal effect of SCs. The survey was sent to state oil companies, international oil companies, international petroleum lawyers, and scholars. The author, eventually, reached some results about SCs in empirical work as detailed below:

First, when asked whether a SC has a legal and functional value in petroleum contracts, 80% of respondents agreed, while 12% disagreed with the question. Over 90% of survey respondents believed that a SC has a legal and functional value, followed by international lawyers at 80.6%. Among the respondents of International Oil Company and of the National Oil Company, respectively, 77.8% and 76.9% felt positively about the legal and functional value of SCs.[221] Second, when asked whether SCs in petroleum contracts are mainly given by governments in a weak bargaining position, 45% of survey

218 Cameron (2006), *supra* note 15, at 15.

219 In some cases, however, the tribunal doesn't give any effect of stabilization clauses for the purpose of compensation. In *Ioannis Kardassopoulos v. Georgia*, the tribunal *Georgia*, in response to Georgia's argument that the stabilization clauses in the joint venture agreement and the Deed of Concession do not affect the measure of damages for expropriation, the tribunal concluded that even if the stabilization clauses were to be applied in this case, the result would be the same due to the application of international law principles of compensation. Accordingly, "the stabilization clauses do[did] not "cap" damages for the purposes of valuing the Claimants' rights nor do[did] they establish a ceiling of compensation beyond which the Claimants could not have legitimately expected to recover in the event of an expropriation." Ioannis Kardassopoulos v. Republic of Georgia, ICSID Case NoNos. ARB/05/18, and ARB/07/15, Award, 471–85 (Mar. 3, 2010), https://www.italaw.com/sites/default/files/case-documents/ita0445.pdf.

220 ERKAN (2010), at 121–138.

221 *Id*, at 121–122.

respondents disagreed, while 40% of respondents agreed with the question.[222] Although, the results found that "there is no clear dominant view overall",[223] Erkan nevertheless believes that the parties' bargaining strength is probably a key point in this issue. When the host state has a strong bargaining power at the time of contract negotiation, a foreign investor can hardly persuade the state to insert SCs in the investment contract. Therefore, the government that has a weak bargaining power, against the foreign investor at the bargaining table, would be more likely to agree to SCs.[224] Third, when asked whether a sovereign state can legally bind itself by a stabilization clause, 58% of survey respondents felt quite strongly that a state can legally bind itself by SCs, and 30% of survey respondents disagreed with the question.[225] Fourth, when asked whether international law recognizes the binding effect of SCs as a limitation on a state's sovereign power, 47% of respondents agreed with the question, and about 27% of survey respondents reported "no". Interestingly, survey participants from developing countries were more supportive of the binding effect of SCs than participants from developed countries. Approximately 52.4% of participants from developing countries said "yes" in answer to this question and 21.4% said "no". While 43% of respondents from developed countries reported "yes" but about 30.2% reported "no" in answer to this question.[226]

Finally, when asked whether SCs are effective in restricting a host state's sovereign rights, 50% of respondents believed that SCs were not effective in fettering sovereign rights of the host state. On the other hand, nearly 40% of survey respondents thought that SCs were effective in restricting a host state's sovereign rights.[227] Most strikingly, Erkan's survey revealed that 61.5% of respondents who represented national oil companies believed the effectiveness of SCs in restricting the host state's sovereign rights, while only 30.8% did not believe that. Nearly 62.1% of survey respondents who were in legal practice believed that SCs have no effective role in restricting the host state's sovereign rights and only 31% did believe this. Crucially, this result raised a fundamental question: why do international lawyers insist on inserting SCs in their clients' contracts with the host states even though a majority of them do

222 *Id*, at 124.

223 Erkan noted that, "one respondent commented that, [it is true that stabilization clauses are more common in such a situation, but they are also sometimes given by governments in a much stronger position but wanting something out of the ordinary from investors.]"

224 *Id.*

225 *Id*, at 125–127.

226 *Id*, at 127–128.

227 *Id.* at 137.

not believe in the effectiveness of SCs?[228] According to Erken "[t]he possible answer is that it does no harm to have one in a contract or alternatively that it is worth a try."[229] Indeed, this practice raised many eyebrows and may reflect rent-seeking behavior by foreign investors and their international lawyers.[230] It also supports the thesis proposition that the effectivness of traditional CSCs is qutestionable.

## 2.9 Conclusion

The examination of these clauses has shown that the validity and legal effect of traditional stabilization clauses are subject to much debate. The disparity between legal scholars and arbitral practice regarding this issue gives an unmistakable indication of the failure of the traditional stabilization clause in achieving its primary objective: from the foreign investor's perspective, as a tool to restrict the host state's legislative power and tie its hands concerning changing the investment contract unilaterally. From a developing host state's perspective, a stabilization clause is a tool to encourage foreign direct investment.

Indeed, the failure of traditional CSCs in achieving their primary objective is made irreparable by the fostering of specific concepts such as "internationalization of contract," which is used to support the idea of the sanctity of contract (*pacta sunt servanda*). The internationalization of contract, as it aims for the absolute applicability of *pacta sunt servanda*, confers complete protection on the foreign investor against the host state, in which foreign investors, *de facto and de jure*, are rarely granted such protection in their home country. The home state of foreign investors often enjoys the right to change or terminate the contract with their national investors unilaterally.

There are several difficulties in accepting the principle of sanctity of contract (*pacta sunt servanda*) applied to state contracts. The concepts of state contracts reflect the necessity of the host state to guard the public interest. Given the fact that the state or state agency is a contracting party, such contracts have different characteristics compared to ordinary private contracts. The manifestations of this distinction are the right of the administration to terminate its contract unilaterally for the public interest.

---

228 *Id.* at 138.

229 ERKAN (2010), at 138.

230 Frank (2015), *supra* note 69, at 106–107.

Moreover, public international law itself allows changing the treaties when the circumstances change fundamentally. Furthermore, even though all domestic laws in different countries adopt the principle of sanctity of contract, they do not accept it in absolute. Instead, they put some restrictions upon it.[231]

While foreign investors experience significant risk when deciding to enter into a state contract, the contractor state is not a traditional party; hence, the importance of stabilization clauses is emerging to mitigate the risks of entering into such agreements. The existence of the stabilization clause in state contracts must not tie the hands of the state to issue nondiscriminatory measures for the public interest. As a logical consequence, the nationalization or expropriation measures of the host state against the foreign investor usually are mandatory rules of that state regardless of the applicable law of the investment contract.

In this connection, it is worth pointing out that the right of the host state to interfere in the investment contract is not absolute. To suggest otherwise is not logical because it would become impossible to convince foreign investors to invest abroad. In other words, if the host state enjoys its power to regulate the new regulations that affect the performance of a contract, it must provide a foreign investor with adequate and fair compensation.

While, the traditional CSCs cannot provide an absolute protection against the host state's intervention if the state has a mind to do so. This does not meant that these clauses have no effect, instead they have some functions. These clauses might nevertheless render nationalization or expropriation an unlawful act and thereby affect the amount of compensation that the arbitral tribunal might grant. They also could support the foreign investor's claims pursuant to the IIAs' provisions such as expropriation, fair and equitable treatment, or umbrella clause.[232] Therefore, it would be rational if today's foreign investors demand that their investment contracts be complemented with a well drafted stabilization clauses.

Inserting traditional SCs in the state contracts creates an inescapable tension between the conflicting interests of the contracting parties. While the host state needs the flexibility of the contract to exercise its regulatory and sovereign powers over its natural resources, the investor seeks firmer stability guarantees. This conflict of interest between a foreign investor and the host state often makes it difficult for traditional CSCs in state contracts to work.

231 *See, e.g.,* the French doctrine of *imprevision,* the corresponding doctrine of *Wegfall der Geschiftsgrundlage* in German law, and the concept of good faith in other civilian systems all provide for limitations on such principle. *See supra* note 179–180.

232 *See infra* Chapter 5.

The stability of state contracts shall not be destroyed, but flexibility must be assured. Against this backdrop, the host states should avoid traditional SCs in state contracts as they can discourage states from passing positive legislation. As an alternative to including traditional CSCs, host states would do well to look to other appropriate legal safeguards for recalibrating the balance of interests and rights between the state and foreign investors.

However, if the traditional SC is included in a state contract, the host state is advised to limit the scope of this clause to cover changes in fiscal policy only so that the state can still regulate non-fiscal issues without fear of contractual repercussions. Furthermore, the traditional SC should be bound in time so that it expires and does not have a chilling effect for the entire term of the investment contract.

CHAPTER 3

# Renegotiation Clauses

## 3.1 Introduction

The pitfalls of traditional contractual stabilization clauses have unleashed a torrent of commentary. This led some scholars to suggest that using adequate renegotiation clauses would be much better to provide contractual stability.[1] Under renegotiation clauses, parties have the right to review and renegotiate certain terms either at the elapsing of a specific time period or the realization of certain conditions or trigger events. The striking feature of inserting renegotiation clauses in the state contract is to help the parties escape from the inflexibility associated with traditional SCs[2] and, more particularly, reduce the risk of the host state's unilateral intervention in the investment project.[3] Unlike traditional SCs, which aim to freeze the host state's legal framework during the lifespan of the contract, renegotiation clauses aim to protect the aggrieved party whose interest was damaged due to a change of circumstances to re-balance the financial equilibrium of their contract. Renegotiation of contractual obligations is commonplace in long-term contracts, particularly in petroleum and mining contracts.[4] Since the 1950s, we have witnessed a burgeoning number of renegotiations in international business.

In most cases, the host states often initiated and forced these renegotiations[5] by threatening nationalization and expropriation of the foreign projects.[6] The reasons for this might be that the host state or its owned-oil company seeks greater participation in petroleum investment projects to ensure its permanent sovereignty over natural resources or to profit from the increase of oil prices.[7] Also, there are renegotiations initiated by foreign investors which

1 PETER (1995), at 229–30; *See also*, Kroll (2004), at 437; ERKAN (2010), at 142.

2 *See* Mohsin Shareef Salih & Akram Yamulki, *Stabilisation and Renegotiation Clauses in Iraqi Kurdistan Oil and Gas Contracts: A Comparative Study*, 100 J.L. POL'Y & GLOBALIZATION 101, 109 (2020).

3 Al Qurashi (2005), at 261 (2005).

4 Kroll (2004), at 425.

5 *See* Wolfgang Peter, *Arbitration and Renegotiation Clause*, 3 J. INT'L ARB. 29, 29 (1986).

6 Salacuse, *Renegotiation International Project Agreements* (*2001*), at 1319; ERKAN (2010), at 146.

7 ERKAN (2010), at 146.

 | DOI:10.1163/9789004692756_004

> [m]ight be shock related, when a devaluation or a recession make the operation of a given concession unsustainable... [t]hey might also be opportunistic, when a firm uses its bargaining power in bilateral negotiation with the government or the regulatory agency to strike a better deal than the initially agreed one.[8]

A party who seeks the renegotiation of the contract due to changed circumstances can rely either on the contract containing a specific renegotiation clause or on the other contractual provisions (*e.g.*, hardship clause and *force-majeure* clause)[9] or applicable law that might provide an appropriate starting point for renegotiation.[10]

Given the fact that the renegotiation mechanism was created to achieve stability and flexibility in long-term investment contracts, one might reasonably ask to what extent renegotiation clauses can effectively undermine stability but provide flexibility that may better sustain the working relationship between the parties? Most significantly, are contractual renegotiation clauses sufficient to achieve contractual stability and diminish the risk of unilateral state intervention? Despite the claimed-trumpeted advantages of renegotiation clauses in long-term investment contracts, why are some foreign investors still skeptical about these clauses and reluctant to insert them in their contracts?

To answer the above-mentioned questions and other related matters, we examine the value and legal effect of renegotiation clauses in state contracts, particularly petroleum contracts, from the perspective of law and practice. We also shed light on the reasons host governments and foreign investors have for including renegotiation clauses in the investment contracts, discuss whether the contract contains a specific renegotiation clause or not and whether the party seeks a renegotiation based on the governing law.

## 3.2 Definition of Renegotiation Clause

In international investment law, the terminology used in the context of renegotiation clauses can be mystifying. Renegotiation can, therefore, exist under a different name, such as review, revision, adaptation, adjustment, restructuring,

8 J. Luis Guach & Stephane Straub, *Renegotiation of Infrastructure Concessions: An Overview*, 77 Annals of Public and Cooperative Economics, 479, 484 (2006).

9 *See infra* part 3.5.1.

10 Al Qurashi (2005), at 262.

rescheduling, and so on.[11] This study will refer to the process as renegotiation. But what does renegotiation mean in the context of an international investment contract?

The literature has given different definitions with the same meaning to the renegotiation clause. For instance, Professor Norbert Horn defined renegotiation as follows:

"Renegotiation describes a common effort by the parties to adapt a contract to a new situation through a material change of its terms."[12] In the words of Professor John Y. Gotanda, "renegotiation clauses are provisions in contracts that, upon the happening of a certain event or events, require all parties to return to the bargaining table and renegotiate the terms of their agreements."[13] Renegotiation clause also could be defined as "a consensual process" of change in the contractual terms and conditions to reconceptualize the rights and duties of the contracting parties.[14] Therefore, the renegotiation clause serves as a tool to provide contractual protection to the parties of the state contract by making such a contract "flexible and dynamic" during its life span, to adapt it to changing circumstances[15] that may occur from unforeseen political, economic, regulatory, and technical circumstances.[16] The crux of this clause is that it offers contracting parties the opportunity to salvage a contract and establish a new equilibrium of their interests that were aggrieved because of fundamental change in circumstances.

The above definition of the renegotiation clause might seem *prima facie,* similar to the adaptation clause, which means adjusting contractual terms to a new situation. Such a situation might result from *force majeure* events or special risks but may also be linked to other new facts.[17]

This led Professor Horn to clarify the differences between both terms, explaining that "renegotiation is more clearly directed to a material change of the contract; that is, not to mere clarification or the filling of gaps, but to the idea of setting aside important clauses of the original contract."[18] Professor

11 Peter (1986), *supra* note 5, at 30; *See also*, ERKAN (2010), at 149–50.

12 NORBERT HORN, ADAPTATION AND RENEGOTIATION OF CONTRACTS IN INTERNATIONAL TRADE AND FINANCE 9 (1985).

13 John Y. Gotanda, *Renegotiation and Adaptation Clauses in Investment Contract, Revisited,* 36 VAND. J. TRANSNAT'L L. 1461, 1462 (2003).

14 Al Faruque (2008), at 120 (noting that the "renegotiation can take place either by way of process prescribed by the provisions of the contract or extra-contract procedures which are generally approved by the legal system followed by the parties.").

15 Salih & Yamulki, *supra* note 2, at 109.

16 Salacuse, *Renegotiating International Project* (*2001*), at 1327.

17 HORN (1985), *supra* note 12, at 7.

18 *Id.* at 9.

Horn also adds that "renegotiation points more clearly to the procedure—the common effort of the parties—than to the result, the adaptation or restructuring of the contract."[19] Likewise, Professor Wolfgang Peter aptly demonstrates the difference between renegotiation and adaptation clauses, stating that "[r]enegotiation clauses in investment agreements are specific contractual provisions which differ from adaptation clauses because they authorize changes in a contract without following an automatic or predetermined pattern. Thus, they serve a purpose that goes beyond the filling of simple gaps."[20] Furthermore, adaptation is often a less time-consuming process compared with renegotiation, which usually necessitates a lengthy consultation process and a comprehensive review of the contractual relationship.[21] Most significantly, while renegotiation clauses often deal with the external events to the contract, the problems that the adaptation clause usually deals with are more contractual in nature that involves technical or financial difficulties. In sum, both renegotiation and adaptation clauses serve conceptually different purposes, and a more complex process is often involved with the operation of the renegotiation clause than the adaptation clause.[22]

---

19 *Id.*

20 PETER (1995), at 239.

21 Al Faruque (2008), at 120 (Al Faruque aptly summarized the differences between renegotiation and adaptation clauses stating that "[t]he expression "adaptation" can be used in a narrow and broader sense. In a narrow sense, it implies a process of contract adjustment through a number of provisions, which are otherwise known as adaptation clauses. On the other hand, adaptation in the broader sense implies readjustment of the contractual relationship which can be achieved by both renegotiation and adaptation clauses. The adaptation clauses allow contract changes by following predetermined procedures and they are designed for the filling of gaps in contracts. Thus, renegotiation can be distinguished from adaptation in the narrow sense in two respects-renegotiation is more clearly directed to a material change of the contract, and it points more clearly to the process of common effort of the parties than to the result. 13 On the other hand, the adaptation clause intends to clarify or fill the gaps in the contract and its application clearly leads to adaptation or also restructures the contract to some extent. Renegotiation can be distinguished from adaptation in narrow sense by the fact that renegotiation usually entails a lengthy consultation process and a reviewing of the whole situation. On the other hand, adaptation in the narrow sense is usually a less time consuming process, and can be carried out through a pre-determined procedure laid down in the contract and even it may be completed without any consultation between the parties in some cases. More importantly, the renegotiation clause often deal with external events to contracts, adaptation clauses deal with problems of a more contractual nature involving technical or financial difficulties. Thus, the renegotiation clause and adaptation clause serve conceptually different purposes and the implementation of renegotiation clause involves often a more complex process than the adaptation clause."

22 *Id.*

## 3.3 History and Background of Renegotiation Clause

The renegotiation of contractual obligations is commonplace in long-term contracts, particularly in petroleum and mining contracts.[23] Since the 1950s, we have witnessed a burgeoning number of renegotiations in international business. For example, in the 1960s and 1970s, there were numerous significant contract renegotiations in the mineral and petroleum industry.[24] The host states often initiated this renegotiation of contracts[25] by threatening nationalization and expropriations.[26] Another example of renegotiations can be found in the loan rescheduling following the debt crisis in many developing countries in the 1980s and restructuring and financing of project agreements following the Asian financial crisis of the late 1990s,[27] and most recently, the financial crisis in 2008. The pattern will undoubtedly continue in the future. For example, in recent years, the governments in Algeria, Bolivia, Ecuador, Russia, and Venezuela have tried to increase their participation in energy projects to profit from high oil prices or ensure permanent sovereignty over their natural resources.[28]

Over these years, several declarations and resolutions issued by the UN General Assembly, OPEC, and other international organizations significantly contributed to furnishing the normative basis of renegotiations.[29] For example, OPEC's Resolution No. XVI. 90 of 1968 declared that host governments have a right to renegotiate contracts when foreign corporations receive "excessively high net earnings after taxes,"[30] Critically, these international declarations, policy statements, and resolutions, which form a "soft law" coupled with the new international economic order by the UN General Assembly had set out the normative basis of the renegotiation of natural resource agreements, especially in developing countries that had a desire to restructure existing legal arrangements in view of the new world order.

---

23 Kroll (2004), at 425.

24 Salacuse, *Renegotiating International Project (2001)*, at 1319; See *infra Appendix*, Part I. tb.1.

25 Peter (1986), *supra* note 5, at 29.

26 Salacuse, Renegotiating International Project (2001), at 1319.

27 *Id.*

28 ERKAN (2010), at 146; *See infra* Appendix, Part I. tb.2.

29 Al Faruque (2008), at 114.

30 Report of the Group of Eminent Persons to Study the Impact of Multinational Corporations on Development and International Relations, United Nations Document E/5500/Rev.l.ST/ESA/6 of 1974.

## 3.4 Types of Renegotiations

The different types of renegotiations have already received a tremendous amount of discussion in the literature. Nevertheless, it is useful to understand these types of renegotiations before embarking upon a detailed consideration of renegotiation clauses. According to Mustafa Erkan, renegotiations can be classified into two groups. The first is the situation-based renegotiation. The second is based on the party that initiates the negotiation.[31]

### 3.4.1 *Renegotiation Based on Situation*

Under this category, there are three types of renegotiations: (1) post-deal renegotiations, (2) intra-deal renegotiations, and (3) extra-deal renegotiations.

#### 3.4.1.1 Post-deal Renegotiation

Post-deal renegotiation simply refers to the situation in which the renegotiation takes place at the end of the original contract when the parties freely decide to renew their original relationship agreement.[32] Therefore, the post-deal renegotiation is sometimes named "contractual renewal."[33]

#### 3.4.1.2 Intra-deal Renegotiation

A long-term agreement itself may provide that during the lifespan of the agreement at a specific time or on the occurrence of certain events, the contracting parties may decide to renegotiate specific provisions of their original agreement.[34] This is called an intra-deal renegotiation because it takes place over the course of the original agreement.[35]

---

31 ERKAN (2010), at 150.

32 Salacuse, Renegotiating International Project (2001), at 1320. The following hypothetical example is clarifying this category of renegotiation clause: "A project company has built an electrical generating station in an emerging market country and has made a twenty-year electricity supply contract with that country's state public utility corporation. At the end of twenty years, when local law considers their legal relationship at an end, the project company and the public utility corporation begin discussions on a second long-term electricity supply contract, thereby "renegotiating" their original relationship." *Id.*

33 *Id.* 1320 n. 8.

34 *Id.* at 1321. The following hypothetical example is clarifying this category of renegotiation clause: "The twenty-year electricity supply contract mentioned above might include a provision calling for the renegotiation of the agreement's pricing terms in the event of dramatic changes in fuel costs. Or in an agreement between a manufacturer and a sales company for the marketing of specific products, the contract may stipulate that if the manufacturer develops new products it will agree to renegotiate its original deal with respect to the marketing of the new products." *Id.*

35 ERKAN (2010), at 151.

#### 3.4.1.3 Extra-deal Renegotiation

Professor Salacuse aptly described this third type of renegotiation, stating that "the most difficult, stressful, and emotional renegotiations are those undertaken in apparent violation of the contract or at least in the absence of a specific clause authorizing a renegotiation. These negotiations take place "extra deal," for they occur outside the framework of the existing agreement."[36] The extra-deal renegotiation is commonplace with petroleum and mining concession contracts, and this was particularly the case in the 1960s and 1970s. Host states often forced foreign corporations to renegotiate by threatening nationalization and expropriation.[37]

### 3.4.2 *Renegotiation Based on the Parties*

Under this second group, the renegotiation can be initiated either by the foreign investor or the host state.

#### 3.4.2.1 Renegotiation by the Investor

In some cases, an occurrence of specific events such as a devaluation of currency or a recession can make the operation of a given concession unsustainable. This might shock the foreign investor and lead them to initiate the renegotiation of the original contract with the host state. In other cases, the foreign investor might be opportunistic and decide to use its bargaining power in renegotiating with the host government to strike a better deal than the original agreed one.[38]

#### 3.4.2.2 Renegotiation by the Government

The host government may seek to renegotiate a state contract with a foreign investor to get greater returns from the foreign project[39] or to restore the economic balance of the contract.[40] To achieve this, the government may use different means to bring the foreign investor back to the negotiating table. This can happen directly when the government explicitly expresses its desire to

---

36 Salacuse, Renegotiating International Project (2001), at 1321. The following hypothetical example is clarifying this category of renegotiation clause: if the state public utility company, without justification in the contract, had insisted on negotiations to reduce the price it was committed to pay for electricity under the contract, such discussions would be categorized as "extra-deal renegotiations," because they would be taking place outside of the legal framework of the original contract.

37 ERKAN (2010), at 146, 151.

38 Guasch & Straub, *supra* note 8, 484.

39 ERKAN (2010), at 151.

40 *Id.* at 152.

renegotiate the contract with the foreign investor, who often refuse the host government's request. In such cases, the host government may resort to indirect methods, such as exercising its sovereign powers by imposing some rigid measures to force renegotiation, such as raising taxes, imposing new restrictions, or unilaterally changing the contract.[41] Government-led renegotiation may also occur opportunisticly, with politicians reneging on previous contracts to appease their constituents "during or after an election compaign."[42]

## 3.5 Contract with and without Renegotiation Clause

The parties in the state contracts may or may not include special mechanisms for dealing with a change in the commercial equilibrium in the contract. These two scenarios will be the subject of the section below.

### 3.5.1 *Contract without Renegotiation Clause*

When the state contract lacks specific provisions for dealing with a change of circumstances that causes an apparent inequality between the parties of the state contract, the aggrieved party would primarily look at other contractual provisions or applicable law to see if they provide an appropriate starting point for renegotiating or adjusting the contract to changed circumstances.[43]

#### 3.5.1.1 Force Majeure and Hardship Clauses

In the absence of an express renegotiation clause, the contracting party who insists on renegotiating the contract may be able to rely on any *force-majeure* clause included in the state contract or the hardship concept of international contract-law.[44] This section will consider the extent to which the contracting party insisting on renegotiation can use these clauses to trigger the renegotiation process.

---

41 *Id.*

42 Guasch & Straub, *supra* note 8, at 484.

43 HORN (1985), *supra* note 12, at 29; Klaus Peter Berger, *Renegotiation and Adaption of International Investment Contracts: The Role of Contract Drafters and Arbitrators*, 36 VAND. J. TRANSNAT'L L. 1347, 1350(2003); PETER (1995), at 240.

44 Berger, *supra* note 43, at 1350; *See also* Alexei G. Doudko, Hardship in Contract: The Approach of the UNIDROIT Principles and Legal Developments in Russia, 5 UNIF. L. REV. n.s. 483, 508 (2000) (noting that, "the tendency to treat hardship as a general rule of law is only just beginning to emerge. The tendency to treat hardship as a general rule of law is only just beginning to emerge.").

3.5.1.1.1 *Force Majeure Clause*

Force majeure in *stricto sensu* is an unforeseen and unavoidable event that is beyond the control of contracting parties. It renders the performance of the contract impossible, whether temporarily or permanently.[45] The UNIDROIT Principles of International Commercial Contracts, a restatement of the currently accepted rules and principles of international contract-law[46] define force majeure and its legal consequences as follows:

> *Article 7.1.7—(Force Majeure)*
> (1) Non-performance by a party is excused if that party proves that the non-performance was due to an impediment beyond its control and that it could not reasonably be expected to have taken the impediment into account at the time of the conclusion of the contract or to have avoided or overcome it or its consequences. (2) When the impediment is only temporary, the excuse shall have effect for such period as is reasonable having regard to the effect of the impediment on the performance of the contract. (3) The party who fails to perform must give notice to the other party of the impediment and its effect on its ability to perform. If the notice is not received by the other party within a reasonable time after the party who fails to perform knew or ought to have known of the impediment, it is liable for damages resulting from such non-receipt. (4) Nothing in this Article prevents a party from exercising a right to terminate the contract or to withhold performance or request interest on money due.[47]

The Force majeure clause has become a common clause in the long-term contract[48] generally, and in petroleum contract

45 PETER (1995), at 235; Al Faruque (2008), at 135. (noting that [t]he Force majeure events may include natural phenomena or calamities, earthquakes, typhoons, fires, wars declared or undeclared, hostilities, invasions, blockades, riots, insurrection, civil disturbance and acts of government, strikes, or industrial disputes, any other act planned by the worker beyond the control of the parties; acts of terrorism; laws, treaties, rules, regulations, decrees, orders, actions or inactions of any governmental authority which prevent, hinder or impede contractors' conduct of operations, or which substantially impairs or threatens contractor's rights under the agreement). *Id.* at 136 n. 55.

46 International Institute for the Unification of Private Law (UNIDROIT), Principles of International Commercial Contracts (2016).

47 *Id.* Art. 7.1.7, at 240.

48 Al Faruque (2008), at 135 (noting that, "[a]n analysis of force majeure clauses in long term contracts reveals that they imply the following procedural steps: the first stage involves defining force majeure either with reference to the catalogue of events that constitute force majeure or the adoption of a definition of force majeure under a legal system; the

particularly,[49] in which foreign investors can rely in case there is no express renegotiation clause contained in the state contract. For example, the Lasmo Group Production Sharing Contract between Vietnam National Oil and Gas Corporation of the Socialist Republic of Vietnam, Lasmo Vietnam Ltd. & C. Itoh Energy Development Co., Ltd for Offshore Block 04–2 (1992) contains the following force-majeure clause:

> 17.7 Force Majeure: The obligations of each of the Parties hereunder, other than the obligation to make payments of money, shall be suspended during a period of Force Majeure and the term of the relevant period or phase of this Agreement shall be extended for a time equivalent to the period of Force Majeure situation. In the event of Force Majeure, the Party affected thereby shall give notice thereof to the other Party as soon as reasonably practical stating the starting date and the extent of such suspension of obligations and the cause thereof. A Party whose obligations have been suspended as aforesaid shall resume the performance of such obligations as soon as reasonably practical after the removal of the Force Majeure and shall notify the other Party accordingly.[50]

Generally, the crux of the force majeure clause is to absolve the contracting parties from the liability of the contractual performance upon the occurrence of events that would otherwise amount to cancellation the contract as a measure of last resort.[51] Therefore, the force majeure is not intended to lead to contract change.[52] However, force majeure clauses usually have a broader meaning

second step deals with the determination of whether the event was reasonably beyond the control of the party invoking the force majeure clause; the third step involves the legal consequences of the events on the performance of the contracts; and the fourth is determining whether the procedural requirements set forth in the force majeure clause have been met."). *Id.* at 136.

49 *Id.* at 136 (noting that "the petroleum contract may define force majeure clauses either illustrating a list of events or adopting its definition under a legal system. Such reference to the legal system may be made to the code or law of the host state applicable to the contract, general principles of law or international law or international commercial practice.").

50 Berger, *supra* note 43, at 1350–51.

51 Al Faruque (2008), at 135; Berger, *supra* note 43, at 1351.

52 Berger, *supra* note 43, at 1352 (noting that, "[h]owever, force majeure clause can also contain an obligation on the parties to negotiate and to search for ways to overcome the situation resulting from intervention by "acts of god." Such a contract is particularly ill-suited for cancellation due to the complexity and financial obligations already incurred by the parties").

in an international business transaction.[53] A study by a group of international lawyers of a significant number of *force majeure* clauses in long-term contracts revealed that: First, most force majeure provisions in such contracts have less strict conditions for the occurrence of force majeure than in the concept of force majeure *stricto sensu*. Second, such clauses are intended to suspend the contract instead of terminating it. Finally, these clauses usually impose a duty on the contracting parties to make their best efforts to overcome the situation of force majeure by subsequent renegotiation.[54] A 1982 Agreement provides a good illustration of force majeure clauses in international contracts:

> Article XIII_ Force Majeure_ 13.1: *Excuse for Non-Performance*. In the event that any party to this Agreement is rendered unable… by Force Majeure to carry out its obligations under this Agreement, such party shalll give notice… to the other parties to this Agreement… setting forth the full particulars of such Force Majeure and the estimated duration thereof… [T]he obligations of such party, insofar as they are affected by such Force Majeure, shall be suspended… during the continuance of any inability so caused, but for no longer period, and such cause shall so far as possible be remedied with reasonable dispatch. The party claiming Force Majeure shall exercise reasonable efforts to mitigate the effects of such Force Majeure on the performance of its obligations under this Agreement.
>
> 13.2: Meaning of Force Majeure… Notwitstanding the foregoing, both Buyers and seller shall make reasonable efforts so that the supply of [Liquefied Natural Gas] shall not be interrupted due to strike, lockout or other industrial disturbance.[55]

#### 3.5.1.1.2 *Hardship Clause*

The force majeure clause seems, *prima facie*, similar to a hardship clause[56] which usually contemplates the situation where the

53 Al Qurashi (2005), at 280.

54 PETER (*1995*), at 235–36.

55 Quoted by PETER (1995), at 236.

56 The UNIDROIT Principles of International Commercial Contracts as a restatement of the currently accepted rules and principles of international contract law define hardship and its legal consequences as follows: Article 6.2.2 Definition of Hardship: There is hardship where the occurrence of events fundamentally alters the equilibrium of the contract either because the cost of a party's performance has increased or because the value of the performance a party receives has diminished, and (a) the events occur or

performance of a contract has not become impossible but extremely burdensome.[57]

A hardship clause is common in long-term commercial contracts, and a notable example can be found in the Nippon Steel-Quintette contract in which the clause in the contract provided under the title "Mutual Cooperation":

> Both Buyer and Seller recognize that circumstances may arise that could not have been foreseen at the time this contract was entered into. Both parties agree to use their best efforts to solve any hardship or difficulties arising from such unforeseeable circumstances in the spirit of mutual good will and cooperation.[58]

According to Schmitthof, there are three significant elements of circumstances in which hardship exists. First, the event in question must arise beyond either part's control. Second, the event in question must be entirely unforeseeable and uncontemplated. Third, change of circumstances must be fundamental and substantial in character.[59]

Ostensibly, both hardship and force majeure clauses are applied in similar circumstances, but they lead to different legal consequences. While the force majeure clause deals with contractual liability arising out of contractual non-performance caused by supervening events,[60] it is not intended to lead

---

become known to the disadvantaged party after the conclusion of the contract; (b) the events could not reasonably have been taken into account by the disadvantaged party at the time of the conclusion of the contract; (c) the events are beyond the control of the disadvantaged party; and (d) the risk of the events was not assumed by the disadvantaged party. *See* International Institute for the Unification of Private Law (UNIDROIT), Principles of International Commercial Contracts. Art. 6.2.2, at 218 (2016). Article 6.2.3 – Effects of Hardship: (1) In case of hardship the disadvantaged party is entitled to request renegotiations. The request shall be made without undue delay and shall indicate the grounds on which it is based. (2) The request for renegotiation does not in itself entitle the disadvantaged party to withhold performance. (3) Upon failure to reach agreement within a reasonable time either party may resort to the court. (4) If the court finds hardship it may, if reasonable, (a) terminate the contract at a date and on terms to be fixed; or (b) adapt the contract with a view to restoring its equilibrium. *Id.* Art. 6.2.3, at 223.

57 PETER (1995), at 237.

58 The Coal Purchase Contract between Nippon Steel Corporation and Quintette Coal Ltd (Oct. 1, 1983) [Cited in William A. W. Neilson, Price Adjustments in Long-Term Supply Contracts: The Saga of the Quintette Coal Arbitration, 18 CAN. Bus. L.J. 76, 85 (1991)].

59 C.M. Schmitthoff, Hardship and Intervener Clauses, *J. Bus. L.* 82,85(1980) (noting that, [t]hese criteria make it clear that the hardship concept is very similar, if not identical, to that of frustration.).

60 Al Faruque (2008), at 136.

primarily to contract change,but rather to excuse liability. However, if the force majeure events lead to the temporary change, impossibility or termination in the event of an absolute and permanent impossibility of performing the contract, the force majeure clause may result in the renegotiating of the original contract.[61] On the other hand, the hardship clause primarily deals with the adjustment of contract conditions and aims to re-establish the original equilbrium of the contract. As a legal consequence of the hardship clause, the contracting parties are obliged to renegotiate their contract.[62] One commentator aptly summarized the underlying concept of the hardship clause, stating that this clause seeks to create a system of “internal regulation” designed to protect the commercial equilibrium of the contract from the undesired effects of a constantly changing economic environment.[63] He further adds that the hardship clause supplements this structure by providing a form of “safety net” designed to mitigate the effects of extraordinary unforeseeable changes in the circumstances surrounding the contract.[64] This led Professor Wolfgang Peter to describe the hardship clause as a specific form of the renegotiation clause which makes contractual obligations more flexible in case of changes the original equilibrium of the contract.[65] Ultimately, the hardship and force majeure clauses are employed as techniques in case of changed circumstances to ensure fairness in the particular situation[66] when the contract lacks a renegotiation clause.

It bears mention that, although the hardship clause is commonlly found in long-term commercial contracts and commodity supply agreements, it is not widely used in petroleum contract. This due to several factors, including the prevalence of force majeure clauses in petroleum contracts, which are designed to address unforessen events that may give rise to hardships. Additionally, many petroleum contracts utilize self-adjusting fiscal mechanisms and economic stabilization clauses to handle windfall profits, price increases, and other economic changes, making the inclusion of a formal hardship clause unnecessary. Finally, some foreign investors are hesitant to include a hardship clause in petroleum contracts due to concerns that it may undermine the stability of the agreement, as the imprecise nature of the clause may allow for

61 *Id.*

62 Berger, *supra* note 43, at 1352.

63 Karen Kemp, *Applying the Hardship Clause*, 1 J. ENERGY & NAT. Resources L. 119,119 (1983).

64 *Id.*

65 PETER (1995), at 242.

66 Al Faruque (2008), at 136.

broad interpretation by the host state, potentially giving the contracting party an opportunity to avoid its contractual obligations.[67]

The preceding analysis of force majeure and hardship clauses reveals that both clauses are applied in very similar circumstances. However, one might ask whether both clauses lead to different results. Theoretically, while the hardship clause aims to adapt the contract to a particular situation, the force majeure clause usually does not describe in detail the procedure to be followed or the adjustments that should be made. Further, while a hardship clause usually describes the sanctions if the contracting parties cannot reach an agreement, the force majeure clause includes elaborate provisos as to the procedure and adjustment. Therefore, the force majeure clause is, in fact, a type of renegotiation clause.[68]

#### 3.5.1.2 Applicable Law to the State Contract in Renegotiations

The issue of the applicable law is one of the critical questions in the resolution of state contracts disputes generally and therefore in relation to renegotiations. Various scenarios may arise regarding the issue of applicable law. First, state contracts may only be governed by the municipal law of the host state. Second, the contract may be governed by the contract itself as an autonomous and exhaustive system (the "*lex contractus*"). Third, a state contract may be governed by international law, general principles of law, or international law of contracts. Fourth, a state contract may be governed by national law with recourse when necessary to international law or by both municipal and international law. Fifth, a contract can be governed by the decisions of an international tribunal. Lastly, the governing law for state contracts may be a combination of these legal sources.[69]

The issue of applicable law is significant for state contract disputes in general, but it becomes particularly crucial when it comes to contract changes. It can determine the conditions under which a contracting party is entitled to change the contract and to what extent, as well as the legal consequences if a contract change fails, or if a party refuses to accept renegotiation. Furthermore, it can also determine the consequences of unilateral changes, such as nationalization or modification of the contract by government decree or legislation.[70]

When the contract lacks provisions that govern the renegotiation or adjustment in case of changed circumstances, the party seeking to renegotiate may

---

67 *Id*, at 128.

68 PETER (1995), at 237–38.

69 Faruque (2006 a), *at* 333; PETER, *supra* note 131, at 130.

70 PETER (1995), at 130.

turn to the objective norms of the applicable law. However, these norms may differ across various legal systems.[71] Thus, this section will examine how the renegotiation of long-term contracts is dealt with under the principal legal systems, including civil and common law systems, as well as under international law. By doing so, we aim to provide a comprehensive overview of the legal framework applicable to state contract renegotiations.

#### 3.5.1.2.1 *Renegotiation under National Legal Systems*

The following brief survey will examine England and the United States as examples of common law systems, and France, Germany, and Egypt as examples of civil law systems.

##### 3.5.1.2.1.1 Common-Law System: Principle of Frustration and Impracticability

Traditionally, in both English and American common law systems, the liability to perform a contract is absolute. This means that even if a party is not at fault for non-performance, they are still required to perform their obligations under the contract.[72] Regardless of how difficult or burdensome performance becomes for a party or how much circumstances change, they must still fulfill their duties. Courts also do not have the authority to modify contract terms to reflect changed circumstances.[73] However, in certain cases where a fundamental change of circumstances renders performance physically or legally impossible, relief from contractual liability may be granted by the court even if the party is not at fault for the breach. In rare cases, the court may grant relief from contractual liability under the principle of frustration and impracticability, even if the performance is still possible,[74] but the contract's purpose has been frustrated due to a supervening event that fundamentally affects the contract's performance.[75] In English law, hardship alone is not enough to grant relief, and the interpretation of frustration is strictly applied by English judges who are often hesitant to use it.[76] English judges typically interpret frustration on

---

71 Horn, *supra* note 12, at 16.

72 *Id.* at 20.

73 Al Qurashi (2005), at 267.

74 Horn, *supra* note 12, at 20–21.

75 Roy Goode, Commercial Law 136 (2004) (noting that, "Among the circumstances which will usually frustrate a contract where there is no fault on either side are: (a) accidental destruction of the subject matter…, (c) supervening illegality; (d) supervening impossibility through government interference; (e) inability to produce a necessary consent of a third party …, (f) a fundamental change in the basis of the contract.") Goode, *supra* note 344, at 137–38.

76 Al Qurashi (2005), at 267.

narrow grounds and are reluctant to apply it in cases where a change in circumstances has made contract performance significantly more burdensome for one party.

For example, in the case *Tasakiroglous v. Noblee*,[77] an English contract-law case concerning the matter of frustration, where the parties had contracted for the sale of Sudanese groundnuts and their transportation from Sudan to Hamburg via the Suez Canal, which was the customary route at the time. On the date of shipment, the Suez Canal closed down for navigation due to the military operations by the British and French armed forces against Egypt. However, on the date of shipment, the Suez Canal was closed due to military operations by the British and French armed forces against Egypt. While an alternative route around the Cape of Good Hope was open, it was almost twice as long and twice as costly for the seller. As a result, the seller refused to ship the goods. The House of Lords held that the contract was not frustrated since the shipping of the goods via the Cape of Good Hope did not fundamentally alter the contract, and the sellers were obligated to transport the goods via a reasonable and practicable route, regardless of the additional cost.[78]

However, English judges may acknowledge the clauses of force majeure and hardship in contracts, which provide some leeway to modify the contract in response to changing circumstances.[79]

To draw a comparison with the narrow approach taken by English courts towards excuses arising from changing circumstances, U.S. courts adopt a broader approach called "frustration and commercial impracticability".[80]

The principle of "frustration and commercial impracticability", which is embodied in sections 2–615 in the Uniform Commercial Code (UCC) and section 268 (2) of the Restatement of Contracts:

77 Tsakiroglou & Co. Ltd. V. Noblee Thorl GmbH [1962] A.C. 93.

78 *Id*; *See also* LawTeacher, Free Law Study Resources, https://www.lawteacher.net/cases/tsakiroglou-and-co-v-noblee-thorl.php; Simple Studying, https://simplestudying.com/tsakiroglou-co-ltd-v-noblee-thorl-gmbh-1962-ac-93/.

79 HORN, *supra* note 12, at 21; Al Qurashi (2005), at 271.

80 As noted by the court in *Mineral Park v. Howard* that "A thing is impossible in legal contemplation when it is not practicable; and a thing is impracticable when it can only be done at an excessive and unreasonable cost." *See* Mineral Park Land Co. v. Howard, 172 Cal. 289, 156 P. 458 (1916); *See also*, Matter of Westinghouse Elec. Corp., Etc., 517 F. Supp. 440 (E.D. Va. 1981). (The court defined the commercial impracticability as "discharge an obligor from his duty to perform a contract where a failure of a basic assumption of the parties produces a grave failure of the equivalence of value of the exchange to the parties.").

> Where, after a contract is made, a party's performance is made impracticable without his fault by the occurrence of an event the non-occurrence of which was a basic assumption on which the contract was made, his duty to render that performance is discharged, unless the language or the circumstances indicate the contrary.[81]

The impracticability doctrine for discharging contractual performance in the US requires a combination of two elements: severity and surprise.[82] Although discharge from unexpectedly onerous contractual obligations is limited in US law, in some cases, courts have adjusted contract terms when changes in circumstances were unforeseen at the time of signing and performance would result in the contracting party's bankruptcy.[83] While some US court opinions recognize the negotiability of long-term contracts in extreme circumstances, the criteria for negotiability remain narrow and strict.[84]

Based on the preceding discussion, the decisions of Anglo-American courts not only reaffirm the principle of *pacta sunt servanda* or the sanctity of contract but also indicate that parties to long-term contracts without renegotiation clauses should not expect being granted relief by the court against bad bargains or simply because they turned out to be onerous.[85] Instead, parties are advised to insert a renegotiation clause in their contract to address changing circumstances, rather than seeking relief in court.

#### 3.5.1.2.1.2 Civil Law System

Civil law systems generally take a more flexible approach to modifying long-term contracts in the face of significant changes in essential circumstances than common law.[86] The *rebus sic stantibus* principle in civil law requires that contracts remain valid as long as the fundamental circumstances that were essential at the time of signing continue to exist.[87] However, if there has been a significant and drastic change in essential circumstances, a party to the contract

---

81 Restatement (Second) of Contracts §261 (1979).

82 R. Buxbaum, *Modification and Adaptation of Contracts: American Legal Developments, in* ADAPTATION AND RENEGOTIATION OF CONTRACTSIN INTERNATIONAL TRADE AND FINANCE 31 (N. Horn ed., 1985).

83 Abba Kolo & Thomas W. Walde, Renegotiation and Contract Adaptation in International Investment Projects – Applicable Legal Principles and Industry Practices, 1 J. World INVESTMENT 5, 35 (2000); *see also*, Al Qurashi (2005), at 267.

84 Kolo & Walde, *supra* note 83, at 35.

85 *Id.*

86 *Id.*

87 *Id.* at 35–36.

may withdraw from its obligations or terminate the contract. While civil law is theoretically based on the principle of sanctity of contract, no major legal system allows for easy withdrawal from contractual commitments. Nevertheless, in practice, the sanctity of contract has never been treated as an absolute and unqualified principle in any major legal system. Civil law courts often recognize the concept of adaptation or modification based on principles such as the German doctrine of *Wegfall der Geschäftsgrundlage*,[88] the French doctrine of *imprevision*,[89] or the principle of good faith in other civil law systems. All of these provide for limitations on the principle of sanctity of contract.[90]

The doctrine of *Wegfall der Geschäftsgrundlage* in German Law allows for termination or judicial adaptation of long-term contracts when there is a fundamental and unexpected change in the necessary circumstances underlying the original contract. However, a mere change in risks and circumstances is

88 Section 313 of German Civil Code provides that "(1) If circumstances which became the basis of a contract have significantly changed since the contract was entered into and if the parties would not have entered into the contract or would have entered into it with different contents if they had foreseen this change, adaptation of the contract may be demanded to the extent that, taking account of all the circumstances of the specific case, in particular the contractual or statutory distribution of risk, one of the parties cannot reasonably be expected to uphold the contract without alteration. (2) It is equivalent to a change of circumstances if material conceptions that have become the basis of the contract are found to be incorrect. (3) If adaptation of the contract is not possible or one party cannot reasonably be expected to accept it, the disadvantaged party may revoke the contract. In the case of continuing obligations, the right to terminate takes the place of the right to revoke." *See* Bürgerliches Gesetzbuch[BGB] [Civil Code],§ 313, *translation at* https://www.gesetze-im-internet.de/englisch_bgb/englisch_bgb.pdf.

89 Article 1195 of French Civil Code provides that "[i]f a change of circumstances that was unforeseeable at the time of the conclusion of the contract renders performance excessively onerous for a party who had not accepted the risk of such a change, that party may ask the other contracting party to renegotiate the contract. The first party must continue to perform his obligations during renegotiation." Ordonnance n° 2016–131 du 10 février 2016 portant réforme du droit des contrats, du régime général et de la preuve des obligations [Law 2016–131 of Feb 10,2016 on the Law of Contract, The General Regime of Obligations, and Proof of Obligations], Art. 1195, Journal Officiel De La Republique Francaise [Official Gazette of France] *translation at* http://www.textes.justice.gouv.fr/art_pix/THE-LAW-OF-CONTRACT-2-5-16.pdf.

90 *See* for a discussion of these doctrines and their differences under various national laws, Hans van Houtte, Changed Circumstances and Pacta Sunt Servanda. In Transnational Rules in International Commercial Arbitration, ed. Emmanuel Gaillard, 105. Paris: ICC Publication, at 113–115 (1993), *available at* https://www.trans-lex.org/117300/_/van-houtte-hans-changed-circumstances-and-pacta-sunt-servanda-in:-gaillard-transnational-rules-in-international-commercial-arbitration-paris-1993-at-105-et-seq/.

not sufficient to justify judicial intervention in the balance of freely negotiated contracts.[91]

Before the 2016 French contract-law reform, French law strictly upheld the principle of sanctity of contract, with excuses from contractual obligations being restricted only to cases of impossibility, mainly due to force majeure, unless there was a contractual clause to the contrary.[92] The French judges were reluctant to apply the theory of imprévision to commercial contracts without a specific agreement between the parties to the contract.[93] The doctrine of *imprévision* (*théorie de l'imprévision*) was initially recognized as an excuse for non-performance only in government contracts (*contrat administratife*).[94] However, in the Gaz de Bordeaux case, the Conseil d'Etat (State Council) applied the doctrine of imprévision for the first time in a government contract. This doctrine allows the French Conseil d'Etat to adapt a contract when unexpected changes in circumstances have made it extremely burdensome for one party.[95]

Similar to the German doctrine of *Wegfall der Geschäftsgrundlage,* the French theory of *imprevision* allows a party to withdraw from contractual obligations in case of occurrence the unforeseeable events that significantly affected the performance of the contract in a way that led to an upheaval of the contract benefits.[96]

---

91 Kolo & Walde, *supra* note 83, at 36.

92 Al Qurashi (2005), at 272.

93 Shearman & Sterling, *Force Majeure and Imprévision Under French Law* (Mar. 26, 2020). Available at https://www.shearman.com/Perspectives/2020/03/Force-Majeure-and-Imprevision-under-French-Law-COVID-19. Since October 1, 2016, *imprévision* is governed by Article 1195 of the French Civil Code: "If a change of circumstances that were unforeseeable at the time of the conclusion of the contract renders performance excessively onerous for a party that had not accepted the risk of such a change, that party may ask the other contracting party to renegotiate the contract. The affected party must continue to perform its obligations during the period of renegotiation. If the renegotiation is refused or fails, the parties may agree to terminate the contract or to turn to a court or arbitral tribunal to adapt the contract. In the absence of such an agreement in a reasonable time, upon the request of any party, a court or tribunal may amend or terminate the contract. In such circumstances, the court or tribunal would determine the date and conditions of the termination." Therefore, for a party to avail itself of the doctrine of *imprévision* under French law, the relevant contract must have been concluded after October 1, 2016. At the same time, the contracting parties are free to exclude or adjust the principle of *imprévision. See Id.*

94 Horn, *supra* note 12, at 18.

95 Shearman & Sterling, *supra* note 93.

96 CE., Mar. 30, 1916.

Interestingly, the French theory of *imprevision* has inspired corresponding provisions in the civil laws of many Arab countries such as Egypt, Iraq, Libya, Sudan, Algeria, and the United Arab Emirates.[97] Article 147 of the Egyptian Civil Code of 1948 is a notable example. While the Egyptian legislature in Article 147 (1) of the Civil Code assured the principle of sanctity of contract (*pacta sunt servanda*), Article 147 (2) provided an exception of the *pacta sunt servanda* principle and established a doctrine of "changed circumstances."[98] To trigger this doctrine, certain conditions must be met. The event must be exceptional and unpredictable, and it must make the performance of the contract so burdensome that it causes exorbitant losses to a contracting party. Upon satisfying the above conditions, a judge is empowered to adapt the contractual undertakings to a reasonable limit considering the interests of contracting parties, but not to terminate the original contract.[99]

It bears mention that the Egyptian civil code in Articles 668–673 recognizes a special type of contract known as administrative contracts. Unlike private contracts, these contracts are more prone to government intervention through renegotiation or termination.[100] This practice is prevalent in Arab countries where the public and administrative law of French tradition has become part of the domestic legal system.[101] Public contracts or administrative contracts, including those related to natural resources development, are governed by a set of public law rules that tailored to meet their objectives.[102] From an administrative law perspective, the government has the inherent and inalienable power to intervene in administrative contracts for public interest considerations by imposing regulations that are beyond the contract's terms.[103]

In sum, in light of the foregoing discussions, the principle of *pacta sunt servanda*, in both private and public law contracts, is widely accepted in

97 HORN, *supra* note 12, at 18.

98 Article 147 (1) stipulates that "*Pacta sunt servanda*, it can be revoked or altered only by mutual consent of the parties or for reasons provided for by the law. (2) Nevertheless, in case of exceptional and unpredictable events that caused the performance of the contractual obligation, even if not impossible, becomes excessively onerous in such way as to threaten the debtor with exorbitant loss, the judge may, according to the circumstances, and after taking into consideration the interests of both parties, reduce to reasonable limits the obligation that has become excessive. Any agreement to the contrary is void." Law No. 131 of 1948 (Civil Code), Al-Waqa'i'a al-Masriya, vol. 108 bis (a), 29 July 1984, art. 147 (*pacta sunt sevanda*) (Egypt). [unofficial translation].

99 *Id.*

100 Al Qurashi (2005), at 268.

101 El-Kosheri & Riad (1986), at 260.

102 *Id.*

103 *Id.* 260–61.

various legal systems worldwide. However, this principle provides for varying exceptions in different legal systems. The validity and legal effect of contracts under all legal systems are lost when the crux purpose of the contract no longer exists.[104] Nevertheless, there are divergent approaches among the various legal systems when the performance of the contract is still to be possible but become extremely onerous to one contracting party due to a drastic and significant change in essential circumstances. In strict common-law of the English tradition, courts are reluctant to intervene in negotiated terms on behalf of the disadvantaged party. In the United States, there are precedents and a legal resoning to help the disadvantage party when "the balance between both parties' performance has been severely distorted and if the change of circumstances was both essential for the original balance of the contract and unforseen at the time of conclusion of the original contract."[105]

Interestingly, this latter concept is widely accepted in all civil law countries, and more so is in governmental contracts or administrative contracts with public law elements.[106] Ultimately, one might reasonably ask whether these doctrines, as alluded to above, would even be helpful and in what circumstances for ordinary contract renegotiations. If the contract lacks a renegotiation clause, a national court will primarily look at the scope of adaptation concepts in the applicable national law. Suppose the concept of adaptation provided in the national law is very narrow (as is the concept of frustration in British law and *imprevision* in French law). In that case, the question will remain open, to say the least, whether the national court will adopt the broader and more flexible concept of adaptation.[107] To circumvent this uncertainty, contracting parties are advised to insert a renegotiation clause in their long-term contract.

#### 3.5.1.2.2 *A Renegotiation under International Law*

If the choice of law provisions explicitly refer to the international law as applicable, then such law shall apply to the state contract. However, it is essential to note that public international law itself does not apply to the investor-state contract.[108] International law, particularly the law of treaties, was created expressly only for relations between countries, not for foreign investors and governments. Nevertheless, certain aspects of international law do relate to

104 Kolo & Walde, *supra* note 83, at 37.
105 *Id.*
106 *Id.*
107 HORN, *supra* note 12, at 29.
108 Waelde & Ndi (1996), at 241.

foreign investor-state agreements.[109] This section will examine generally recognized principles of international law, the law of treaties, decisions of the international tribunal, and literature on state contracts.

In the international law of treaties, the principle of *pacta sunt servanda* is affirmed by Article 26 of Vienna Convention on the Law of Treaties of 1969.[110] However, Article 62 recognizes the doctrine of *rebus sic stantihus*, which allows for the termination or withdrawal from a treaty on the basis of a change in circumstances.[111] Certain conditions must be met for the doctrine of *rebus sic stantihus* to be applied as a valid base for terminating or withdrawing. In the *Gabickovo-Nagynaros* case,[112] the International Court of Justice (ICJ) tackled the issue of change of circumstances on which Hungary relied as ground to withdraw from its treaty undertakings. These events included "profound changes of a political nature, the Project's diminishing economic viability, the progress of environmental knowledge and the development of new norms and prescriptions of international environmental law."[113] The court acknowledged that new norms and standards have been developed since the Treaty was signed in 1977. Nonetheless,

> The Court does not consider that new developments in the state of environmental knowledge and of environmental law can be said to have been completely unforeseen... The changed circumstances advanced by

---

109 Professor Horn argued that Article 62 of the Vienna Convention "is a strong argument for the existence of a general legal principle which might also be relevant to transnational contracts with or between private parties." *See* HORN, *supra* note 12, at 25.

110 Article 26 stipulates that "[e]very treaty in force is binding upon the parties to it and must be performed by them in good faith."

111 Article 62 stipulates that "Fundamental change of circumstances: 1. A fundamental change of circumstances which has occurred with regard to those existing at the time of the conclusion of a treaty, and which was not foreseen by the parties, may not be invoked as a ground for terminating or withdrawing from the treaty unless: (a) the existence of those circumstances constituted an essential basis of the consent of the parties to be bound by the treaty; and 21 (b) the effect of the change is radically to transform the extent of obligations still to be performed under the treaty. 2. A fundamental change of circumstances may not be invoked as a ground for terminating or withdrawing from a treaty: (a) if the treaty establishes a boundary; or (b) if the fundamental change is the result of a breach by the party invoking it either of an obligation under the treaty or of any other international obligation owed to any other party to the treaty. 3. If, under the foregoing paragraphs, a party may invoke a fundamental change of circumstances as a ground for terminating or withdrawing from a treaty it may also invoke the change as a ground for suspending the operation of the treaty."

112 GabCikovo-Nagymaros Project (Hungary/Slovakia), Judgment, ICJ Reports (1997).

113 *Id.* 104.

> Hungary are, in the Court's view, not of such a nature, either individually or collectively, that their effect would radically transform the extent of the obligations still to be performed in order to accomplish the Project. A fundamental change of circumstances must have been unforeseen; the existence of the circumstances at the time of the Treaty's conclusion must have constituted an essential basis of the consent of the parties to be bound by the Treaty. The negative and conditional wording of Article 62 of the Vienna Convention on the Law of Treaties is a clear indication moreover that the stability of treaty relations requires that the plea of fundamental change of circumstances be applied only in exceptional cases.[114]

While the above decision of the ICJ reinforced the traditional principle of *pacta sunt servanda*, it also suggests that an unexpected drastic change of circumstances that essentially affects the agreement basis could be a valid ground for renegotiating the original agreement.

Although this case involved two sovereign states, it nonetheless can provide a perfect analogy as the nature of the disputed project (a long-term development of natural resources) is typical of the type of investor-state contracts, and the issues involved are also common (*e.g.*, SPP *v. Egypt*).[115] In this vein, Professor Horn has reaffirmed that while the Vienna convention applies only to treaties between sovereign states, it does not apply to private contracts or state contracts. However, Article 62 mentioned above is a strong argument for the existence of a general legal principle that may also be relevant to transnational contracts with or between private parties.[116] Over the past forty years, the question of state sovereignty versus protection of foreign investments has been the primary concern in international investment law. This view has been based on various United Nations General Assembly Resolutions supported by developing countries seeking to review their previously concluded long-term investment agreements. In their report on Multinational Companies, the UN Group of Eminent Persons recommended that long-term contracts include a renegotiation clause.[117] Moreover, the UN Economic and Social Council

---

114 *Id.*

115 Kolo & Walde, *supra* note 83, at 39.

116 HORN, *supra* note 12, at 25.

117 13 I.L.M. 800, at 818–19 (2014) (noting that "[t]he Group recommends that in the initial agreement with multinational corporations, host countries should consider making provision for the review, at the request of either side, after suitable intervals, of various clauses of the agreement. The review by the host country should be carried out by the negotiating services or co-ordinating groups recommended above.").

(ECSOC) Drafted Code of Conduct on Transnational Corporations (section 5) that recommends multinational corporations engage in renegotiation with the governments in case of a fundamental change of circumstances leading to inequity between the contracting parties in the absence of contractual clauses providing for review or renegotiation.

Furthermore, in 1968, the members of OPEC made an explicit declaration supporting the states' right to renegotiate their long-term petroleum contracts with multinational corporations.[118] In this vein, the inescapable consequence, however, is that the existence of the duty to negotiate long-term agreements did not find unanimous support among the countries.[119] While developed countries, on the one hand, did uphold the principle of *pacta sunt servanda* (sanctity of contract), they did not explicitly or implicitly reject the application of contract-law concepts such as the principle of *rebus sic stantihus* (change of circumstances doctrine). Developed countries, however, rejected the right to unilaterally change the long-term investment contracts claimed by developing countries on the ground of sovereignty and new economic policy alone.[120]

From the above discussion, it can be concluded that the doctrine of *rebus sic stantihus* can only be invoked when truly unforeseeable and grave consequences occurs, making it of little use in most ordinary situations where a party is trying to renegotiate or terminate its obligations. Therefore, it is advisable to include a renegotiation or revision clause in the long-term contracts to avoid the need to rely on the doctrine of *rebus sic stantihus.*

### 3.5.2 *Contract with Renegotiation Clause*

Due to the principle of *pacta sunt servanda* on the one hand, and the failure of a *force-majeure* clause and hardship doctrine to provide adequate support in a substantial change of circumstances, the necessity of including state contracts specific provisions is apparent if the investor requires contractual flexibility. Plainly, foreign investors, through the inclusion of renegotiation clauses in their investment contracts, have tried to secure their investment against adverse changes to the commercial balance of the contract.[121] Equally, host states have employed these clauses to increase their participation in energy projects to profit from high oil prices or to ensure permanent sovereignty over their natural resources.[122] Therefore, in practice, the drafting of PSAs reveals

118 Declaratory Statement of Petroleum Policy in Member Countries, Res. No. XVI. 90 of the Sixteenth OPEC Conference, 7 I.L.M. 1183 (1968).

119 Kolo & Walde, *supra* note 83, at 40; Al Qurashi (2005), at 278.

120 Kolo & Walde, *supra* note 83, at 40.

121 Berger, *supra* note 43, at 1357.

122 ERKAN (2010), at 146.

that the inclusion of renegotiation clauses has become common in modern times.[123]

An early and instructive example of the traditional renegotiation clause can be found in the Article 9 of supplementary agreement (July 29, 1961) to the concession agreement between the state of Kuwait and the American Independent Oil Company (June 28, 1984) (AMINOIL Contract):

> If, as a result of changes in the terms of concessions now in existence or as a result of the terms of concessions granted hereafter, an increase in benefits to Governments in the Middle East should come generally to be received by them, the Company shall consult with the Ruler whether in the light of all relevant circumstances, including the conditions in which operations are carried out, and taking into account all payments made, any alterations in the terms of the agreements between the Ruler and the Company would be equitable to the parties.[124]

Another example of traditional renegotiation clauses can be found in article 47(b) of the Ghana/Shell Clause (The Petroleum Production Agreement between the Government of Ghana and Shell Exploration and Production Company of Ghana Ltd., of 1974):

> It is hereby agreed that if during the term of this Agreement there should occur such changes in the financial and economic circumstances relating to the petroleum industry, operating conditions in Ghana and marketing conditions generally as to materially affect the fundamental economic and financial basis of this Agreement, then the provisions of this Agreement may be reviewed or renegotiated with a view to making such adjustments and modifications as may be reasonable having regard to the Operator's capital employed and the risks incurred by him always provided that no such adjustments or modifications shall be made within 5 years after the commencement of production of petroleum in commercial quantities from the production area and that they shall have no retroactive effect.[125]

---

123 Berger, *supra* note 43, at 1357–58.

124 Kuwait v. American Indep. Oil Co. (Aminoil), 21 I.L.M. 976, at 18 (1982). For a more detailed analysis of Aminoil renegotiation see PETER (1995), at 90–103 (noting that "... the Aminoil renegotiations were an excellent illustrative case of the general issues arising in connection with investment contracts."); *see also* Berger, *supra* note 43, at 1358–59; *see* Aminoil Clause, *infra*, Appendix, Part I.A.

125 Asante (1979), at 417.

Additional renegotiation clauses can are included in the Ok Tedi Clause, the Lasmo Clause, and the Qatar Clause as listed in the Appendix.[126] By examining these examples of renegotiation clauses, the divergences between stability and renegotiation clauses become apparent. While the traditional stabilization clause aims to protect the foreign investor by freezing the host state's regulatory framework applicable to the contract during the lifespan of their investment project, this inevitably comes into conflict with the host state's sovereignty.[127] In contrast, as cited above, the renegotiation clause aims to protect foreign investors by providing flexability to the state contract and adapting to changed circumstances caused by the host state's sovereign acts.[128] This comparison highlights the inherent conflict of interests between foreign investors and host states.[129]

Moreover, under the traditional renegotiation clauses mentioned above, the renegotiating of contractual terms does not occur automatically. Its application is subject to certain conditions. This raises several questions that are crucial to the effectivness and enforcement of such clauses: What are the specific events that must occur to trigger the duty to renegotiate? What are the obligations of the contracting parties during the renegotiation process? What are the exact procedures for renegotiation? And if the renegotiation process fails to achieve its primary goal, what is the solution?

#### 3.5.2.1 Triggering Events for Renegotiation

When drafting a renegotiation clause, contracting parties should clearly identify and define any triggering events for renegotiation.[130] The significance of this element stems from the fact that the parties, upon meeting the provisions on renegotiation, may decide to commence renegotiations relying on the framework provided by the renegotiation clause.[131] The renegotiation

126 *See infra* Appendix, Part I.A.

127 Berger, *supra* note 43, at 1360.

128 *Id.* at 1361.

129 Asante (1979), at 404 (noting that "[a] major source of conflict between host governments of developing countries and transnational corporations derives from the preoccupation of transnational corporations with stability and predictability in contractual relations on the one hand, and the persistent demands of host governments for a more flexible contractual regime on the other hand.").

130 Piero Bernardini, *Stabilization and Adaptation in Oil and Gas Investments*, 1 J. World Energy & Bus. 98, 103 (2008).

131 Cameron (2010), at 85; Berger, *supra* note 43, at 1362 (noting that "[t]he ability of a renegotiation clause to function in practice is dependent, above all, on the prerequisites for initiating a consensual procedure being clearly defined in the clause.").

boundary depends upon the scope of triggering events provided in the renegotiation clause.[132]

There is no set formula in practice that can be adapted to determine the triggering events on renegotiation. Instead, divergent approaches can be found in this vein depending on the duration and complexity of each contract.[133] This thesis opines that these different approaches can be divided into three categories. The first category is a simple renegotiation clause that indicates a possibility of renegotiating without providing for any event as a trigger.[134] A notable example here can be found in The OK Tedi Papua New Guinea Agreement of 1976, in which clause 42 provided that "[t]he parties may from time to time by agreement in writing add to, substitute for, cancel or vary all or any of the provisions of this Agreement."[135]

The central concerns about renegotiation clauses like The Ok Tedi Clause articulated above are that they do not mandate or otherwise require parties to renegotiate. Indeed, they often add little to the contract since the agreements with or without such clauses can always be subsequently modified by the agreement of the parties-so what exactly would such noncompulsory language add remains an open question.

The second category is a general renegotiation clause that provides for broad and general triggering events for renegotiation. Article 9 of the AMINOIL contract is probably one of the best known of such clauses, which makes the obligation to renegotiate dependent on the existence of an "increase in benefits to Governments in the Middle East ... generally to be received by them."[136] Another example of this type of renegotiation clause can be found in Article 47 (b) of the Ghana/Shell contract, which requires that "such changes in the financial and economic circumstances relating to the petroleum industry, operating conditions in Ghana and marketing conditions generally as to materially affect the fundamental economic and financial basis of this Agreement."[137]

It might be argued that it is difficult to formulate such a general renegotiation clause that defines specifically when a change of circumstances and its impact is serious enough to trigger a renegotiation.[138] Additionally, even when

---

132 Al Faruque (2008), at 122.

133 *Id*; Berger, *supra* note 43, at 1362; Al Qurashi (2005), at 289.

134 PETER (1995), at 242.

135 Ok-Tedi, Copper Agreement between the State of papua New Guinea and Dampier Mining Co. Ltd. Art. 42 (1976); *See infra*-Appendix, Part I.A and accompanying text.

136 Kuwait v. American Indep. Oil Co. (Aminoil), 21 I.L.M. 976, at 18 (1982); *See infra*-Appendix, Part I. A. and accompanying text.

137 Asante (1979), at 417; *see infra*-Appendix, Part I.A. and accompanying text.

138 Kolo & Walde, *supra* note 83, at 47.

the parties can agree on and identify the trigger event, they are phrased so broadly to invite disagreement on the facts-for example, what counts as "materially" or even "benefits"? For this reason, parties in the state contracts do not often focus on including a general renegotiation clause in their contracts.[139]

The third and final category is the particular event clause, which requires a specific occurrence of a specific event or set of events to occur as defined precisely in the clause before triggering renegotiation. Examples of such events include tax increases, changes in raw materials prices, or the materialization of a specific risk (special risk clause).[140] Although this category has the advantage of clearly defining the beginning of the renegotiation process, it may also be seen as a disadvantages as it only allows for overcoming the concept of *pacta sunt servanda* for a specific type of risk.[141]

As the elaboration of triggering events in the renegotiation clause provides the legal framework for the renegotiation process, a well-defined set of triggering events must be carefully worded in the contract to avoid contradiction between the parties regarding the point at which renegotiation should occur.[142] However, depending on the the parties' ability to anticipate potential problems, the types of triggering events may vary from contract to contract. Therefore, the scope of renegotiation may depend on the formulation of triggering events.[143] If the triggering events are phrased imprecisely, the renegotiation may occur in unforeseen circumstances, reducing contractual flexability.[144] Conversely, an imprecise draft of triggering events may be broadly interpreted, causing instability in the contract. Thus, the contracting parties are advised to define triggering events in a way that protect contract stability. Additionally, trivial events with no significant economic consequences should not lead to a renegotiation of the contract.[145]

#### 3.5.2.2 Effects of the Change of Circumstances on the Contract

A renegotiation clause clause should be reserved for a rare and extraordinary situations.[146] For example, a change of circumstances that triggers a renegotiation should only be considered if it causes significant harm or imbalance to

139 *Id.*
140 Berger, *supra* note 43, at 1362.
141 *Id; But cf.* Horn, *supra* note 12, at 129 (noting that "[t]he parties are well advised to be quite specific as to the adaptation mechanism.").
142 Al Faruque (2008), at 122.
143 *Id.*
144 *Id*; CAMERON (2010), at 85.
145 Al Faruque (2008), at 122.
146 Bernardini (2008), *supra* note 130, at 104.

one of the parties or if its consequences are fundamentally different from what the parties had anticipated when entering the agreement. One commentator proposed that triggering events should involve "disproportionate prejudice", "substantial detriment" or a material impact on the economic and financial basis of the agreement.[147]

### 3.5.2.3 Objective and Standards of Renegotiations

Renegotiation clauses often defines standards and sometimes contains a guideline for changing the contract.[148] For example, the Contract of Work between the Government of Indonesia and P.T.RIO Tinto Indonesia, concluded in 1977, includes a guideline for the extent of contract change.[149] The specific wording of the renegotiation clause determines the extent of change that can be made.[150] Such wording may be adopting an objective standard such as original contractual equilibrium.[151] One example of an objective standard is the original contractual equilibrium, as seen in the Vietnam Production Sharing Agreement.[152] Under Article 17(8) of this agreement, the contracting parties much consult each other and "make the necessary change to ensure that the contractor is restored to the same economics which would have prevailed if the new law/or regulation or amendment had not been introduced."[153]

On the contrary, some renegotiation clause use generic wording and adopt subjective standards by using open-ended phrases like "removing the unfairness" or "adopting an equitable revision."[154] The subjective standard of change was explained by Professor Clive M. Schmitthoff, who argued that it is an unnecessary for negotiators to adopt the old equilibrium as their guiding criterion. Instead, they should aim to establish a situation that is fair and equitable to both parties in the new circumstances.[155] Professor Wolfgang Peter shared this view, suggesting that an accurate interpretation of a subjective criterion

---

147 *Id.* at 105.

148 PETER (1995), at 244; Al Qurashi (2005), at 290 (noting that "[t]he importance of this issue stems from the fact that it will determine the result to be achieved by the renegotiation process.").

149 *See infra*-Appendix, Part I.A. and accompanying text.

150 Bernardini (2008), *supra* note 130, at 105.

151 *Id*; PETER (1995), at 246.

152 The Production Sharing Contract between the Vietnam National Oil and Gas Corporation of the Socialist Republic of Vietnam, Art. 17(8) (Aug. 19, 1992) [Cited in Berger, *supra* note 43, at 1359–60].

153 *Id.*

154 Bernardini (2008), *supra* note 130, at 105.

155 Schmitthoff, supra note 59, at 87.

such as "fairness" requires reference to the agreement's objectives and the parties' intent. However, these elements are difficult to determine, so using an objective criterion like "restoring the financial balance of obligations of the parties" may be more useful. This is because it is easier to quantify the financial aspects of the contract than to determine what the parties should consider "fair" under new circumstances.[156]

Furthermore, some renegotiation clauses may include language that aims to safeguard both parties by using an objective standard such as "restoring the original contractual equilibrium".[157] An example of such an objective standard can be seen in the Qatar Model Exploration and Production Sharing Agreement of 1994. Where Article 34.12, also known as "Equilibrium of the Agreement," states that:

> Whereas the financial position of the Contractor has been based, under the agreement, on the laws and regulations in force at the Effective Date, it is agreed that, if any future law, decree or regulation affects Contractor's financial position, and in particular if the customs duties exceed … percent during the term of the Agreement, both Parties shall enter into negotiations, in good faith, in order to reach an equitable solution that maintains the economic equilibrium of this Agreement. Failing to reach agreement on such equitable solution, the matter may be referred by either Party to arbitration pursuant to art 31.

Moreover, certain renegotiation clauses may have limitations on the degree of change allowed, which can be achieved by incorporating suitable restrictions. These restrictions may include limiting the number of years before renegotiation can take place or excluding specific outcomes, such as prohibiting retroactive effects of contract changes.[158] An instance of such restrictions is clause 47(b) of the 1974 Petroleum Production Agreement between Ghana and Shell:[159]

> *Article. 47(b)*: It is hereby agreed that if during the term of this Agreement there should occur such changes in the financial and economic circumstances relating to the petroleum industry, operating conditions in Ghana and marketing conditions generally as to materially affect the

156 Peter (1995), at 246.
157 Bernardini (2008), *supra* note 130, at 105.
158 *Id*; Al Qurashi (2005), at 290.
159 *See infra*-Appendix, Part I.A. and accompanying text.

> fundamental economic and financial basis of this Agreement, then the provisions of this Agreement may be reviewed or renegotiated with a view to making such adjustments and modifications as may be reasonable having regard to the Operator's capital employed and the risks incurred by him always provided that no such adjustments or modifications shall be made within 5 years after the commencement of production of petroleum in commercial quantities from the production area and that they shall have no retroactive effect.[160]

### 3.5.2.4 Procedure for Renegotiation

#### 3.5.2.4.1 *Occurrence of Triggering Events*

In order for the renegotiation process to begin, the parties must first agree on the events that trigger the renegotiation as defined in the contract, and those events must have occurred.[161] However, there may be disagreements between the parties as to whether a particular event qualifies as a trigger, especially if the renegotiation clause is drafted at a high level of generality.[162] This underscores the importance of including a clearly defined set of triggering events in the contract to prevent any contradiction or confusion about the specific point at which renegotiation should commence. Careful drafting of these triggering events in the contract can help avoid potential disputes and facilitate a smooth renegotiation process.

In a similar vein, if a dispute arises regarding the occurrence of triggering events, the parties typically meet and attempt to come to an agreement on the matter in good faith.[163] However, if the parties fail to reach an agreement, the contract typically requires that any dispute concerning renegotiation be resolved by an arbitrator. The arbitrator will be required to render a decision on the matter only if the dispute amounts to a legal issue that arises out of the contract.[164] This emphasizes the significance of having clear and well-defined clauses in the renegotiation process to avoid misunderstandings or disagreements that could potentially escalate into legal disputes.

160 The Petroleum Production Agreement between the Government of Ghana and Shell Exploration and Production Company of Ghana Ltd., of 1974 (Cited in Asante (1979), at 417).

161 Peter (1995), at 247.

162 Cameron (2010), at 85.

163 *Id.*

164 Peter (1995), at 247; Cameron (2010), at 85.

### 3.5.2.4.2 *Precise Obligations to Renegotiate*

After the triggering events have occurred and all the conditions for implementing the renegotiation clause are met, the next step is for the parties to fulfill their obligation to renegotiate and restore the original financial circumstances of both parties. However, this stage can give rise to several questions such as whether the parties are obligated to negotiate or agree, and whether a party is in breach of contract if they refuse to participate in the renegotiation process. The renegotiation clause typically imposes an obligation on the parties to renegotiate in good faith to restore the original contractual balance once the conditions for implementing the renegotiation clause are met. In this sense, the parties are obligated to negotiate, but not necessarily to agree. However, the parties must approach the negotiation process with a genuine intention to reach an equitable solution. If one party refuses to participate in the renegotiation process, they would be in breach of their obligations under the contract. As a result, the party refusing to renegotiate could face legal sanctions or damages for any loss suffered by the other party due to their refusal to participate in the renegotiation process.[165]

The arbitral jurisprudence The arbitrators have provided insight into the level of obligation that parties have to renegotiate. In the AMINOIL case, the arbitral tribunal emphasized that the duty to negotiate carries significant meaning and may involve specific requirements if it is established within a clear legal framework.[166] A comparable explanation can be found in ICC award No.4727 of 1987, where the arbitral tribunal defined the duty to negotiate as an obligation for the parties to actively participate in negotiations in good faith, with the intention of reaching an agreement while adhering to the framework established by the parties and without attempting to alter previously agreed-upon provisions.[167]

---

165 PETER (1995), at 247 (noting that, "[i]f a party refuses to renegotiate or unreasonably fails to agree, the violation of its duty has to be sanctioned: a) either by the procedure provided for in the renegotiation clause, or failing such proviso (which would be the most frequent situation), b) by litigation or arbitration. This is a very delicate problem, since the task amounts to nothing less than to evaluate the result of the renegotiation which the parties should have reached under the clause."); R. Bishop, *The Duty to Negotiate in Good Faith and the Enforceability of Short-Term Natural Gas Clauses in Production Sharing Agreements*, CEPMLP Discussion Paper No. DP 13, 26 (1997) *Available at* https://www.ogel.org/article.asp?key=1745; E. Farnsworth, *Pre-contractual Liability and Preliminary Agreements: Fair Dealing and Failed Negotiations*, 87 Colum. L. Rev. 217, 240 (1987); *See generally* F. Kessler & E. Fine, *Culpa in Contrahendo, Bargaining in Good Faith, and Freedom of Contract: A Comparative Study*, 77 Harv. L. Rev. 401 (1964).

166 Kuwait v. American Indep. Oil Co. (Aminoil), 21 I.L.M. 976, at 24 (1982).

167 Unpublished ICC Award No. 4727, Sec. 85 (1987), cited in PETER (1995), at 247.

It is highly recommended that the parties use precise language to define their obligations during the renegotiation process. Vague wording such as "best efforts" or "utmost to reach an agreement" does not create an obligation to agree on revised terms.[168] Thus, if the renegotiating parties fail to reach an agreement, neither party can be held responsible for breaching the existing contract.[169] The arbitral jurisprudence supports this view, as illustrated by the AMINOIL award, which emphasizes that an obligation to negotiate is distinct from an obligation to agree, but it is not without content, and may entail specific requirements within a well-defined legal framework. In cases where a party's conduct causes the failure of the negotiation, the matter may be transformed into a responsibility issue that must be addressed accordingly.[170]

Although the arbitral tribunal explicitly stated that the parties' duty to negotiate their original contract does not necessitate an obligation to agree, they added that "the matter becomes transposed onto the plane of responsibility" if the failure of negotiations can be attributed to one party.[171]

In the same vein, the tribunal addressed the parties' obligation during renegotiation and referred to the International Court of Justice's (ICJ) position on the content of an obligation to negotiate in the *North Sea Continental Shelf Case*.[172] The tribunal pointed out that the ICJ emphasized the general principles that should be followed in fulfilling an obligation to negotiate, including good faith in its true sense, maintaining negotiations for an appropriate period based on the circumstances, taking into account the other party's interests, and diligently seeking an acceptable compromise.[173]

Parties are obligated to conduct their renegotiations in good faith, which means they must sincerely search for possibilities of agreement, look for a compromise between their diverging interests, and demonstrate a genuine willingness to reach a resolution. The obligation of good faith applies regardless of whether it is specifically included in the renegotiation clause. This was confirmed by the ICC tribunal in an unpublished award involving Madagascar and Societie des Grands Moulins de Dakar.[174]

---

168 *Id*; Bernardini (2008), *supra* note 130, at 105.
169 Bernardini (2008), *supra* note 130, at 105.
170 Aminoil Award, 24 (1982).
171 *Id.*
172 North Sea Continental Shelf (Federal Republic of Germany v. Denmark), ICJ rep 1969, 4, 47 et seq.
173 Aminoil Award, at 70 (1982).
174 The Government of the Madagascan Republic and the Société des Grands Moulins de Dakar, at pp. 65–66 (May 1, 1972). Unpublished award cited in PETER (1995), at 248.

In the event of a failed renegotiation process, any tribunal proceedings to settle the resulting dispute will take into account the parties' obligation to negotiate in good faith.[175] The case of *Venture Associates Corp v. Zenith Data Systems Corp*[176] is relevant in this regard. The Federal court in this case held that if a party unreasonably insists on a condition outside the scope of the parties' preliminary agreement, especially as a pretext for scuttling the deal due to unfavorable market conditions, that party may be deemed to have breached its obligation to bargain in good faith. The court further noted that if it can be shown that a deal would have been reached but for the other party's improper conduct, the aggrieved party may be entitled to recover the difference between the agreed-upon sale price and the market value of the asset at the time of the breach.[177]

The case of *Wintershall, A.G. v. Government of Qatar*[178] is the only known case where an arbitral tribunal has addressed the enforcement of a short-form gas clause. The tribunal held that Qatar had not breached any duty to agree with Wintershall, as the parties' duty to negotiate in good faith did not include an obligation to reach an agreement on the proposals made. Qatar's refusal was justified as a normal commercial judgment made in good faith.[179] This decision sheds light on three key points. First, the duty to negotiate is vague and provides a lot of leeway for the defendant to act reasonably, making it difficult to prove a breach. Second, the duty to negotiate does not equate to an obligation to agree. Finally, obtaining a remedy for breach of the duty to negotiate can be challenging, and the AMINOIL case represents a rare exception rather than the rule. Therefore, it is suggested that arbitral tribunals should model their remedies after the AMINOIL case.

Based on the analysis of both national and international arbitration cases, a duty to negotiate in good faith is present in a PSA. This duty requires the contracting parties to:

1) Engage in negotiations with the aim of reaching an agreement;
2) Behave in a way that ensures the negotiations are meaningful by not being overly rigid in their position without considering any modifications;

175 *Id*; Bernardini (2008), *supra* note 130, at 105.
176 Venture Assocs. Corp. v. Zenith Data Sys. Corp., 887 F. Supp. 1014 (N.D.III. 1995).
177 *Id.*
178 28.I.L.M. 795 (July, 1989).
179 *Id*, 814–15; *See also* Sangwani Patrick Ng'ambi, *Efficient and Flexible: The Case for Renegotiation Clauses in Concession Agreements*. 45 Zam. L.J. 1, 24.n134 (2014), available at SSRN: https://ssrn.com/abstract=3233764.

3) Sustain the negotiations for an appropriate period of time given the circumstances;
4) Approach negotiations with an understanding of the interests of the other party;
5) Make a good faith attempt to reach an acceptable compromise.

The renegotiation duty must be fulfilled within a reasonable time frame, as delaying contractual obligations could lead to a breach of contract.[180] The renegotiation clause is meant to adapt the contract to the changed circumstances and not to completely restructure the contract unless expressly agreed upon by both parties.[181] The "no profit no loss rule" also applies, which means that the equilibrium of the original contract should be maintained, and neither party should be allowed to profit or suffer a loss as a result of the renegotiation.[182]

#### 3.5.2.5 Failure of Renegotiations and Its Solution

In long-term investment contracts, it's common for the contracting parties to renegotiate their original agreement during the project's lifespan. However, it's often difficult for them to reach an agreement.[183] Neither national nor

180 Peter (1995), at 247, n. 138.

181 Berger, *supra* note 43, at 1365.

182 Horn, *supra* note 12, at 28; Berger, *supra* note 43, at 1365 (Professor Berger lists 19 obligations that should govern the contracting parties during a contract renegotiation process as follows: "1. Keeping to the negotiation framework set out by the clause, 2. Respecting the remaining provisions of the contract, 3. Having regard to the prior contractual practice between the parties, 4. Making a serious effort to reach agreement, 5. Paying attention to the interests of the other side, 6. Producing information relevant to the adaptation, 7. Showing a sincere willingness to reach a compromise, 8. Maintaining flexibility in the conduct of negotiations, 9. Searching for reasonable and appropriate adjustment solutions, 10. Making concrete and reasonable suggestions for adjustment instead of mere general declarations of willingness, 11. Avoiding rushed adjustment suggestions, 12. Giving appropriate reasons for one's own adjustment suggestions, 13. Obtaining expert advice in difficult and complex consensus proceedings, 14. Responding promptly to adjustment offers from the other side, 15. Making an effort to maintain the price-performance relationship taking into consideration the parameters regarded as relevant by the parties, 16. Avoiding an unfair advantage or detriment to the other side ("no profit – no loss" principle), 17. Prohibition on creating established facts during negotiations except in emergency situations (ban on "escalation" strategies), 18. Maintaining efforts to reach agreement over an appropriate length of time, and 19. Avoiding unnecessary delays in the consensus proceedings.") Berger, *supra* note 43, at 1365–66.

183 Peter (1995), at 247; Al Qurashi (2005), at 292.

international law explicitly requires the parties to come to an agreement, so neither can be held responsible for the failure to do so.[184]

Additionally, even when a renegotiation clause is present in the contract, it doesn't necessarily imply a duty to reach an agreement. For example, in the Bauxite Agreement between Indonesia and Asahan Hydroelectric and Aluminium Project of 1975, clause 26.4 states that "neither party shall unreasonably refuse to agree to any change, modification, amplification, deletion, or addition proposed by the other party."[185] This clause limits the obligation to reach an agreement and may require third-party evaluation of the problem.[186]

The parties may fail to renegotiate for various reasons, including: (1) when the contract specifies the terms and conditions of renegotiation, such as when a new law affects the contractor's rights or interests, financial position, or net economic results, as seen in clauses like the Azerbaijan,[187] Qatar,[188] and Turkmenistan clauses;[189] and (2) when there are conditions that need to be revised to restore the economic balance of the parties, to reach a fair solution that maintains the agreement's economic equilibrium, or to ensure that the contractor achieves the expected economic results, as seen in clauses like the ones in Azerbaijan, Qatar, and Turkmenistan.[190]

---

184 Al Qurashi (2005), at 292; Bishop, *supra* note 434, at 26; PETER (1995), at 247; P. Bernardini, *TheRenegotiation of Investment Contract*, 13 ICSID REV. 411, 419 (1998); Jeswald W. Salacuse, *Renegotiating International Business Transactions: The Continuing Struggle of Life against Form*, 35 INT'L L. 1507,1513 (2001) [hereinafter Salacuse, *Renegotiating International Business Transactions*].

185 Bauxite Agreement between the Government of the Republic of Indonesia and the Investors for Asahan Hydroelectric and Aluminium Project, clause 26.4 (1975).

186 PETER (1995), at 249.

187 For example, a Petroleum Production Sharing Agreement of 1995 between the State Oil Company of the Azerbaijan Republic and a consortium of oil companies provides: "In the event that any Government Authority invokes any present or future law, treaty, intergovernmental agreement, decree or administrative order which contravenes the provisions of this Agreement or adversely or positively affects the rights or interests of Contractor hereunder,..., the terms of this Agreement shall be adjusted to re-establish the economic equilibrium of the Parties, and if the rights or interests of Contractor have been adversely affected, then the State entity shall indemnify the Contractor (and its assignees) for any disbenefit, deterioration in economic circumstances, loss or damages that ensue therefrom." *See* Petroleum Production Sharing Agreement between the State Oil Company of the Azerbaijan Republic and a consortium of oil companies (Nov. 10, 1995) [cited in Bernardini (1998), *supra* note 184, at 416].

188 *See infra*-Appendix, Part I.A.

189 *Id.*

190 *Id; see also* Bernardini (1998), *supra* note 184, at 416.

It is expected that if parties fail to renegotiate their contract, a dispute will arise, especially if they have an arbitration clause. There are two possible scenarios that could occur: First, if the arbitrator decides that the conditions for renegotiation are not met, then the contract will remain in effect as it was initially agreed upon. Second, if the arbitrator decides that the conditions for renegotiation are met, then there are different consequences depending on the parties' demands. The arbitrator might encourage the parties to renegotiate the disputed terms based on their findings. If the renegotiation does not work, or if the parties do not attempt to renegotiate, the arbitrator may decide that only the parties, and not the arbitrator, can proceed with the revision of the contract. If the arbitrator finds that one party acted in bad faith, they may declare the contract terminated and award compensation to the affected party. Lastly, the arbitrator may determine how to modify the contract to comply with the parties' wishes and issue an award accordingly.[191]

The first two solutions mentioned earlier fall within the arbitrator's jurisdiction, but the third option presents some challenges.[192] The arbitrator is typically not authorized to modify or rewrite the parties' contract as it conflicts with the principle of cooperation between the parties. In the AMINOIL case, the arbitral tribunal acknowledged this and stated that arbitral tribunals have limited powers and cannot replace the parties in completing or modifying a contract unless authorized by law or the express agreement of the parties. While courts in some countries may have the authority to complete a contract, an arbitral tribunal, cannot modify or complete a contract unilaterally. Any modification would require the consent of both parties.[193]

In addition to the above, many legal scholars have expressed concern about allowing an arbitrator to modify a contract, even a long-term one, in case of a change in circumstances. They argue that an arbitrator lacks the necessary background knowledge and may exercise its power arbitrarily, leading to one party's refusal to recognize and enforce the decision. Furthermore, giving the arbitrator the power to modify the contract is seen as contrary to the parties' autonomy, as they are in the best position to judge their interests and reach an optimal solution.[194]

---

191 Bernardini (1998), *supra* note 184, at 421.

192 Bernardini (2008), *supra* note 130, at 107.

193 Kuwait v. American Indep. Oil Co. (Aminoil), 21 I.L.M. 976 (1982), 74.

194 Bernardini (2008), *supra* note 130, at 107; Al Faruque (2008), at 140; *See also* Angeliki E. Moysidou, Changed Circumstances in Oil and Gas Contracts, Master Thesis, University of Piraeus 16 (2021).

Moreover, it is important for parties to clearly specify the scope of the arbitrator's power to modify the contract when drafting their arbitration clause. Merely including an arbitration clause in the agreement is not enough to confer such power to the arbitrator.[195] Therefore, parties must expressly outline how the contract can be adapted and the extent of the arbitrator's authority in the event of a renegotiation. This is particularly significant given the widely held view that only legal disputes can be arbitrated. As such, any disagreement between the parties during a renegotiation phase may not be considered a legal dispute and therefore, may not be arbitrable unless expressly provided for in the arbitration clause.[196]

## 3.6 The Significance of Renegotiation Clause in the State Contract

Renegotiation and renegotiation clauses in state contracts and petroleum contracts are of significant importance due to several crucial reasons, as discussed below.

### 3.6.1 *Salvage the State Contract*

State contracts are characterized by long-term durations, and profitability is typically achieved only after extended periods of operation.[197] Thus, it is imperative to maintain a balance between the parties involved throughout the lifespan of the investment project.[198] One way to achieve this is by incorporating a renegotiation clause in the state contract, which provides the parties with an opportunity to address any unforeseen events that may render the contract impractical or inefficient, and avoid termination or withdrawal from the contract altogether.[199]

---

195 Bernardini (2008), *supra* note 130, at 107; Al Faruque (2008), at 141.

196 Al Faruque (2008), at 140.

197 U.N. IFC report, *supra* note 35, at 14–18.

198 ERKAN (2010), at 167; *See also* Kolo & Walde, *supra* note 83, at 5 (noting that, the long-term nature of the contracts at issue makes them vulnerable to disruption from unforeseen events or events which the parties-for whatever reason-did not, and perhaps could not, deal within the contract with sufficient time and in sufficient detail. The longer term an agreement and the more exposed to geological, commercial and political risk, the more it becomes vulnerable to external events. Such events can make the operation of the contract partially impracticable or, from a commercial and financial perspective, no longer viable for one party. One consequence is for the parties to terminate the agreement or for one party to withdraw).

199 Tade Oyewunmi, Stabilization and Renegotiation Clauses in Production Sharing Contracts: Examining the Problems and Key Issues, 9 Oil, Gas & Energy L. Intelligence 1, 11

### 3.6.2 *Changing Circumstances*

Long-term investment agreements, particularly in the petroleum and mining sectors, operate in unstable and unpredictable conditions. In case of substantial changes in circumstances, parties should have the right to renegotiate their original contract.[200] Such changes can manifest in various forms, such as changes in economic conditions, regulatory frameworks, or political environments of the host state. For instance, if economic conditions change negatively, such as cost inputs or returns,[201] making contract performance onerous or unfair, the parties may consider renegotiation.[202] Similarly, if the host state imposes new regulations that negatively impact the financial equilibrium of the contract, or if there is a change in the political environment due to a new government or regime change, renegotiation may be necessary.[203] Though a change of government does not typically provide legal grounds for renegotiation,[204] the new government may force renegotiation if allegations of corruption surround the initial contract[205] or if there are doubts about the legitimacy of the previous regime that signed the original contract.[206]

---

(2011) *Available at* https://www.ogel.org/article.asp?key=3184 ERKAN (2010), at 167; Bede Nwete, *To what extent Extent Can Renegotiation Clauses Achieve Stability and Flexibility in Petroleum Development Contracts*, I.E.L.T.R. 59 (2006).

200 M. Bartels, Contractual Adaptation and Conflict Resolution: Based on Venture Contracts for mining Projects in Developing Countries 55 (1985) (noting that, "[l]egal commentators often express the opinion that initial inequality in a contract, together with a subsequent fundamental change of circumstances, gives rise to a right to negotiate."); ERKAN (2010), at 167.

201 ERKAN (2010), at 167–168.

202 Nwete, *supra* note 199, at 60.

203 ERKAN (2010)*, at* 172; Waelde & Ndi, *supra* note 2, at 231 (noting that [e]nvironmental measures imposed on energy and resource projects can have a significant negative impact on the financial viability-and can force the closure-of a particular project or eliminate altogether the profitability of an operation. All these factors of sensitivity for an investor will ultimately translate into a disruption of the financial equilibrium envisaged at the time of project proposal and negotiation.); Al Qurashi (2005), at 266.

204 Kolo & Waelde, *supra* note 83, at 29.

205 *Id.*

206 ERKAN (2010), at 173 [noting that "renegotiation may be due to doubts about the legitimacy of the former government on objective grounds by the new government. Currently, this topic is hotly discussed in the literature. In Iraq, after the Saddam regime, several petroleum contracts have been made by the administration set in place by the U.S. and the UK without any United Nations authority. Moreover, in Northern Iraq, the local Kurdish Government has signed several petroleum contracts without getting any or sufficient authority from the central government in Baghdad. Now, one needs to ask whether the Iraqi administration and the local government in Northern Iraq have the legal capacity to sign a binding contract? This question is likely to be discussed frequently in the near

### 3.6.3 *Filling Gaps*

Long-term investment contracts, particularly those in the petroleum and mining sectors, involve geological uncertainty and a limited amount of information available at the time of signing the contract.[207] This makes it difficult to cover all possible scenarios that may arise during the lifespan of the contract.[208] Therefore, the parties typically leave some terms open for negotiation at a later stage when more information becomes available.[209] Renegotiation clauses provide an opportunity for the parties to fill in the gaps and allocate risks that were not previously considered, ultimately enabling them to complete an incomplete contract.[210]

### 3.6.4 *Providing Flexibility for Differing Cultural Attitudes*

Renegotiation can be necessitated due to the contrasting cultral beliefs of the parties involved in the contract.[211] These differences can affect their perspectives and expectations of the state contract and ultimately influence their stance on renegotiation.[212] Western nations, primarily Anglo-Saxon ones, generally prioritize signing the contract and strictly adhering to it.[213] They place great importance on the sanctity of the contract and the certainty it provides in knowing precisely what they have agreed to commit to.[214]

The differing cultural attitudes of contracting parties can lead to the need for renegotiation. While western negotiators generally view a signed contract as strictly binding and expect long-term business transactions to be set in concrete with no possibility of modification,[215] parties from eastern and Asian

---

future. The validity of contracts made by the administration of the Iraqi oil industry and the local government in Northern Iraq will be questioned."].

207 Al Faruque (2008), at 133.

208 ERKAN (2010), at 177.

209 Al Faruque (2008), at 133.

210 Nwete, *supra* note 199, at 60.

211 Al Faruque (2008), at 116.

212 ERKAN (2010), at 178–179.

213 Jeswald W. Salacuse, *After the contract, What? Negotiating to Work Successfully with a Foreign Partner*, 2 CANADIAN. INT'L. LAW, 195, 197 (1997) [hereinafter, Salacuse, *After the Contract* (1997)] (noting that "[f]or North Americans, the goal of a business negotiation, first and foremost, is usually to arrive at a signed contract between the parties. They consider a signed contract as a definitive set of rights and duties that strictly binds the two side, an attitude succinctly summed up in the statement "a deal is a deal."").

214 William Alfred Stoever, Renegotiations in International Business Transactions: The Process of Dispute-Resolution between Multinational Investors and Host Societies 35 (1978).

215 Salacuse, *Renegotiating International Business Transaction* (2001), at 1515.

cultures place a greater emphasis on the relationship between the parties. Businessmen from these cultures often assume that long-term transaction relationships[216] include an implicit principle that in the event of a change in circumstances, parties should meet to discuss how to adjust their relationship accordingly.[217]

Professor Salacuse conducted a study on how culture affects negotiating style,[218] in which he surveyed 310 executives and lawyers of 12 different nationalities.[219] According to the survey results, 74% of the Spanish respondents viewed a contract as the negotiating goal, while 67% of the Indians favored establishing a relationship as the negotiating goal.[220] These findings demonstrate how different cultures have varying understandings and expectations regarding contracts.[221] Therefore, the study supports the idea that significant differences exist between nationalities regarding whether their negotiating goal is to contract or establish a relationship.

The success of long-term contracts heavily relies on the cooperation between the contracting parties. If the parties come from different cultures, it is important to recognize and consider their differing perspectives during contract negotiations, and strive to find a mutually satisfactory compromise.[222] To this end, some experts have suggested that a renegotiation clause can serve as a middle ground between overly rigid contracts and overly flexible ones. By doing so, the renegotiation clause can promote stability in a long-term contract, which is inherently prone to instability due to various risks.[223]

## 3.7 Limitations and Constraints of Renegotiation Clauses

Although renegotiation clauses play an important role in long-term contracts, they are subject to limitations and constraints. First, the nature of a renegotiation clause, whether specific or general, can impact its flexibility

216 Al Qurashi (2005), at 268.

217 Salacuse, *Renogotiating International Business Transactions* (2001), at 1514.

218 Jeswald W. Salacuse, *Ten Ways that Culture Affects Negotiating Style: Some Survey Results.* 14 Neg.J. 221 (1998) [hereinafter, Salacuse, *Ten Ways* (1998)].

219 *Id*, at 221.

220 *Id*, at 226.

221 Salacuse, *Ten Ways* (1998), *supra* note 218, at 221.

222 *Id*, at 1515; Al Qurashi (2005), at 268.

223 Sornarajah, The Settlement of Foreign Investment Disputes 55 (2000); Salacuse, *Renegotiating International Business Transactions* (2001), at 1515; Al Qurashi (2005), at 268.

and effectiveness. Specific clauses only allow for renegotiation when certain events, as specified in the contract, occur. As a result, their flexibility is limited. On the other hand, general clauses provide more flexibility, but can also lead to parties requesting renegotiation on flimsy grounds, which can jeopardize the stability of the contract.[224]

For instance, the host state cannot rely on a specific renegotiation clause to request renegotiation for windfall profits resulting from recent increases in prices. Conversely, a general renegotiation clause, such as Clause 23C of the 1977 Contract of Work between Indonesia and P.T.RIO Tinto Indonesia, allows for consultation between the government and the company at any time to assess whether the financial or other provisions of the agreement operate equitably and without major detriment to either party.[225]

Secondly, a significant issue arises when a renegotiation occurs either upon the occurrence of a specified event or upon request by one party: what will happen to the renegotiated contract if another specified event occurs or another party requests a new renegotiation? The likely outcome is that the parties will need to initiate a new renegotiation, leading to a potentially endless cycle of renegotiations.[226] This raises concerns about the stability and certainty of the contract, and underscores the importance of drafting clear and comprehensive renegotiation clauses that establish the specific triggers for renegotiation and the scope of any changes that may be made to the contract. Without such provisions, the renegotiation process may become overly burdensome and lead to ongoing uncertainty and disputes between the parties.

Thirdly, from the perspective of foreign investors, once the investment project commences after signing a contract with the host state, it becomes vulnerable to the status of a hostage. As a result, the bargaining power may shift in favor of the host state, thereby resulting in an unfair renegotiation when the host state has strong bargaining power.[227] Additionally, the inclusion of

---

224 *Id.*

225 Clause 23C of the 1977 Contract of Work between Indonesia and P.T.RIO Tinto Indonesia, states that "[A]t any time during the terms of this Agreement the Government and the Company may consult with each other to determine whether in the light of all relevant circumstances the financial or other provisions of this Agreement operates equitably and without major detriment to the interests of either party." Cited in PETER (1995), at 245.

226 Nwete, *supra* note 199, at 5.

227 ERKAN (2010), at 192. Perhaps the following excerpts from Erkan's survey can help to clarify foreign investors' view: "[foreign investors] would always prefer to avoid renegotiating contracts as host government[s] always have [the] stronger position in renegotiations unless the request by the host government is very reasonable… Renegotiations always open the door or set precedent to future renegotiations and usually the host government has a stronger positions in renegotiations due to the threat of expropriation or unilateral

a renegotiation clause can be detrimental to the foreign investor's contractual stability, particularly when it affects other contractual obligations of the investor. For instance, foreign project lenders usually require long-term investment contracts to be stable and predictable. However, with the renegotiation clause, the investor's obligations to the lenders will be contingent on the results of future renegotiations, which may negate the stability guarantee by the lenders.[228]

Fourthly, the renegotiation clause does not create an obligation for the contracting parties to agree. Consequently, if a party is uncooperative, the absence of a mandatory obligation to agree undermines the stability and predictability of the contract. However, imposing a duty to agree within the contract may not be advisable, as it could lead to the referral of the matter to an arbitrator or judge who will have the power to fill the gap, review or rewrite the contract with little or no guidance or criteria. This could result in a reduction of contract stability.[229]

Fifthly, there is a high cost to the host state when renegotiating contracts to obtain flexibility. The renegotiation clause can create uncertainty surrounding state contracts, increasing the transaction costs and ultimately passed onto the host state by foreign investors in the form of capital costs or other expenses.[230] Finally, it is challenging to determine the effectiveness of renegotiation clauses in practice due to a lack of data on whether such clauses have led to successfully renegotiated agreements or whether parties have avoided arbitration.

## 3.8 Recalibration and Recommendations

Some commentators[231] suggested that the criticism towards specific renegotiation clauses might be overcome by having a general renegotiation clause. This clause would outline triggering events and limit the ability of contracting parties to seek renegotiation on frivolous grounds, thereby reducing the risk

changes in terms. Of course, renegotiation is always preferable to expropriation or unilateral change in terms… The original deal best reflects the terms of a fair agreements. Both parties bargained from a position of risk. For example, the investor assumed the risk that exploration would uncover no resources or that those resources could not be extracted for profit. Changing the bargain after risks dissipate or are mitigated does not adequately compensate an investor for assuming the risks up front." *Id.*

228 Nwete, *supra* note 199, at 6.

229 *Id.*

230 *Id.*

231 *See eg.*, Nwete, *supra* note 199, at 6.

of contracts becoming an endless game. To further promote stability and predictability, drafters should include a time frame for renegotiation and specify that failure to renegotiate will result in a dispute. This approach would create an implicit obligation to agree, as parties would want to avoid the potentially unfavorable outcome of arbitration.[232] Additionally, the role of the arbitrator should be limited to restoring parties to their original rights and obligations. Finally, emphasizing the need for good faith negotiations and the necessity of reaching an agreement reinforces the importance of the renegotiation process.

The aforementioned measures outlined above have the potential to enhance both the flexibility and stability of state contracts. However, if the primary goal is to safeguard foreign investment projects from intervention by the host state, then utilizing what this dissertation refers to as Contractual Legislative Stability Clauses (LSCs) would be a more effective alternative to renegotiation clauses or traditional Contractual Stability Clauses (CSCs). Contractual LSCs provide investors with stability guarantees through contracts that are typically contingent on satisfying specific investment criteria specified in legislation. The deliberate legislative approval of these contracts confers a stronger legal foundation, rendering them superior to the host state's domestic laws. Consequently, for the host state to modify the provisions of such contracts, it must undergo the cumbersome process of obtaining legislative approval (as expounded in the next Chapter).

## 3.9 Conclusion

In conclusion, the analysis of nationwide legal systems shows that the worldwide recognized principle of *Pacta Sunt Servanda* (Sanctity of the contract) is indispensable for contractual stability. Therefore, every request or claim for renegotiating a contract must be weighed against this principle.[233] However, the study shows that the sanctity of contract has never been treated as an absolute and unqualified principle in any major legal system. The French doctrine of *imprevision*, the corresponding doctrine of *Wegfall der Geschäftsgrundlage* in German law, and the concept of good faith in other civilian systems all provide for limitations on such principle. Yet depending on the law applicable to the contract, the changes in the contractual environment may, only in

232 *Id*, at 7.
233 HORN, *supra* note 12, at 6.

exceptional circumstances, lead to renegotiation of the contract or excuse of non-performance.[234]

Also, the study revealed how the inclusion of force majeure and hardship clauses in a long-term investment contract could promote contractual flexibility and provide a starting point for renegotiation. But a caveat must be made here: the parties in state contracts and particularly petroleum contracts should not expect relief from arbitral tribunals or domestic courts simply because the performance of obligations becomes onerous for a party to the contract. Unless the contract contains specific provisions that provide for the contract's adaptation, neither the *force majeure* nor the hardship clauses can provide any protection against unfavorable change in the contractual equilibrium. Long-term agreements, especially petroleum development contracts, need stability and flexibility to achieve the desired outcomes for both parties (a foreign investor and the host state). Traditional stabilization clauses aim for contractual stability by fettering the host state's hands not to enact legislation inconsistent with the state contract.[235] Although the stabilization clauses are still of application in many state contracts, the effectiveness of such provisions may be doubtful. This has led some commentators to propose that incorporating appropriate renegotiation clauses may be more effective than traditional CSCs in achieving contractual stability and predictability.[236] Theoretical analysis suggests that the inclusion of a renegotiation clause in the state contract would potentially promote the contractual stability and flexibility by allowing the parties to negotiate a new equilibrium in situations where the terms of the contract have become onerous. However, in practice, renegotiation clauses may be of limited effectiveness in achieving these goals, and the lack of available data on whether such clauses have resulted in successful renegotiations or avoided arbitration further complicates the evaluation of their efficacy. Moreover, there is a risk that renegotiation clauses could prolong disputes unnecessarily and increase costs, potentially undermining the very goals they are intended to achieve. Given these considerations, it may be necessary to explore alternative approaches to promoting contractual stability and flexibility in state contracts.

---

234 Al Qurashi (2005), at 299.

235 Waelde & Ndi, *supra* note 2, at 260.

236 ERKAN (2010), at 196; Nwete, *supra* note 199, at 59.

CHAPTER 4

# Reconceptualizing the Legislative Stabilization Clause

## 4.1 Introduction[1]

In its contractual form, the stabilization clause is ubiquitous in the world of foreign investment.[2] CSCs are frequently deployed in investment contracts in developing countries vulnerable to political and economic crises.[3] More recently, various countries have gone further and provided legislative stabilization clauses (LSCs), i.e., stability provisions in their domestic laws, such as constitutions, statutes, regulations, and administrative issuances like governmental permits and licenses.[4] Although the mechanics of LSCs varies distinctly from that of CSCs, the unspoken assumption is that they both attract and promote FDI in host states in much the same way. The minimal scholarly debate around LSCs focuses on whether LSCs are or should be enforceable on account of their unilateral nature.[5] There has been next to no discussion on the significant question of whether LSCs—as opposed to CSCs or stabilization clauses in general—facilitate FDI and are thus constructive for host states.

This conflation between CSCs and LSCs is unwarranted given the more tenuous nature of LSCs and the ability on the part of the host state unilaterally to withdraw legislation containing the LSCs at any time.[6] Expecting the informed investor to rely exclusively on LSCs is unrealistic when the investor often has access to CSCs—which provide more secure stability guarantees—and investment treaties. If LSC does not in fact attract and increase FDI, they represent a singularly poor proposition for host states since the states remain potentially

1 This Chapter is predominantly based on *Legislative Stabilization Clauses*, 55 NYJILP. 67 (2023). In this article, I was a co-author with my supervisor, Professor Jarrod Wong, at McGeorge Law.

2 *See* Halabi (2011), at 290; O'Connor & Franck (2014), 1631; *See* ERKEN, *supra* note 2, at 103; GJUZI (2018) at 14; BISHOP, *supra* note 20, at 23.

3 DOLZER (2018), at 192.

4 Gjuzi (2018) at 34 (2018); *see also* Neuhaus (2015).

5 *See, e.g.*, Neuhaus (2015), at 318; Jarrod Hepburn, *Domestic Investment Statutes in International Law*, 112 AM. J. INT'L. L.658 (2018).

6 CAMERON (2010), at 62–64; Abdullah Al Faruque, *The Rationale and Instrumentalities for Stability in Long-Term State Contracts*, 7 J. WORLD INVESTMENT & TRADE 85, 105–107 (2006 b).

 | DOI:10.1163/9789004692756_005

liable for any subsequent regulations, they pass that violate their own legislative stability guarantees. Regardless of whether there was actual initial reliance by the investor on the LSC in establishing its investment, the investor may look to the LSC after the fact to ground or bolster its investment claims in any subsequent dispute with the host state.

To investigate the connection between LSCs and FDI, this study closely examines a number of national investment case studies and commentary that have considered the extent to which stabilization clauses in general impact FDI in-flows, but parsing out to the extent possible the findings in relation to LSCs specifically.[7] It turns out to be difficult after the fact to isolate the impact of any LSC on FDI levels, and what evidence there is looking backwards is generally inconclusive on whether LSCs impact FDI inflows.

LSCs come in various stripes, however, with certain LSCs being more forward-looking than others. What this study calls Contractual LSCs allow for the operation of a governmental mechanism to recognize, track and monitor the stability obligations created under the LSC. Host states as such are much better equipped to evaluate the utility and value of the LSC, and make appropriate adjustments. From this perspective, the chapter construct a new taxonomy of LSCs that divides them into three fundamental categories according to their structural form and utility: Aspirational LSCs, Standard LSCs and Contractual LSCs.

Aspirational LSCs contain hortatory language about, or ostensibly authorize states to provide, stability guarantees but without committing the states to grant them; an example is Article 6 of Madagascar's Investment Law (2008) "[t]he state *uses its best endeavours* to set up and maintain a favourable climate for investment by establishing a simple, fair and growth-conducive tax system for investors within the context of carrying out investment projects referred to in this Act."[8]

Standard LSCs are stock LSCs that promise to stabilize particular national laws or regulations applicable to foreign investments upon their establishment; an example is Article 7 of Armenia's law on foreign investment (1994) "[i]n the event of amendments to the foreign investment legislation of the Republic of Armenia, the legislation that was effective at the moment of implementation of investments *shall be applied, upon the request of a foreign investor*, during a five year period from that moment."[9]

7 *See infra* Part 4.2.2.2, 4.2.3.3.
8 *See infra* Appendix, Part II.1 (emphasis added).
9 *See infra* Appendix, Part II.2 (emphasis added).

Finally, Contractual LSCs grant investors stability guarantees through contracts approved by the government, often conditional on meeting particular investment profile criteria; one example is Colombia's Legal Stability Contracts Law No. 963 of 2005:

> Article 1. Legal Stability Contracts: Legal stability contracts are established in order to promote new investments and expand existing ones in the national territory. ... *Through these contracts*, the State guarantees the investors who sign them, that if during their validity any of the regulations that have been identified in the contracts as a determinant of the investment is modified in an adverse way, the investors will have the right to be continue to apply these rules to them for the duration of the respective contract.
>
> Article 2: National and Foreign Investors: National and foreign investors be they natural or legal persons, as well as consortia, who make new investments or expand existing ones in the national territory, for an amount equal to or greater than 150,000 UVT, may be party to the legal stability contracts.[10]

Host states should on balance steer clear of Aspirational LSCs, which contain hortatory language plainly providing no stability guarantee and little purpose, as well as reconsider Standard LSCs, which have not been shown to influence FDI in-flows but yet potentially impose onerous stability obligations on host states. In their place, we recommend that host states adopt Contractual LSCs. Unlike Aspirational and Standard LSCs, the architecture of Contractual LSCs accommodates an administrative system to approve investment contracts that enables the host state to monitor and directly tie the number and nature of such contracts created under the particular LSC. Further, this framework not only permits the host state to better target investment projects and manage its stability obligations, it presents investors with a more transparent and reliable process to access enhanced stability guarantees than would be the case through individual negotiations with the government for standalone stability contracts. By going back to the LSC's contractual roots, the Contractual LSC thereby turns the unilateral paradigm of the LSC on its head, minimizes the uncertainty surrounding its enforceability, and locks down an assured, stabilized contract between the investor and host state.

---

10 *See infra* Appendix, Part II.3 (emphasis added).

In comparison to traditional CSCs, Contractual LSCs provide a more transparent and dependable mechanism for investors to obtain enhanced stability guarantees through stabilization contracts created under the legislation. This makes Contractual LSCs more effective than traditional CSCs, which exclusively benefit foreign investors at the expense of the host state's public interest. Thus, Contractual LSCs can be an important tool for host states to rebalance the interests and rights between them and foreign investors. Unlike renegotiation clauses, which lack practical evidence of their effectiveness in achieving stability and flexibility, case studies on Contractual LSCs have demonstrated their effectiveness in recalibrating the delicate balance.

Next section illustrates the original taxonomy of LSCs by noting the distinctive characteristics of the three categories of LSCs. This taxonomy is based on a security of the relevant jurisprudence and various national case studies. This analysis provides the foundation for the recommendation that host states avoid Aspirational LSCs, reevaluate Standard LSCs, and enact Contractual LSCs. This chapter concludes by reflecting on the analogy between LSCs and investment treaties, and on the potential benefits that Contractual LSCs in particular can bring to the table for investors and host states alike, thereby restoring a measure of equilibrium between them.

## 4.2 A New Taxonomy of Legislative Stabilization Clauses

To proposed taxonomy of LSCs reconceptualizes based on the structural form and utility of their respective stability guarantees. This taxonomy leaves behind the traditional classification of stabilization clauses into freezing, equilibrium and hybrid clauses, which focuses and is based on the particular operational mechanisms of contractual stabilization clauses.[11] Whatever value this differentiation may have for CSCs, it fails to address the legislative nature of LSCs. This more holistic taxonomy accounts for both the legislative and contractual form of the stability guarantees implicated, and divides the various LSCs into three categories:[12]

11 *See* Jernej Letnar Černič, *Corporate Human Rights Obligations under Stabilization Clauses*, 11 GERMAN L.J. 210, 213 (2010); Halabi (2011), at 292–94. Certain scholars would even classify "good faith" as a fourth type of stabilization clauses. *See, e.g.*, Curtis (1988), at 346.

12 The author includes in the Appendix select examples from each of the three categories of LSCs. *See infra* Appendix.

| | |
|---|---|
| Aspirational LSC | An LSC that speaks in hortatory or general terms about, or ostensibly authorizes the host state to provide, stability guarantees but without committing the state to grant them. |
| Standard LSC | A stock LSC that promises to stabilize national laws or regulations applicable to foreign investments upon their establishment. |
| Contractual LSC | An LSC that grants investors stability guarantees through contracts approved by the government, often conditional on meeting investment profile criteria. |

### 4.2.1 *Aspirational LSCs*

The host state national law may contain provisions authorizing the government to furnish a foreign investor with stability guarantees, and perhaps even aver that the government will so endeavor to provide. For instance, the Madagascar LSC states that the government will "use[] its best endeavours to ... establish[] a simple, fair and growth-conducive tax system for investors."[13] However, if such LSCs do not require the government to provide stability guarantees, but instead grant it broad discretion on whether to award them, they cannot be relied upon to stabilize the relevant national rules. Because they often contain hortatory language that appear to promise stability, we term such provisions Aspirational LSCs. Included in that category are provisions in the investment laws of Albania, Madagascar, and Papua New Guinea.[14]

In appearing to promise stability, Aspirational LSCs might also be seen as indicating that the investor's stability concerns will be safeguarded in a regulatory environment set up under the legislation. Yet, as the tribunal in *AES v. Hungary* noted, "[a] legal framework is by definition subject to change as it adapts to new circumstances day by day and a state has the sovereign right to exercise its powers which include legislative acts," and "any reasonably informed business person or investor knows that laws can evolve in accordance with the perceived political or policy dictates of the times."[15] Aspirational LSCs do not require the government to provide stability guarantees, but instead grant it broad discretion on whether to award them, and thus cannot be relied upon to stabilize the relevant national rules. Accordingly, regional and international

13 *Id.* at Part II.1.

14 *Id.*

15 AES Summit Generation Limited & AES-Tisza Erömü Kft v. Hung., ICSID Case No. ARB/07/22, Award, 9.3.29, .34, .35 (Sept. 23, 2010) [hereinafter AES v. Hungary Award].

legal instruments like the E.U. energy directives 2005/89—which encourages Member States to create a stable environment for electricity investments, but does not impose any binding stability requirement[16]—and 2009/72—which regulates the internal electricity market but does not explicitly prevent Member States from interfering with liberalized electricity prices[17]—"fall short of providing clear and directly enforceable guarantees to investors that the regulatory framework governing their investments will remain unchanged."[18] Similarly, Article 10(1) of the Energy Charter Treaty, which directs Contracting States to "*encourage* and create *stable*, equitable, favourable and transparent conditions for Investors,"[19] was found to "provide[] no specific directions on the particular elements that such conditions are to embody" and like other similar investment treaty provisions, are "far too general" to be enforceable as a stability guarantee by investors.[20]

Under these circumstances, it is difficult to imagine that Aspirational LSCs will attract and increase FDI. Rather, and more broadly, any weak signaling function in the market that Aspirational LSCs might serve might will be immediately undermined by their manifest lack of commitment to provide stability guarantees. Further, while a host state would appear to have little to lose in enacting an Aspirational LSC that does not bind the government but may yet draw in a less savvy investor, this would be an unwise gamble, since

16 2005 O.J. (L89/EC), Art. 3. *available at* http://data.europa.eu/eli/dir/2005/89/oj.(Article 3 provides that "Member States shall ensure a high level of security of electricity supply by taking the necessary measures to facilitate a stable investment…2. In implementing the measures referred to in paragraph 1, Member States shall take account of: a) …b) the importance of a transparent and stable regulatory framework."

17 2009 O.J. (L72), Art. 57–59, *available at* http://data.europa.eu/eli/dir/2009/72/oj ("57. Promoting fair competition and easy access for different suppliers and fostering capacity for new electricity generation should be of the utmost importance for Member State in order to allow consumers to take full advantage of the opportunities of a liberalised internal market in electricity. 58. With a view to creating an internal market in electricity, Member States should foster the integration of their national markets and the cooperation of system operators at Community and regional level, also incorporating isolated systems forming electricity islands that persist in the Community. 59. The development of a true internal market in electricity, through a network connected across the Community, should be one of the main goals of this Directive and regulatory issues on cross-border interconnections and regional markets should, therefore, be one of the main tasks of the regulatory authorities, in close cooperation with the Agency where relevant.").

18 Anatole Boute, *The Quest For Regulatory Stability in the EU Energy Market: An Analysis Through the Prism of Legal Certainty*, 37(6) EUR. L. REV. 675, 686 (2012).

19 The Energy Charter Treaty (ECT), Dec. 17, 1994, 2080 U.N.T.S. 95, Art. 10 [hereinafter *ECT*].

20 Stadtwerke München GmbH, RWE Innogy GmbH and Others v. Spain, ICSID Case No. ARB/15/1, Award, 196–197 (Dec. 2, 2019) (emphasis added).

the line between Aspirational and Standard LSCs is not always clear. If the state attempts to strengthen the apparent promise to stabilize—as it must, to increase the chances of enticing the investor—the state runs the risk of crossing over and being bound as a Standard LSC. For example, some tribunals like the one in *Frontier v. Czech Republic* have taken a broad view of legislative promises, stating in dicta that investors are entitled to rely on representations or undertakings made "explicitly or *implicitly*" by the host state through "*legislation*, treaties, decrees, licenses, and contracts."[21] Conversely, if the state employs manifestly hortatory language in crafting its Aspirational LSC so as to avoid this danger, the LSC is that much less likely to ensnare even the unsophisticated investor. In that event, an Aspirational LSC would prove only as useful as a handsome trade brochure that is discarded after it is read.[22]

### 4.2.2 *Standard LSCs*

In contrast to Aspirational LSCs, Standard LSCs promise to stabilize particular national laws or regulations applicable to foreign investments upon their establishment. Standard LSCs typically provide for stabilization of the laws affecting the investment for a fixed duration of time from its establishment, and can apply to a specific sector or area of law, such as mining, energy, commercial, tax, labor, or environmental law.[23] For example, the Georgia LSC provides that: "[a] new legislative act which worsens investment conditions established under this law shall not apply to the already realized investments within ten years from the date of its entry into force."[24]

Standard LSCs can be found in the investment laws of many developing countries, including Armenia, Bosnia and Herzegovina, Cuba, Georgia, Guinea-Bissau, Kazakhstan, Kyrgyzstan and Vietnam.[25]

---

21 Petroleum Servs. Ltd. v. Czech Republic, UNCITRAL, Final Award 285 (Nov. 12, 2010).

22 For a pithy take on the limits of signaling in the law, *see* Geoffrey Manne, *A Signaling Theory of Law* 1 (2012), *available at* https://papers.ssrn.com/sol3/papers.cfm?abstract_id=2180698.

23 CAMERON (2010), at 62.

24 *See* Georgia LSC, *infra*, Appendix, Part II.2.

25 *See infra* Appendix, Part. II. Harder to classify are the provisions in state constitutions such as Brazil's constitution that secure contractual rights, including those derived from state contracts. These provisions can provide a high degree of stability and protection for foreign investors' contractual rights as they are insulated from ordinary legislative procedure and cannot be as readily withdrawn by state governments. *See* A. F. M. Maniruzzaman, *National Laws Providing for Stability of International Investment Contracts: A Comparative Perspective*, 8 J. WORLD INVESTMENT & TRADE 233 (2007).

### 4.2.2.1 The Enforceability of Standard LSCs

When a host state extends enforceable stability guarantees to investors, it renders itself potentially vulnerable to claims by investors with respect to any subsequent governmental measure that breaches those guarantees and adversely impacts their investments.[26] To challenge such measures, an investor typically relies on an applicable investment treaty (or investment chapter of a free trade agreement) entered into between the host state and home state of the investor. In particular, the investor often looks to central investment treaty provisions: the fair and equitable treatment (FET) clause and umbrella clause.

The FET requires the host state to accord fair and equitable treatment to foreign investments in its territory, and is "closely tied" to the notion of legitimate expectations which is, in the context of international investment law practice, the dominant element of that standard (see Chapter 5).[27] While the FET standard "necessarily embraces an obligation to provide fundamental stability in the essential characteristics of the legal regime relied upon by investors in making long-term investments,"[28] the protection of such a legitimate expectation under the FET standard is not absolute.[29] Rather, the FET standard standing alone protects only the investor's legitimate and reasonable expectations, which must be balanced against the host state's regulatory interest so as to preserve the state's continuing ability to regulate in the public interest.[30] As such, the investor's legitimate expectations would have "to include the real possibility of reasonable changes and amendments in the legal framework,

---

26 *See* for example the cases discussed in Part. 4.2.2.2.

27 Saluka Invs. BV (Neth.) v. Czech Republic, UNCITRAL, Partial Award 301 (Mar. 17, 2006) [hereinafter Saluka Partial Award].

28 Eiser Infrastructure Limited and Energy Solar Luxembourg S.A R.I. v. Spain, ICSID Case No. ARB/13/36, Award, 382 (May 4, 2017); *see also* AES v. Hungary Award, *supra* note 552, 9.3.29; Mamidoil Jetoil Greek Petroleum Products Société S.A. v. Republic of Albania, ICSID Case No. ARB/11/24, Award, 617–618 (Mar. 30, 2015)[hereinafter Mamidoil Award]; *Novenergia II – Energy & Environment (SCA) (Grand Duchy of Luxembourg), SICAR v. Spain*, SCC Case No. 2015/063, Final Award, 646 (Feb. 15, 2018).

29 The AES Corporation and TAU Power B.V. v. Kazakhstan, ICSID Case No. ARB/10/16, Award, 401 (Nov. 1, 2013) (emphasis added) [hereinafter AES v. Kazakhstan Award].

30 Saluka Partial Award (2006), 305–06; Methanex Corp. v. United States, UNCITRAL, Final Award, pt. IV, ch. D, P 7 (Aug. 3, 2005) (stating that economic injury caused by bona fide regulation within the police powers of a state does not require compensation); Marvin Feldman v. Mexico, ICSID Case No. ARB(AF)/99/1, Award 103 (Dec. 16, 2002) (stating that customary international law recognizes that "governments must be free to act in broader public interest" and must be able to undertake "[r]easonable governmental regulation"); SURYA P SUBEDI, INTERNATIONAL INVESTMENT LAW, RECONCILING POLICY AND PRINCIPLES (2008) (contending that the FET standard requires arbitrators to "balance" the competing rights of states and investors).

made by the competent authorities within the limits of the powers conferred on them by the law."[31]

Should the investor be granted a firm stability guarantee whose terms clearly provide for the freezing of applicable regulations at the time of the establishment of the investment, the investor's reasonable and legitimate expectations would be elevated and transformed accordingly: "Stability is not an absolute concept; *absent a clear stabilization clause*, it does not equate with immutability."[32]

The reasonable expectation of the investor holding a clear stability guarantee is that the investment will be categorically stabilized in line with the terms of the guarantee, and the host state violates its FET obligations if and when it subsequently passes regulations adversely impacting the investment contrary to those terms.[33]

In addition to the FET clause, investors have also sought to rely on the so-called umbrella clause in investment treaties, to enforce stability guarantees.[34] A typical formulation of the umbrella clause is that found in Article 10(1) of the Energy Charter treaty: "Each Contracting Party shall observe any obligations it has entered into with an Investor or an Investment of an Investor of any other Contracting Party."[35]

The umbrella clause converts any independent obligations the host state has assumed with respect to the investor and investment—notably contractual obligations—into international obligations under the relevant treaty.[36] A breach of the independent obligation (meaning a breach of the investment

31 El Paso Energy Award (2011), 400.

32 *See* RREEF Infrastructure (G.P.) Limited and RREEF Pan-European Infrastructure Two Lux S.à r.l. v. Republic of Spain, ICSID Case No. ARB/13/30, Decision on Responsibility and on the Principles of Quantum, 315 (Nov. 30, 2018) [hereinafter RREEF Decision].

33 *See* the cases discussed in 4.2.3.

34 On umbrella clauses generally, *see* Jarrod Wong, Umbrella Clauses in Bilateral Investment Treaties: Of Breaches of Contract, Treaty Violations, and The Divide Between Developing and Developed Countries in Foreign Investment Disputes, 14 GEO. MASON L. REV. 137 (2006); Anthony C. Sinclair, *The Origins of the Umbrella Clause in the International Law of Investment Protection,* 20 ARB. INT'L 411(2004); *See also* Stephan Schill, *Enabling Private Ordering: Function, Scope and Effect of Umbrella Clauses in International Investment Treaties*, 18 MINN. J. INTL L. 1 (2009); Christoph Schreuer, Travelling the BIT Route: Of Waiting Period, Umbrella Clauses and Forks in the Road, 5 J. World Inv. & Trade 231, 249–55 (2004); Thomas W. Wälde, *The "Umbrella Clause" in Investment Arbitration: A Comment on Original Intentions and Recent Cases*, 6 J. WORLD INV. & TRADE 183 (2005).

35 ECT, *supra* note 91, Art. 10(1).

36 Wong (2006), *supra* note 34, at 143 ("Its purpose is to create an inter-state obligation to observe investment agreements that investors may enforce when the BIT confers a direct right of recourse to arbitration. More specifically, the history of the umbrella clause makes clear that it was designed to allow for any breach of a relevant investment contract

contract if that is the source of the independent obligation) represent a breach of the treaty, which allows the investor to bring a claim against the host state under the treaty through its dispute resolution provisions.[37] Investors looking to enforce stability guarantees would argue that the alleged stabilization obligations are elevated to treaty obligations by virtue of the umbrella clause, and actionable accordingly.

Whether the investor seeks to challenge subsequent legislative regulations through an FET or umbrella clause, the question remains as to whether the stabilization guarantee itself is valid. While the firmness and clarity of the asserted guarantee's language are of important elements, its structural form matters as well. It is well established that contractual stability clauses are enforceable, but legislative stability clauses (LSCs) are a more recent invention and there are conflicting views as to their enforceability due in part to their unilateral nature. Unsurprisingly, the relevant caselaw on the enforeceability of LSCs is far thinner and less coherent.[38]

On one view, some commentators argue that LSCs standing alone should not be enforceable based on a broad reading of the state's sovereign power to legislate and regulate. For example, Thomas Wälde and George Ndi contend that a purely legislative stabilization promise does not have the character and substance of an explicit, formal, and binding stabilization agreement.[39] At least one tribunal appears to agree that Standard LSCs are inherently unenforceable, although based on the unspecific nature of legislation, even as to LSCs applicable only to investors in a particular sector who have met preconditions specified in the legislation. In *Charanne v, Spain*, the investor claimants contended that Spain, in reforming its renewable energy regime, had breached stability guarantees contained in prior regulations, specifically Royal Decrees (RD) 661/2007 and 1578/2008, freezing remuneration rates for electricity generated by qualified renewable energy producers.[40] In rejecting the claimants' arguments, the majority of the tribunal held that:

---

to be resolved under the treaty in an international forum."). *See also* Sinclair, *supra* note 34, at 413–18.

37 *See id.*

38 Neuhaus (2015), at 319.

39 *See, e.g.*, Waelde & Ndi (1996), at 240 ("[I]n view of the sensitivity of the issue and the principle of interpreting waivers of sovereignty restrictively, we contend that a stabilization promise made only in legislation is not sufficient to assume an explicit, formal, and binding stabilization agreement.").

40 *See* Charanne B.V. and Construction Investments S.A.R.L. v. Kingdom of Spain, SCC Case No. 062/2012, Award, 478–9, 487 (Jan. 21, 2016) [hereinafter Charanne Award].

> Even if RD 661/2007 and 1578/2008 were addressed to a limited group of investors, that does not turn them into commitments specifically addressed to each of those investors. Having a specific scope does not mean that the disputed provisions lose the general nature that characterizes any legislative or regulatory measure. Turning a regulatory provision, due to the limited number of persons that may be subject thereto, into a specific commitment entered into by the State towards each and every one of those persons would be an excessive limitation of the capacity of States to regulate the economy according to the public interest.[41]

*Charanne* was the first in a similar string of cases brought against Spain under the Energy Charter Treaty in which investors sought to rely on the stability promises in RD 661/2007. While not going as far as *Charanne*, other tribunals have also concluded that RD 661/2007 does not provide an enforceable stability guarantee, albeit on different grounds. One of the complications here was that the relevant provision in RD 661/2007 (article 44.3) was ambiguously drafted, providing that:

> During the year 2010, on sight of the results of the monitoring reports on the degree of fulfilment of [certain applicable energy plans and] new targets as may be included in the subsequent Renewable Energies Plan 2011–2020, there shall be a review of the tariffs, premiums, supplements and lower and upper limits defined in this Royal Decree with regard to [associated costs, demand and impact] *and a reasonable rate of profitability shall always be guaranteed* with reference to the cost of money in the capital markets.
>
> Subsequently a further review shall be performed every four years, maintaining the same criteria as previously. The revisions to the regulated tariff and the upper and lower limits indicated in this paragraph shall not affect facilities for which the deed of commissioning shall have been granted prior to 1 January of the second year following the year in which the revision shall have been performed.[42]

41 *Id.* 493. *See also* Masdar Solar & Wind Cooperatief U.A. v. Spain, ICSID Case No. ARB/14/1, Award, 507–508(May. 16, 2018) [hereinafter Masdar Award] (noting that for the Charanne tribunal, "stabilisation provisions offered in general legislation, or political announcements, like press releases and others, cannot create legitimate expectations").

42 Masdar Award (2018), *supra* note 41, 116 (quoting Article 44.3 of RD 661/2007) (emphasis added).

The tribunal in *RREEF v. Spain* interpreted this language to "show that adjustments were to be envisaged" and thus determined that this Standard LSC was not enforceable as a firm stability guarantee.[43] It emphasized that in the absence of a clear stabilization clause, the investment was not immutably stabilized.[44]

The tribunal in *Stadtwerke v. Spain* similarly rejected claimants' reliance on the RD 661/2007. The primary legislation contemplated that the premiums, which had to generate a reasonable rate of return, would be established by regulations that had themselves been amended in the interim. As such, the *Stadtwerke* tribunal determined that "it would have been unreasonable for the Claimants to have interpreted Article 44(3) of RD 661/2007 as constituting a stabilized regime for the calculation of the premium that would be impervious to any future modification regardless of a change in the market conditions."[45]

As a striking illustration of how uncertain and even contorted the law is, a different tribunal in *Masdar v. Spain* decided in favor of investor claimants seeking to rely on RD 661/2007. The decision was not made on the basis of Article 44.3, but rather of letters issued by the government to investors that expressly affirmed the application of RD 661/2007 to the investments for their operational lifetime.[46] The *Masdar* tribunal first acknowledged that there were different schools of thought on the enforceability of LSCs, including the view expressed in *Charanne* that the unspecific legislative nature of RD 661/2007 rendered its stability promise unenforceable.[47] The tribunal however distinguished the facts in *Masdar*, stating that because of the "specific commitments" provided by the government in the letters, "and irrespective of whether the general provisions of RD661/2007 would be sufficient ... the Tribunal concludes that, in any event, Claimant had legitimate expectations that the benefits granted by RD661/2007 would remain unaltered."[48]

National courts may also independently rule LSCs to be invalid, thereby deepening the uncertainty over their enforceability. For example, the Federal High Court of Nigeria determined that the stabilization clause (Standard LSC) in the Nigeria Liquefied Natural Gas Act of 1990 was unconstitutional and therefore invalid.[49] Specifically, the court found that the LSC restricted Nigeria's

43 RREEF Decision (2018), *supra* note 32, 319.
44 *Id.*, 315.
45 Stadwerke Award (2019), *supra* note 19, 282.
46 Masdar Award (2018), *supra* note 41, 516–522.
47 *Id*, 490, 507–08.
48 *Id.*, 521.
49 Niger Delta Case (Judgment 2007), *supra* note 147; GJUZI (2018), at 194, n. 43. For the text of the Nigeria LSC, *see infra* Appendix at Part II.

power to regulate and was inconsistent with the Nigerian constitution, which empowered the legislature to enact laws for the good of all Nigerian citizens.[50]

Apart perhaps from *Charanne,* the tribunals in the arbitral cases discussed above appear to allow for the possibility of enforcing Standard LSCs provided there is sufficient firmness and clarity of the stability guarantees in the relevant legislation. There is caselaw affirmatively determining that investors may reasonably and legitimately rely on the stability guarantees in LSCs.[51] For example, tribunals have upheld the stability guarantee in Article 6(1) of Kazahstan's 1994 Foreign Investment Law (FIL), which provides that:

> Should a foreign investor's position be adversely affected as the result of change in legislation and/or the enactment and/or amendment of the terms and conditions of international treaties, the legislation which was in effect at the moment of the investment was made shall apply to foreign investments for a period of 10 years, and with respect to investments made under long-term contracts (more than 10 years) with authorized state agencies, until the expiration of the term of the contract unless the contract stipulates otherwise. ... These requirements shall not apply to changes in the legislation ... in the area of ensuring defense potential, national security, ecological safety and public health and morals. If a change in legislation adversely affects the position of a foreign investor in these areas, the foreign investor must be paid immediate adequate and effective compensation in the currency of the investment or in the foreign currency established by the foreign investor's agreement with the Republic of Kazakhstan.[52]

The tribunal in *AES Corporation and Taupower B.V. v. Kazakhstan* determined that the claimant investors could reasonably rely on the guarantee in Article 6(1) to stabilize their investment for ten years:[53]

---

50 Oshionebo (2010).

51 *See, e.g.,* Ioan Micula v. Romania, ICSID Case No. ARB/05/20, Award 674 (Dec. 11, 2013) (determining that "the legislative framework in Romania between the years 1998–2002 ... together with [Permanent Investor Certificates issued by the relevant agency to investors who qualified for benefits under the LSC], instilled in the Claimants a legitimate expectation that they would be entitled to the [stability guarantees in the LSC] in substantially the same form as when they received their [Permanent Investor Certificates], until [the end of the promised stabilization period]").

52 Law No. of 1994 (Foreign Investment Law), Dec. 27, 1994.

53 *See id.* and accompanying text.

> At the time claimants made their investment, the 1994 FIL was effective, and claimants were therefore entitled to expect to be granted the protection afforded by the 1994 FIL and that … such protection could not simply be revoked unilaterally without due regard to claimants' expectations as raised under such law.[54]

The tribunal in *Rumeli Telekom AS v. Kazakhstan* took the same view, noting that "Article 6(1) grants foreign investors protection against adverse changes in legislation for a period of ten years from the date they made their investment."[55]

Comparing the respective stabilization provisions in Kazahkstan and Spain's legislation, Article 6(1) of the 1994 FIL articulates its stability promise far more concretely than does Article 44.3 of RD611/2007, both in specifying a time duration for the stabilization ("period of ten years") and its scope of protection (against any "change in legislation" that "adversely affected" the investor).[56] Whether a Standard LSC is enforceable may turn then on the firmness, clarity, and scope of the stability promise in the applicable legislation.

Given its potential enforceability, a state should provide a Standard LSC and thereby circumscribe its regulatory freedom only if the Standard LSC positively influenced FDI inflows. Otherwise, without the *quid pro quo*, the investor is a free-rider at the host state's expense.

#### 4.2.2.2 Standard LSCs and FDI: Kazakhstan Case Study

Since gaining independence in 1991, the new Republic of Kazakhstan has prioritized establishing a legal and commercial framework aimed at attracting FDI.[57] In that process, the Kazakhstani government enacted several basic laws: A Foreign Investment Law in 1994 (1994 FIL), a Tax Code in 1995, and a Petroleum Law along with a Subsoil Law in 1996. Through these laws, Kazakhstan provided a range of legislative stability guarantees.[58] Most prominently for investors across the board, Article 6 (1) of the 1994 FIL, as elaborated

---

54 AES v. Kazakhstan, Award, *supra* note 29, 253.

55 Rumeli Telekom AS & Telsim Mobil Telekomunikasyon Hizmetleri AS v. Kazakhstan, ICSID Case No ARB/05/16, Award, 333 (July. 29, 2008).

56 For the text of Article 44.3 of RD661/2007, *see supra* note 42 and accompanying text.

57 Org. for Econ. Co-operation and Dev. (OECD), *Investment Policy Reviews: Kazakhstan* 39 (1998), *available at* https://read.oecd-ilibrary.org/finance-and-investment/investment-guides-kazakhstan-1998_9789264163546-en#page40 [hereinafter OECD, *Kazakhstan 1998*].

58 CAMERON (2010), at 320.

above, shields otherwise "adversely affected" investors from any "change in legislation" for at least ten years.[59]

Article 57 of the Petroleum Law 2350[60] and Article 71 of the Subsoil Law[61] also provided similar general stability guarantees against subsequent changes in the regulatory framework adopted after the conclusion of state contracts.[62] Similar to Article 6(1) of the 1994 FIL, these LSCs apply on their terms to relevant state contracts; they do not appear to introduce or else require stabilization clauses in the contracts themselves, unlike the LSCs in Chile, Peru and Colombia. Separately, Kazakhstan has offered stabilization clauses in their petroleum production sharing agreements with foreign investors.[63] Additionally, between 1995 and 2003, Kazakhstan signed international investment agreements (IIAs) with over 30 countries including the US, the UK, France, Germany and Italy.[64] It is also a party to the Energy Charter Treaty.[65]

---

59 Law No. of 1994 (Foreign Investment Law), Dec. 27, 1994. For a more extensive excerpt of Article 6(1), see *supra* note 56 and accompanying text.

60 Article 57 of the Petroleum Law provides that the"[c]ontractor is guaranteed the protection of his rights in accordance with the legislation of the Republic of Kazakhstan. Changes and additions to legislation that worsen the position of the Contractor shall not apply to Contracts concluded before such changes and additions. The guarantees established by this article do not apply to changes in the legislation of the Republic of Kazakhstan in the field of ensuring defense capability, national security in the field of environmental safety, as well as healthcare." [Unofficial translation]. Law No2350 of 1996 (Petroleum Law), 28 June 1996 (Kaz).

61 Article 71 of the Subsoil Law provided that "[s]ubsurface Users shall be guaranteed the protection of their rights in accordance with legislation. Amendments and additions to legislation, which deteriorate the position of Subsurface Users, shall not apply to the Licences and [...] Contracts which were issued and concluded prior to such amendments and additions. contracts concluded prior to the introduction of such amendments and additions. [..] The guarantees established by this Article shall not apply to changes in the legislation of the Republic of Kazakhstan concerning providing for the defence capacity, National security, concerning the ecological safety and health protection. [unofficial translation]". Law No. 2828 (Law on Subsoil and Subsoil Use), 27 Jan. 1996 (Kaz).

62 *See* Law No. 2350 (Petroleum Law), 18 June 1996 (Kaz); Law No. 2828 (Law on Subsoil and Subsoil Use), 27 Jan. 1996 (Kaz).

63 CAMERON (2010), at 320.

64 *See* UNCTAD, *Investment Policy Hub, Kazakhstan, available at* https://investmentpolicy.unctad.org/international-investment-agreements/countries/107/kazakhstan.

65 *See* details about the signing and ratification of CET *available at* https://www.energycharter.org/process/energy-charter-treaty-1994/energy-charter-treaty/.

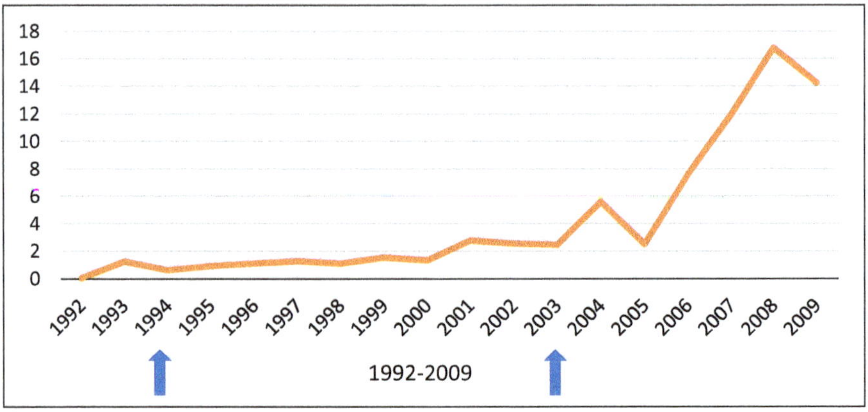


1994 LSC 2003 Withdrawal of LSC

FIGURE 2 FDI net inflows (US$ Billions)-Kazakhstan
WORLD BANK DATA, *FOREIGN DIRECT INVESTMENT, NET INFLOWS (BOP, CURRENT US$)-KAZAKHSTAN, AVAILABLE AT* HTTPS://DATA.WORLDBANK.ORG/INDICATOR/BX.KLT.DINV.CD.WD?END=2009&LOCATIONS=KZ&START=1992&VIEW=CHART

Despite these efforts, as the chart below reflects, Kazakhstan's FDI levels remained low in the years following the spate of legislation, although it did pick up a step at the end of the decade.[66]

Beginning in 1999, Kazakhstan's GDP increased due to growth in the petroleum sector, and increased prices on world markets for oil, metals, and grain, which are Kazakhstan's leading exports.[67] Starting in 2003, to protect national and economic interests, Kazakhstan began to dismantle many legislative protections of investor, including the LSC in the 1994 FIL.[68]

Instead of falling off as one might expect, between 2004 and 2009, the rate of FDI inflows into Kazakhstan—much of it going into its extractive

66 *See* Kubat Umurzakov, *Investment Climate in Kazakhstan Country Report, United Nations Economic and Social Commission for Asia and the Pacific, Regional Round Table on Foreign Direct Investment for Central Asia*, 4 (Feb. 2003).

67 Umurzakov, *supra* note 66, at 4–5 (noting that Kazakhstan's GDP "grew 9.6 per cent in 2000, up from 1.7 per cent in 1999. Rising oil 5 production supported by the official opening of the Caspian Pipeline Consortium (CPC) in November 2001 and surge of FDI inflows, despite decline in world prices on mineral resources, drove growth in 2001 to 13.2 per cent. GDP growth in 2002 was expected to again be close to 10 per cent.").

68 CAMERON (2010), at 321. *See also* SOTONYE FRANK, STABILISATION CLAUSES AND SUSTAINABLE DEVELOPMENT IN DEVELOPING COUNTRIES. PhD thesis, University of Nottingham (2014), *available at* http://eprints.nottingham.ac.uk/14466/1/PhD_Thesis.pdf.

sector—increased by about 25% a year.[69] Sotonye Frank has argued that this result indicates that the stabilization guarantees provided by Kazakhstan, including the LSC in the 1994 FIL, did not play any significant role in attracting FDI.[70] Along those lines, one might point conversely to the relatively flat FDI levels in the years following the introduction of the Standard LSC in the 1994 FIL as evidence supporting the same conclusion.

While it may be tempting to draw conclusions from any fluctuation (or the lack thereof) in the state's overall FDI levels at the time Kazakhstan's LSC was introduced and then withdrawn respectively, the reported FDI levels could of course have been significantly impacted by any number of governmental measures in addition to the LSC, or by external market events. For example, the flat FDI levels through the 1990s might perhaps be better attributed to "low domestic and export energy prices, [Kazakhstan's] transport constraints and inability to diversify export markets, and the lack of commercial orientation of energy companies."[71] Additionally, there was an acute problem of non-payment by end-users as the previous exchange mechanisms of the country and the purchasing power of consumers collapsed. This non-payment proved especially detrimental for the finances of the gas sector with Kazakhgas, the largest gas pipeline company, reported to be owed 24 billion tenge at the beginning of 1997.[72] Conversely, the jump in FDI levels beginning in 2004 might be better explained by the surge in both oil production and prices during that period.[73]

---

69 *See* OECD, *Competitiveness and Private Sector Development: Kazakhstan 2010 (Sector Competitiveness Strategy)*,19 (2011), *available at* https://www.oecd-ilibrary.org/finance-and-investment/competitiveness-and-private-sector-development-kazakhstan-2010_9789264089792-en.

70 Frank (2015), at 113–114.

71 OECD, Kazakhstan 1998, *supra* note 70, at 108 (noting that low energy prices and Kazakhstan's infrastructure deficiencies led to a strong decline in the size and quality of Kazakhstan's oil and gas production a "consequent inadequate cash generation for maintenance and replacement investment").

72 *Id.* at 108–109.

73 *See* Serik Orazgaliyev, *State intervention in Kazakhstan's energy sector: Nationalisation or participation?* 9 J. OF EURASIAN STU. 143, 146 (2018), *available at* https://doi.org/10.1016/j.euras.2018.06.001 ("Following the privatisation reforms in the 1990s, Kazakhstan's economy prospered, and between 2000 and 2007 the annual GDP growth was consistently above nine percent. This remarkable economic growth was attributed to increased oil exports, which coincided with high oil prices. Oil production doubled within ten years from under 0.8 million barrels per day in 2000 to just over 1.6 million bpd in 2011 (EIA, 2012). This was due to the progress in the development of the two largest fields, namely Tengiz and Karachaganak.").

For good measure, Frank also points to a survey of a small group of foreign investors in Kazakhstan conducted in 2010.[74] The survey had found that the government's removal of fiscal stability from petroleum contracts had sent a negative signal to investors.[75] It also found that notwithstanding the challenges encountered in Kazakhstan's business environment, 81% of the mere 41 investors surveyed had indicated they would still have invested if they had a chance to reconsider their investment decision.[76] In Frank's view, this statistic supports his conclusion that stabilization clauses "play little if any role in influencing the decision to invest."[77]

Such an inference is overstated, however, as it would recognize stabilization clauses as a factor only if it were always determinative of the decision to invest. As the survey itself indicates, any investment decision is necessarily impacted by a complex host of factors such as the state of the country's transport and telecommunications infrastructure, the transparency of the administrative and legal regime, and the cost and skills level of local labor, with the security and stability of contracts being but one element.[78] None of these factors—significant as they all may be—is necessarily determinative of the decision to invest. Indeed, according to the survey, in addition to the removal of fiscal stability of petroleum contracts, the investment conditions in Kazakhstan that were perceived to have deteriorated included the increase in the administrative bureaucratic burden, the disproportionate penalization of non-compliance with tax laws, growing nationalization tendencies, corruption, lack of flexibility in the labor market in terms of the ability to bring in qualified foreign labor and the critical lack of relevant skills in the local workforce.[79] But because most of the small group of 41 foreign investors surveyed would nonetheless have invested, all of these factors would, by Frank's calculations, "play little if any role in influencing the decision to invest." Yet, as reflected by the fact that the survey explicitly flags these factors as concerning to the investors, they are plainly important considerations for any foreign investor.

Ultimately, where one is unable to desegregate the impact of the LSC from other factors on FDI levels, it is not possible to reliably draw conclusions on the

---

74 *See* Frank (2015), at 114.

75 *See* Ernst & Young's Investor Opinion Survey, Kazakhstan Investment Attractiveness, at 6, 8, (2011), *available at* https://www.mpo.cz/assets/dokumenty/43916/49303/577174/priloha001.pdf [hereinafter Ernst & Young's Investor Opinion Survey, *Kazakhstan 2011*].

76 *Id.* at 6.

77 Frank (2015), at 69.

78 *See* Ernst & Young's Investor Opinion Survey, *Kazakhstan 2011, supra* note 76, at 8.

79 *Id.* at 13.

relationship between the two. After all, it is entirely possible that Kazakhstan's FDI levels might have been even lower than they were in the 1990s had the state not introduced its LSC in 1996, or conversely even higher than they were in the 2000s had the same LSC not been withdrawn in 2003.

#### 4.2.2.3 The Uncertain Bargain of Standard LSCs

It is unclear whether the Standard LSC increases FDI, even as it constrains the state's regulatory powers and exposes the state to the risk of attracting liability for adversely impacting foreign investment in its territory. As such, the standard LSC may be a poor deal for the host state, which could end up bargaining away stability benefits with little proof of return.

In comparison, consider international investment treaties, which are far more established legal instruments relied upon by states to attract foreign investment. As of 2020, there were nearly 3,300 international investment agreements in place and over 1,000 treaty-based investor-state arbitration cases that have been initiated.[80] In 2019 alone, arbitral tribunals rendered 71 substantive decisions in investor–state disputes.[81] Notwithstanding this impressive body of law and the sprawling jurisprudence it has generated, there is little consensus on whether investment treaties attract FDI. The many empirical studies conducted on the question have notoriously yielded inconsistent results.[82] If it is unclear despite their ubiquity and familiarity whether investment treaties increase FDI, how likely are LSCs, their relatively exotic cousins, to be known and appreciated by investors? Even if investors were fully apprised of LSCs, it is doubtful that they would be advised to rely solely on Standard LSCs given their limited legal provenance, and the thin and uneven caselaw on their enforceability. Investors looking to obtain stability guarantees would surely seek out a more reliable way to access those guarantees, namely through the time-tested mechanism of contracting.[83] As described in the next section, Contractual

---

80 UNCTAD, *World Investment Report 2020*, at xii (Jun. 16, 2020).

81 *Id.* at xii.

82 *See* Jason Webb Yackee, *Do Bilateral Investment Treaties Promote Foreign Direct Investment? Some Hints from Alternative Evidence*, 51 VA. J. INT'L L. 397, 399 (2011) (noting that "the results of these various statistical exercises are inconsistent"); Christopher M. Ryan, *Meeting Expectations: Assessing the Long-Term Legitimacy and Stability of International Investment Law*, 29 U. PA. J. INT'L L. 725, 741 (2008) (noting that "empirical studies have found mixed results regarding the link between the BITs and FDI"); Susan D. Franck, *Empirically Evaluating Claims About Investment Treaty Arbitration*, 86 N.C. L. REV. 1, 5 n. 11 (2007) ("The literature on [the issue of whether BITs increase FDI] is mixed.").

83 *See infra*-Appendix, Part. II.3. and accompanying text.

LSCs provide one such (potentially supercharged) vehicle for securing stability contracts.[84]

### 4.2.3 *Contractual LSCs*

The proposed taxonomy characterizes a Contractual LSC as an LSC that grants investors stability guarantees through contract, often conditional on meeting particular investment profile criteria set out in the legislation. The Contractual LSC dates back to at least 1974, when Chile introduced its first LSC in Decree-Law 600.[85] The LSC did not, however, gain traction until the 1990s and after Chile revised and updated Decree-Law 600.[86] Around the same time, Peru, Ecuador, Panama, Venezuela, and later on, Colombia, enacted legislation containing Contractual LSCs modeled after Chile's LSC.[87] Many foreign investors relied on such Contractual LSCs as detailed in the case studies of Peru, Chile and Colombia below.[88] Halfway across the globe, Azerbaijan was also including Contractual LSCs in its legislation. To assure investors after its post-communist transition, the Azerbaijan government provided petroleum agreements with stability provisions to be submitted to and approved by its parliament in certain cases.[89] Following in Azerbaijan's footsteps, Sierra Leone introduced LSCs, which stabilized major petroleum and mining agreements that were submitted to its parliament for approval.[90] These examples show that a broad range of developing countries have experimented with Contractual LSCs, providing insights into their success.

#### 4.2.3.1 The Enforceability of Contractual LSCs

The core distinction between a Contractual and Standard LSC is that the former grants stability guarantees through investment contracts, which must typically be authorized or granted by the government. For example, in

---

84 *See infra*-Part 4.2.3.

85 *See supra*-Part 4.2.3.3.2.

86 *Id.*

87 *See* Peter D Cameron, *Stability of Contract in the International Energy Industry*, 27 J. ENERGY & NAT. RESOURCES L. 305, 312 (2009).

88 *See infra* Part 4.2.3.3.

89 Al Faruque (2006 b), at 106 n. 56 (noting that "Azerbaijan has no legislation on investment law on the energy sector and PSCs do not have the legal status of a contract, but each agreement signed requires approval of the Parliament prior to its implementation and has the status of the law of Azerbaijan. An important provision for the ratification law for each PSC is that specific guarantees are given regarding the precedence of the PSC over any future amendments or new legislation").

90 *Id.*

Chile, contracts with stabilization provisions were generated under Decree-Law 600, which contained a Contractual LSC, upon the relevant investments being reviewed and approved by the Foreign Investment Committee (FIC), an agency established under the legislation.[91] It should be emphasized that as defined in the new taxonomy, the stability guarantees provided under a Contractual LSC are not just promised in the legislation. Rather, the stability guarantees are expressed in the resulting investment contract itself, meaning that a Contractual LSC ultimately leads to a contractual stabilization clause. This astute reliance on contract is key to understanding how Contractual LSCs are received by investors.

Stability contracts are ubiquitous, and far more established and familiar to both investors and states, than LSCs.[92] Indeed, when presented with LSCs, investors will often still reach for stabilization clauses in their contracts. For instance, UNCTAD noted in its discussion of Colombia's LSC that "[m]ajor investors in regulated industries (including oil and gas, mining, power generation and infrastructure concessions) will seek to negotiate development or concession agreements with the government in any event."[93] This makes eminent sense since "arbitral practice has explicitly and repeatedly confirmed the validity of stabilization clauses in the past" in relation to "modern contracting practice" and "contractual stabilization techniques."[94] As the tribunal in *Aguatiya v. Peru* noted of the CSC generated by the Peru LSC:

> It freezes the laws, rules and regulations applicable to it, as they were in existence at the time the Agreement was concluded. This means that no new law may be passed which would state that [certain rules in existence then] would no longer apply to the Claimant.[95]

The legislative blessing of such stability contracts through Contractual LSCs may elevate the stability guarantees in the resulting contracts above those in standalone stability contracts. Some commentators have even offered that the deliberate and particular legislative approval of these contracts means that they "enjoy a stronger legal platform than stabilisation clauses."[96]

---

91 *See infra* part 4.2.3.3.2 and accompanying text.

92 Halabi (2011), at 290; O'Connor & Franck (2014), at 1631; DOLZER (2018), at 192 (2018).

93 UNCTAD, *Investment Policy Review of Colombia*, 23 (2006) *available at* https://unctad.org/system/files/official-document/iteipc200511_en.pdf [hereinafter UNCTAD, *Colombia 2006*].

94 Verhoosel (1998), at 456.

95 Aguatiya Energy Award (2018), 95.

96 Cameron (2009), *supra* note 88, at 312 (quoting D E Vielleville, B S Vasani, *Sovereignty over Natural Resources Versus Rights under Investment Contracts: Which One Prevails?*, (2006)

Consistent with such layered protection, tribunals have found Contractual LSCs valid because of the reinforcing effect of the various expressions of stability commitment by host states. In *Greentech Energy v. Italy*, the claimants initiated arbitration under the Energy Charter Treaty (ECT) against Italy for enacting measures they claimed diminished the incentives, including premium tariffs, that the government had previously provided to Photovoltaic (PV) facility operators pursuant to Legislative Decree No. 387.[97] The tariff incentives were operationalized through a series of "Conto Energia" (Energy Account) ministerial decrees, and paid by GSE, a state-owned company that confirmed the right to a specific tariff rate in both a letter to as well as a contract entered into with the qualified investor.[98] Claimants alleged that their expectation that the tariff incentives would be stabilized for twenty years were legitimately premised on various state representations, including in:

(i) the Conto Energia decrees, each of which specified certain tariff rates for a twenty-year period;
(ii) the GSE Agreements, which also specified certain tariff rates for certain PV facilities for a twenty-year period;
(iii) the GSE letters informing PV operators of their eligibility under particular Conto Energia decrees;
(iv) declarations of and publications by Italian national and regional authorities and officials regarding the Conto Energia regime; and
(v) the declared purposes and policies underlying the Conto Energia regime.[99]

---

Oil, Gas & Energy L J (2006)). *But cf.* Al Faruque (2006 b), at 106. The value of legislative stability provisions, in the legal hierarchy, may have a greater legal platform than the contractual stabilization clause. Practically, however, the above assumption could be erroneous because the legislative stability's continuing effect is in the hands of the host state's legislature, as the state can revoke the relevant law to renege its obligation to stability. Accordingly, the legal stability guarantee is precarious and based on unsteady ground.

97 Greentech Energy Systems A/S, NovEnergia II Energy & Environment (SCA) SICAR, and NovEnergia II Italian Portfolio SA v. Italy, SCC Arbitration V (2015/095), Final Award (Dec. 23, 2018) [hereinafter Greentech Award].

98 *Id.*

99 *Id.* 408. To illustrate the specificity of the representations, the claimants pointed as an example to the GSE agreements, one of which provided that "[f]or a 20-year period as of 9 February 2011, the incentive tariff, in regular installments in the applicable currency, to be recognized to the photovoltaic plant mentioned in this Agreement, is equal to 0,3460 Euro/kWh …." *Id.* 410.

The *Greentech* claimants compared their circumstances to *Masdar*, discussed above, in which the tribunal unanimously held that Spain had made a specific commitment that investors' plants would benefit from certain incentives throughout their operating lives.[100] The *Greentech* claimants argued that "Italy's commitments to PV investors are '*significantly stronger and more specific*' than those which the Masdar tribunal found Spain to have made" in part because "*Spain did not use contracts* under its incentive regime, whereas each eligible PV producer benefitting from the Conto Energia regime entered into GSE Agreements providing for an exact tariff rate, fixed for twenty years."[101]

The *Greentech* claimants also highlighted the fact that notwithstanding there being "*no specific contractual arrangement* like the GSE Agreements," the tribunal in *Micula v. Romania* had found that Romania defeated legitimate expectations by offering a ten-year tax holiday to investors only to revoke them after only four-and-a-half years.[102] Accordingly, the claimants argued "that their case presents an even stronger showing of legitimate expectations."[103] A majority of the *Greentech* tribunal agreed, noting that given the specificity and contractual nature of the assurances Italy offered, "those assurances bear the hallmarks of … "an agreement, in the form of a stabilisation clause or otherwise.""[104] The tribunal concluded that Italy had breached its obligation to provide fair and equitable treatment (FET) of foreign investments under the ECT.

The contractual form of the stability guarantee may also bolster the investor's claims under an umbrella clause (and not just the FET clause) in an investment treaty. Recall that the umbrella clause in the ECT extends to "any obligations [the host state] has entered into with an Investor or an Investment of an Investor of any other Contracting Party."[105] The *RREEF* tribunal opined that

> the phrase 'it has entered into' seems to refer exclusively to bilateral relationships existing between the Respondent and the Claimants, to the exclusion of general rules; and the Spanish … or French [articulations of the umbrella clause] … lead to the conclusion that the last sentence of Article 10(1) ECT *only applies to contractual obligations*.[106]

100 *Id*; Masdar Award (2018), *supra* notes 41 and accompanying text.
101 Greentech Award (2018), *supra* note 98, 413.
102 *Id.* 411.
103 *Id.*
104 *Id.* 453 (quotation omitted).
105 *See* ECT (1994), Art. 10(1), and accompanying text (quoting umbrella clause in Article 10(1) of the ECT).
106 RREEF Decision (2018), *supra* note 32, 284.

Likewise, the tribunal in *Noble Ventures v. Romania* held with respect to a similarly-worded umbrella clause that "it is difficult not to regard this as a clear reference to investment contracts."[107] Other tribunals like the *Greentech* tribunal, however, choose instead "to interpret 'obligations' referred to in the ECT's umbrella clause as sufficiently broad to encompass not only contractual duties but also certain legislative and regulatory instruments that are specific enough to qualify as commitments to identifiable investments or investors."[108] The point remains that while all tribunals upholding the umbrella clause would apply it to contractual obligations, not all will apply it to legislative promises.

For all of these reasons, then, Contractual LSCs would far more likely be welcomed by investors than Standard or Aspirational LSCs.

#### 4.2.3.2 The Forward-looking Nature of Contractual LSCs

What is additionally distinctive about Contractual LSCs is their future-oriented architecture. With Contractual LSCs, host states are primed to put in place an administrative system for approving the resulting stability contracts promised in the legislation. This system technically permits the host state to monitor carefully and keep precise track of the number and value of the stability contracts generated under—and therefore the investments associated with—the Contractual LSC. The unique ability to drill down to such specific data provides the host state with far more pertinent information to evaluate the utility and desirability of the Contractual LSC. The tracking of these investments also enables the host state to better anticipate potential investor claims against future legislation. A host state may also target certain kind of investments by specifying the criteria for eligible investments in the legislation. Taken together, these features of the Contractual LSC not only empowers the host state to make a much more informed decision on whether to maintain, adjust or even repeal the LSC, it provides the means through which to implement and supervise any necessary changes to the LSC.

#### 4.2.3.3 Contractual LSC Case Studies

Colombia, Chile and Peru provide case studies involving model Contractual LSCs that extend stability guarantees through stability contracts that are approved and granted by the respective governments in line with specified investment criteria. The concomitant system for governmental approval in

107 Noble Ventures, Inc. v. Romania, ICSID Case No. ARB/01/11, Award 51 (Oct. 12, 2005).

108 Greentech Award (2018), *supra* note 98, 464.

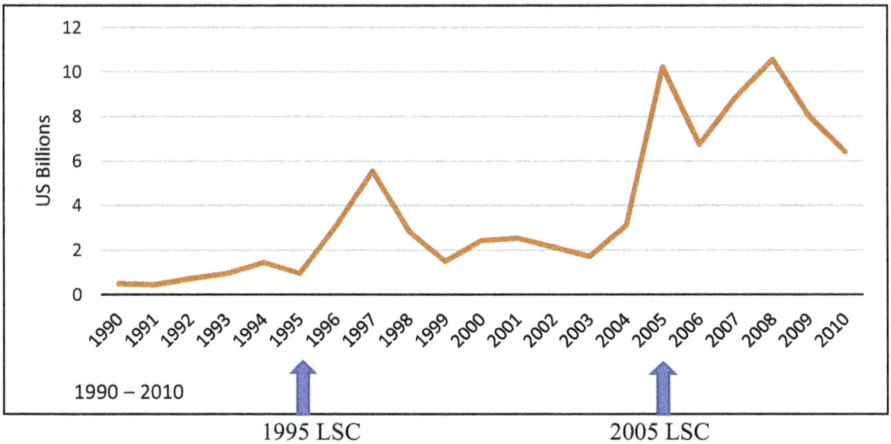


FIGURE 3 Foreign Direct Investment, net inflows (US$-Billions)-Colombia
THE WORLD BANK DATA, *FOREIGN DIRECT INVESTMENT, NET INFLOWS* (*BOP, CURRENT US$*)-*COLOMBIA*, *AVAILABLE AT* HTTPS://DATA.WORLDBANK.ORG/INDICATOR/BX.KLT.DINV.CD.WD?END=2019&LOCATIONS=CO&START=1976

each state may, in turn, offer direct evidence on on the relationship between the Contractual LSCs and the foreign investments established under them.

#### 4.2.3.3.1 *Colombia*

Colombia first experimented with LSCs in 1995, albeit in a limited way. Article 169 of Law 223 apparently authorized the government to enter into contracts with investors to stabilize tax regulations.[109] Law 223 constituted part of the national tax regime, and was enacted to facilitate deep tax collection in Colombia in 1995.[110] This LSC does not appear to have been particularly successful in attracting investment, as less than ten stability contracts were inked over the five years the LSC was in force, even as FDI levels rose over the period as a result of an extensive national privatization program.[111]

When the former president Alvaro Uribe Velez assumed office in 2002, he prioritized increasing FDI in-flows through a policy he called "Convianza Inversionista" (Investors' Reliance).[112] The following year, a survey conducted

109 *See* Alvaro Pereira, *Legal Stability Contracts in Colombia: An Appropriate Incentive for Investments: Historical Causes and Impact Analysis of Law 963 of 2005*, 12 RICH. J. GLOBAL L. & BUS. 237, 254–55 & n. 104 (2013).

110 *Id.*

111 *Id.* at 255–256; *See also* UNCTAD, *Colombia 2006*, *supra note* 94, at 4.

112 Pereira, *supra* note 110, at 258–59.

by UNCTAD of foreign investors in Colombia indicated that the high level of legal instability arising from the frequent issuance of regulations and administrative rulings impacting day-to-day business, was the most important FDI determinant after the potential local market size.[113] To address such instability concerns, the Colombian government enacted Laws 962 and 963 in 2005. Law 962 simplified administrative procedures for foreign investors, and Law 963 introduced an LSC introducing stabilization clauses but through contract.[114] Under Law 963, investments of over US$1.2 million could obtain contractual protection from adverse changes in national legislation through CSCs. Law 963 designates particular sectors as eligible for such treatment, although any activity outside these sectors could be approved by a special committee convened for this purpose.[115] Further, and unlike similar schemes in Chile and Peru described below, Law 963 adopts a negative approach, meaning that the Colombian government is authorized to stabilize any regulation, unless expressly excluded by law.[116]

In contrast to the 1995 LSC, which led to only 10 stability contracts over the 5 years it was in operation, the 2005 LSC (Law 963) generated 66 stability contracts, between 2006 and 2010 worth over US$12.731 billion, with the vast majority (91%) established between 2008 and 2010, according to an OECD study.[117] A separate study reported even more elevated numbers, stating that the 2005 LSC (Law 963) generated an average of 25 stability contracts a year between 2006 and 2012, with the vast majority (88%) established between 2008 and 2010.[118] Overall FDI inflows increased from 3.1 billion in 2004 to a peak of 10.6 billion in 2008, with the average FDI level from 2006–2010 going up by 105% as compared to that from 2001–2005 (Figure 4).

Other measures have been credited with increasing FDI inflows into Colombia towards the end of that decade include the Colombia Productive Transformation Program adopted in 2008 to accelerate growth of value-added sectors, and the initiatives undertaken by Proexport (Colombia's investment promotion agency) to streamline administrative procedures and produce a

113 UNCTAD, *Colombia (2006)*, *supra* note 94, at 46, 67.
114 *Id.* at 39.
115 *Id.* at 23.
116 *Id.* at 23, n. 31.
117 *See* Org. for Econ. Co-operation and Dev. (OECD), *Investment Policy Reviews: Colombia* 90–91 (2012), *available at* https://read.oecd-ilibrary.org/finance-and-investment/oecd-investment-policy-reviews-colombia-2012_9789264167742-en#page1 [hereinafter OECD, *Colombia 2012*].
118 Pereira, *supra* note 110, at 264.

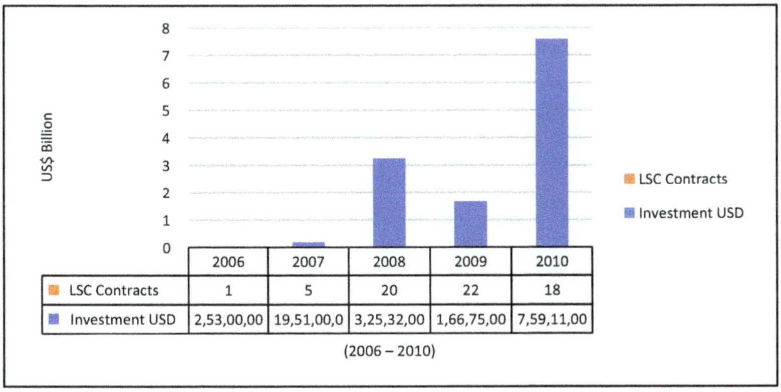


FIGURE 4 Colombia's 2005 LSC (Number of Contracts & Investment US$)
SOURCE: OECD INVESTMENT POLICY REVIEW: COLOMBIA (2012), *SUPRA* NOTE 119, AT 91.

comprehensive guide on "doing business and investing in Colombia" in 2009 and 20010 respectively.[119]

Over this time period, there were only a handful of international investment agreements in force, namely the Andean Community Treaty, the Treaty on Free Trade between Colombia, Mexico and Venezuela (G-3 treaty), the bilateral investment treaties (BITs) Colombia concluded with Spain in 2005 (replacing a 1995 BIT), and with Chile in 2000, and the Central America Northern Triangle (Guatemala, Salvador, and Honduras) Free Trade Agreement.[120]

Against this background, foreign investors in Colombia entered into at least sixty-six stability contracts relying on the 2005 LSC between 2006 and 2010 constituting investments worth over USD$12.7 billion.[121] More critically for the dissertation purposes, what is having here is meaningful investment data that is tied directly to the 2005 LSC. Indeed, consider the revealing granularity of the data on these sixty-six stability contracts:

It is particularly instructive to compare this data both to that for the 1995 LSC (which generated only 10 stability contracts over its lifetime) as well as the overall FDI inflows into Colombia. As between Colombia's two LSCs, the 2005 LSC generated more six times the number of stability contracts worth significantly more in value than the 1995 LSC. As between Colombia's overall

119 *Id*, at 92–97.
120 UNCTAD, *Colombia (2006)*, *supra* note 94, at 22; *See also* OECD, Colombia 2012, *supra* note 119 at 99.
121 OECD, *Colombia 2012*, *supra* note 119, at 90–91.

TABLE 2 Legal stability contracts 2006–10 (Colombia)

| Year | Economic sector | Number of contracts | Investment (USD million) |
|---|---|---|---|
| 2006 | Manufacturing industry | 1 | 25.3 |
| 2007 | Wholesale and retail trade | 2 | 165.1 |
| | Manufacturing industry | 3 | 30.0 |
| 2008 | Real estate, leasing and business activities | 2 | 556.3 |
| | Wholesale and retail trade | 1 | 49.2 |
| | Construction | 1 | 38.0 |
| | Mining and quarrying | 1 | 9.8 |
| | Hotels and restaurants | 3 | 91.3 |
| | Manufacturing industry | 8 | 927.7 |
| | Other community, social, and personal | 1 | 27.7 |
| | services | 2 | 1253.2 |
| | Electricity, gas and water supply | 1 | 300.0 |
| | Transport, storage and communications | | |
| 2009 | Wholesale and retail trade | 2 | 48.0 |
| | Construction | 1 | 78.0 |
| | Manufacturing industry | 12 | 241.2 |
| | Financial intermediation | 4 | 622.4 |
| | Social and health services | 1 | 0.0 |
| | Electricity, gas and water supply | 1 | 38.8 |
| | Transport, storage and communications | 1 | 603.1 |
| 2010 | Real estate, leasing and business activities | 1 | 20.6 |
| | Wholesale and retail trade | 2 | 46.3 |
| | Mining and quarrying exploitation | 1 | 2762.5 |
| | Manufacturing industry | 9 | 243.0 |
| | Financial intermediation | 1 | 797.5 |
| | Electricity, gas and water supply | 2 | 2655.2 |
| | Transport, storage and communications | 2 | 1066.0 |
| Total | | 66 | 12731.9 |

SOURCE: OECD INVESTMENT POLICY REVIEW: COLOMBIA (2012), *ID.* AT 91.

FDI (Figure 3) and 2005 LSC-specific FDI (Figure 4), while the former reflects overall FDI declining from 2008 to 2010 and at levels below that in 2005, the 2005 LSC-specific FDI data indicates that FDI levels associated with the LSC increased progressively from 2006 to its highest level in 2010. Although there was a slight dip in LSC-associated FDI in 2009 from 2008, the LSC-associated FDI level in 2009 remained markedly above those in 2006 and 2007.

The contrast between overall and LSC-associated FDI levels illustrates how ill-advised it is to look to the former as a proxy for the latter. Sotonye Frank relied on overall FDI levels in Colombia (in Figure 3) to conclude that stability contracts did not impact FDI levels given that between 2005 and 2010, with the exception of 2008, FDI inflow into Colombia was at its highest level in 2005 before the first stability contract was signed.[122] In contrast, the 2005 LSC-associated FDI data (in Figure 4) indicates that, consistent with the ramp-up time expected with any new initiative, FDI levels attributable to the stability contracts rose between 2006 and 2010, peaking at the end of the stretch in 2010.[123] From the latter and arguably more germane perspective, the 2005 LSC presents as a far more successful initiative in Colombia's efforts to attract FDI.

Likewise, the LSC-associated data more reliably indicates that many more investors relied on the 2005 LSC than the 1995 LSC. This contrast between the performance of what appears to be two similarly-structured LSCs brings home the point that the complicated business of attracting foreign investment turns on a complex interaction of multiple factors. The question of whether any LSC influences FDI in-flows is not necessarily binary, and is better approached as one of a matter of degree. Further, an LSC that is successful at one point in time may well be regarded as unnecessary later when investments in that host stabilize. In 2012, the Colombian Congress approved Law 1607 (tax reform), which expressly repealed Law 963 of 2005 and apparently did away with stability contracts.[124] In explaining this course of action, commentators have offered that the Colombian government had established the 2005 LSC with the aim of "maximizing investment levels in the short term by offering tax stability, though it was known this measure could not be sustainable over time, which can be understood as a problem of intertemporal consistency of the tax authority."[125]

---

122 *See* Frank (2015), at 111.

123 *See supra* Figure 3.

124 Azuero Zúñiga et al., *Legal Stability Contracts in Colombia: An Analysis from Information Economy and Political Economy*, 27 Innovar 125, 125 (2017), *available at* http://www.scielo.org.co/scielo.php?script=sci_abstract&pid=S0121-50512017000100125.

125 *Id.*

Ultimately, for a host state to make an informed decision on whether and when to offer and maintain LSCs, it cannot just look to overall FDI levels. Evaluating the merit of any LSC requires the kind of targeted information provided through the governmental approval mechanism accompanying Contractual LSCs.

#### 4.2.3.3.2 *Chile*

Inbound FDI in Chile virtually came to a halt after the government nationalized major copper transnational corporations in the early 1970s with little or no compensation.[126] In 1974, the government enacted Decree-Law 600 (DL 600), which opened the door again to foreign capital, and provided to foreign investors the right to non-discriminatory treatment, and to transfer capital and net profits overseas.[127] Among other features, the law contained innovative LSCs that furnished stabilization guarantees by way of contract. Specifically, Article 7 authorized state contracts fixing for ten years the corporate income tax rate at 42% (which was higher than the then standard 35% rate for remitted profits that might however fluctuate), whereas Article 8 permitted state contracts stabilizing the VAT and charges for imported machinery and equipment, pending the establishment of the investment.[128] Foreign investors were permitted to enter into such contracts upon the review and approval of their proposed investments by the Foreign Investment Committee (FIC), an agency established under Decree-Law 600.[129] Notwithstanding the passage of Decree-Law 600, FDI did not pick up until the late 1970s, and even then only in a limited fashion.[130]

Things took a positive turn soon after 1993, when DL 600 was amended to offer additional benefits to foreign investments over US$50 million pursuant to a new Article 11 bis. For the mining industry, such benefits included permission to hold accounts in foreign currency, an extension of the 42% fixed income tax under Article 7 for a period of 20 years, and the stabilization of other tax incentives also for up to 20 years.[131] FDI levels increased dramatically in the latter

126 *See* UNCTAD, *Best Practice in Investment for Development: How to Attract and Benefit from FDI in Mining: Lessons from Canada and Chile*, 89 (2011), *available at* https://unctad.org/system/files/official-document/diaepcb2010d11_en.pdf [hereinafter UNCTAD, *Chile* (2011)].

127 *Id.* at 62.

128 *Id.* at 65.

129 *See* Rodrigo Polanco Lazo, *Legal Framework of Foreign Investment in Chile*, 18 LAW & BUS. REV. AM. 203, 210 (2012).

130 *See* UNCTAD, *Chile* (2011), *supra* note 130, at 56; *see also infra* Figure 5.

131 UNCTAD, *Chile* (2011), *supra* note 130, at 65; *see also* Lazo, *supra* note 133, at 211.

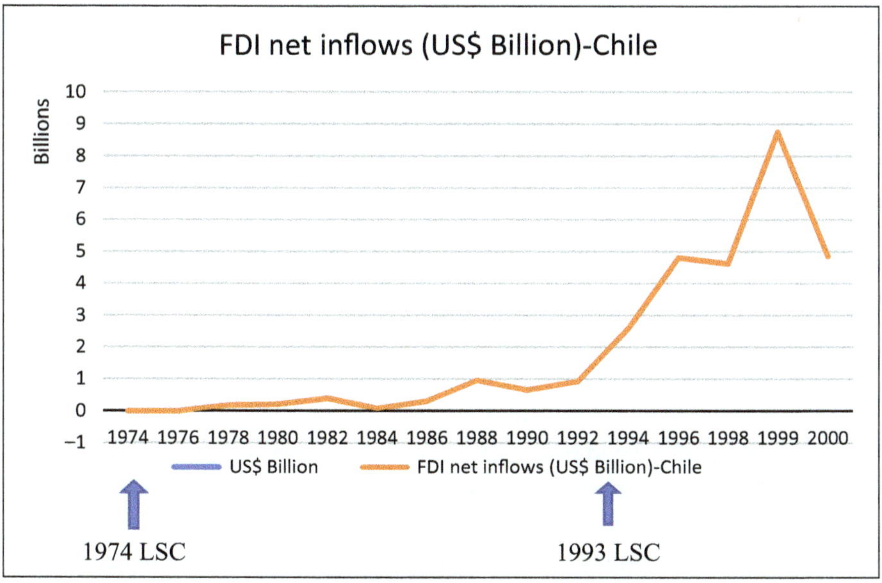


FIGURE 5 FDI net inflows (US$ Billion)-Chile
THE WORLD BANK DATA, *FOREIGN DIRECT INVESTMENT, NET INFLOWS (BOP, CURRENT US$)-CHILE, AVAILABLE AT* HTTPS://DATA.WORLDBANK.ORG/INDICATOR/BX.KLT.DINV.CD.WD?END=2000&LOCATIONS=CL&START=1973&VIEW=CHART

half of 1990, going from US$1.034 billion in 1993 to US$4.815 billion in 1996 to its peak of US$8.761 billion in 1999.[132]

FDI once again became the dominant driver of the development of Chile's mining industry, the success of which is attributed in part to the amended LSCs.[133] A World Bank analysis of Zambia's copper mining industry not only

132 *See* The World Bank Data, *Foreign direct Investment, Net inflows* (*Bop, Current US$*)-*Chile*, *available at* https://data.worldbank.org/indicator/BX.KLT.DINV.CD.WD?end=2000&locations=CL&start=1973&view=chart; *infra* Figure 5.

133 UNCTAD, *Chile* (*2011*), *supra* note 130, at 89–90 (counting the amended LSCs as among the important policy tools used to achieve Chile's goal of attracting FDI). Another significant factor may have been the appreciable number of BITs that Chile signed with countries across the globe in the 1990s. *See* Lazo, *supra* note 133, at 221–222. *But cf.* Frank (2015), at 107–108. In challenging the UNCTAD study's conclusion that LSCs attract FDI, Frank states that "the study acknowledged [that] a significant number of mining investors in Chile do not have stability contracts." *Id.* However, the author is not able to find any such acknowledgement in the study; it certainly is not on the page (page 62) that Frank cites to for that proposition. Frank also attributes the rise in FDI levels instead to the fact that Chile "already possesses the key determinants of FDI location in addition to its liberal fiscal regime." *Id.* However, many of these other key determinants are longtime features

reports that the Chilean 1993 LSC's "invariability guarantee is credited with the surge in FDI that took place after the law was passed," but that it also "influenced the mining companies to negotiate similar tax stability clauses in their Development Agreements with the Zambian government."[134] In 2006, DL 600 was amended yet again to adjust for the introduction of a new specific mining tax. As revised, Article 11 ter of DL 600 allowed investments equal or higher than US$50 million to fix this new mining tax rate for 15 years, and to avoid being subject to any increase in start-up or organizational licensing expenses. However, to be eligible, the investor had to opt out of any other stability agreements it was party to under Articles 7 and 11 bis.[135]

From 1974 until 2011, the majority of foreign investors in Chile chose to rely on DL 600.[136] One report documents that by 2009, foreign investment worth almost US$74.9 billion had been put through the paces of DL 600, representing 67.3% of the foreign capital effectively entering Chile during that period.[137] Chile had the ability to monitor closely the investments directly relying on DL 600—and thus evaluate the utility of DL 600—because of the centralized administrative system set up under the legislation. All investments under DL 600 required prior approval from the Foreign Investment Committee (FIC), the only agency authorized to accept the entry of foreign capital received under this decree.[138] The FIC established the terms and conditions of the respective contracts including their stability provisions and if the investment was approved, a foreign investment contract would be executed with the Republic of Chile. The oversight of these investments took place at a high level, with the FIC comprised of the Minister of Economy, Development and Reconstruction (who chaired the Ministry of Finance), Minister of Foreign Affairs, the Minister for Planning and Cooperation, the President of the Central Bank of Chile and

---

of Chile's investment profile that predate the 1993 amendment of Decree-Law 600, and do not explain why FDI levels rose appreciably over the period from 1994 to 1996 as compared to 1991to 1993. *See* UNCTAD, *Chile (2011)*, *supra* note 130, at 89–90.

134 *See* World Bank, *What would it Take for Zambia's Copper Mining Industry to achieve its Potential?* 21 (Jun. 2011), *available at* http://documents1.worldbank.org/curated/en/461971468170956129/pdf/623780ESW0Gray0e00only0900BOX361532B.pdf [hereinafter World Bank, *Zambia 2011*].

135 *Id.*

136 *See* Lazo, *supra* note 133 at 210; *Trade Policy Review: Chile, Report by the Secretariat,* WTO. WT/TPR/S/315, at 40 (May. 5, 2015), *available at* https://www.wto.org/english/tratop_e/tpr_e/tp415_e.htm (noting that until 2011, over US$82 billion constituting 56.5 percent of Chile's capital inflow entered Chile under the DL 600 regime).

137 *See* Lazo, *supra* note 133 at 210.

138 *Id.*

the minister of the relevant sector in the case of investment applications linked with ministries not represented on the committee.[139]

Although the procedure under DL 600 involved additional bureaucracy and costs for investors, its framework allowed foreign investors to make investments in the country under a stable tax regime, which not only encompassed income tax and VAT but also mining tax and customs duties on imports of capital goods for the development of mining projects.[140] That framework also yielded the important benefit of allowing the government to track the investments arising under DL 600, giving unusual insight into their status, and thereby to adjust the structure of its stability incentives accordingly. Like Colombia, Chile's first stab at the LSC in 1974 led to less than inspired results, and in 1993, the government successfully retooled DL 600 with revised stability guarantees that are credited by both UNCTAD and World Bank Reports with helping to significantly boost FDI levels in the years that followed. Also like Colombia, when Chile determined that DL 600 had run its course and was unnecessary given its strengthened and stable investment conditions,[141] it withdrew the LSC. In 2014, the Chilean government enacted law No. 20,780, a coprehensive tax reform that abrogated DL 600.[142] The next year, the government enacted Law 20,848 (the New Regime), establishing a new legal framework for FDI in Chile starting January 1, 2016.[143]

---

139 *Id.*

140 Juan Pabloe Menna, *Tax Stability in the Mining Industry*, LEXOLOGY (Nov. 29, 2021), https://www.lexology.com/library/detail.aspx?g=56b017b7-5bbb-4473-8aea-594dddde69c9.

141 *See* Martín Aylwin Fernández, *Regulating Foreign Direct Investment in Chile: Is the New Regime a Step towards the Right Track? A Comparative Analysis after a Year of Application*, 33 ICSID REVIEW 702, 712 (2019) Fernandez also refers to a statement in the legislative record indicating that the stability incentive available under Article 7 was accessed by only one company, offering it as the second reason for the repeal of DL 600. *See id.* The authors are unable to verify the authority cited by Fernandez, but note that the statement is contrary to the findings in UNCTAD's 2011 Chile report, which notes that "[m]any foreign investors opted for this regime [under Article 7], paying a slight premium in corporate tax rates to protect themselves against future taxes or royalties and to secure the use of accelerated depreciation and other tax incentives." *See UNCTAD, Chile (2011)*, at 130. At any rate, the stabilization regime under DL 600 ranged far beyond Article 7, turning significantly on Articles 8, 11 bis and 11 ter.

142 *See* Menna, *supra* note 145.

143 Under the new foreign investment law, foreign investors continue to enjoy the rights and obligations granted in existing contracts under the DL600 to the date it was repealed as of January 1, 2016. After January 1, 2016, foreign investors would have the opportunity to enter into four-year contracts with the Chilean government as outlined in the DL 600 with limited benefits. *Id.*

Chile's experience with its Contractual LSC parallels Colombia's in presenting a complex investment portrait of a non-linear relationship between the LSC and FDI that ranges over time. At the height of its success, however, Chile's Contractual LSC appeared not only to exert a considerable pull on investors and investments, but also inspire other developing host states to offer similar hybrid stability guarantees. At the same time, the ability the government would have had through FIC to monitor the quantity and quality of investments established under DL 600 conceivably put Chile in a better position to make the necessary adjustments to its LSC, including both the successful enhancement of the instrument in 1993 and its retirement in 2014 when its investment profile stabilized.

#### 4.2.3.3.3 *Peru*

In the 1980s, Peru experienced economic turmoil, civil upheavals, and political instability. When the former president Alberto Fujimori assumed office in 1990, he adopted extensive structural reforms as a part of his economic reform program to attract and increase FDI in-flows.[144] In that decade alone, the government aggressively privatized its economy, and divested most of its holdings in the fisheries and financial sectors and more than two thirds of its holdings in mining, oil and telecommunications.[145] To eliminate any legal or administrative hurdles hampering private initiatives, the Peruvian government in 1991 enacted two laws: Legislative Decree 662 (the Law to Promote Foreign Investment) and Legislative Decree 757 (the Framework Law for Growth in Private Investment).[146] Under Law 662, the Peruvian government is authorized to contract with an investor that assures national treatment and stabilizes for ten years sectoral regulation, foreign exchange matters, and income tax payable on dividends or other forms of profit-sharing. To qualify for such a stability agreement, an investor must invest at least (i) US$2 million; or (ii) US$500,000 and either create 20 jobs or generate US$2 million worth of exports over the first three years.[147] Unlike the LSC in Colombia,[148] Law 662

---

144 *See* Suzanne Wilhelm, *Peru and the Myth of Independent Statehood,* 15 THIRD WORLD LEGAL STUD. 153, 160 (1999) (noting that Fujimori's program for economic reform involved three phases: first, 'shock therapy' to stabilize the economy; second, structural reforms to attract foreign investment; and third, massive privatization and debt restructuring).

145 UNCTAD, *Investment Policy Review: Peru* 3 (2000), *available at* https://unctad.org/system/files/official-document/iteiipmisc19_en.pdf [hereinafter UNCTAD, *Peru 2000*].

146 Wilhelm, *supra* note 149, at 162.

147 UNCTAD, *Peru* (2000), *supra* note 150, at 21.

148 *See infra* Part 4.2.3.3.1.

adopts a predetermined list of favorable matters, and there is no negotiation of the contract's provisions, drafting, or duration.[149]

Between 1991 and September 1998, Law 662 generated 230 tax stabilizing contracts,[150] or an average of 33 CSCs per year. From an annual average of US$30 million in the 1980s, FDI inflow rose to around US$2 billion per annum in the second half of the 1990s.[151] By 1996, Peru was one of the top 10 recipients of FDI among developing states, and in 1998, the FDI inflows into Peru were the sixth largest in Latin America.[152] Overall, some 35 per cent of registered FDI inflows into Peru in the 1990s came in through the government's privatization program.[153] Also, since 1991, Peru had signed international investment agreements with over 30 countries, including the United States, Chile, Canada, Singapore, China, and the European Union.[154] Note, however that, in 1999, almost two thirds of inward FDI originated in just three countries[155]—Canada, the United Kingdom and the United States—and Peru did not have any investment agreements in force with any of the three countries at the time.

In September 2000, a new law (Law No. 27341) covering the stability agreements established under DL Nos. 662 and 757 was enacted that stabilized the income tax payable on dividends at two percentage points above the applicable rate. In addition, to qualify for a stability agreement an investor now had to invest at least US$5 million (US$10 million in mining and hydrocarbons), as opposed to the earlier US$2 million threshold.[156] Following its revision in 2000, and as Peru's policy framework has stabilized, investors' interest in the LSC naturally waned, although Law 662 continued to generate stability contracts, albeit at a slower pace.[157] Between 2000 and 2008, investors relied on Law 662 to establish 174 stabilizing contracts for investment projects worth over US$5.2 billion.[158]

---

149 UNCTAD, *Colombia* (2006), *supra* note 94, at 39 & Annex Table A.2.

150 Wilhelm, *supra* note 149, at 162.

151 UNCTAD, *Peru (2000)*, *supra* note 150, at 3.

152 *Id.* at 3.

153 *Id.*

154 *See* Benjamin Chavez & Jaime Dupuy, *Inward FDI in Peru and its Policy Context*, COLOMBIA UNIVERSITY LIBRARIES (Aug. 2010), *available at* https://doi.org/10.7916/D8GB29WZ.

155 UNCTAD, *Peru (2000)*, *supra* note 150, at 9.

156 *Id*, at 21.

157 *See* Org. for Econ. Co-operation and Dev. (OECD), *Investment Policy Reviews: Peru* 29 (2008), *available at* https://read.oecd-ilibrary.org/finance-and-investment/oecd-investment-policy-reviews-peru-2008_9789264053755-en#page1.

158 *Id.*

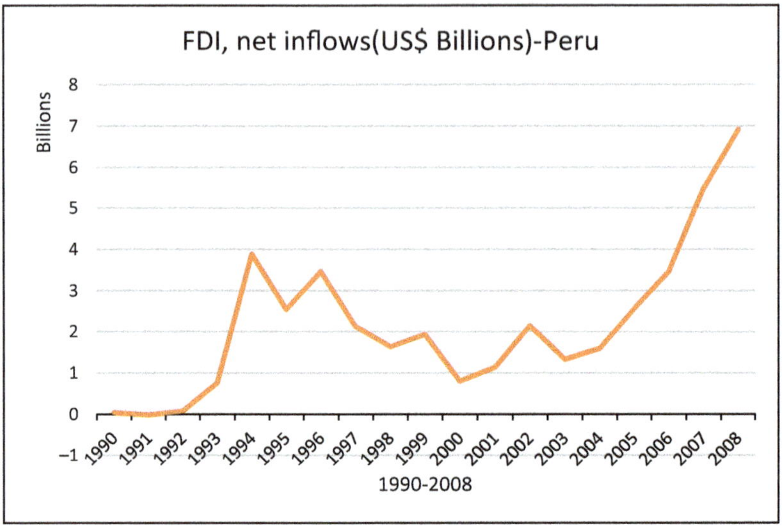


FIGURE 6 FDI net inflows (US$ Billion)-Peru
SOURCE: WORLD BANK DATA

While the sharp increase in FDI levels in the mid to late 1990s is attributable in part to the government opening up to pent-up demand and privatizing Peru's economy—note though that close to two-thirds of the registered FDI did not come through its privatization program[159]—the fact that a significant number of tax stabilization contracts were concluded pursuant to Law 662 over that time period suggests that the LSC played an instrumental part in promoting foreign investment in Peru. FDI levels increased dramatically in the latter half of 1990, going from—US$700 million in 1991 to US$3.47 billion in 1996 to its peak of US$6.92 billion in 2008.[160]

As with Colombia and Chile, the framework of the stabilization regime established under the Contractual LSC in Law 662 allows the Peruvian government to better survey and monitor the investments generated under Law 662. That in turn has better positioned Peru to evaluate the utility of its LSC and to make any necessary adjustments to the stability commitments it provides to foreign investors.

159 UNCTAD, *Peru (2000)*, *supra* note 150, at 3.

160 *See* The World Bank, Foreign Direct Investment, Net inflows (Bop, Current US$)-Peru, *available at* https://data.worldbank.org/indicator/BX.KLT.DINV.CD.WD?end=2008&locations=PE&start=1991&view=chart%20[hereinafter%20The%20World%20Bank,%20Peru%20FDI];%20See%20also%20infra%20Figure%205.

## 4.3 Recalibration and Recommendations

The particular construct of the LSC impacts the validity and potential appeal of the clause. Most significantly, because it leads to a contract, the Contractual LSC should be preferred over the Standard LSC (and the Aspirational LSC) by both the investor and the host state. The mutually reinforcing effect of contract and legislation renders the Contractual LSC more reliably enforceable than the purely legislative Standard LSC or a standalone stability contract. Notably, when presented with a Standard LSC, the investor would nonetheless seek out a stability contract.[161]

The administrative system that a host state would institute for approving stability contracts under the Contractual LSC provides the state with the means to monitor much more closely those foreign investments in its territory that it is obligated to stabilize under the LSC. That information in turn places the host state in a better position to evaluate the value and utility of the LSC in real time, and thus to react promptly in making any necessary adjustments to the LSC. As was elaborated with the investment case studies of Colombia, Chile and Peru, the ability to make an informed decision to revise or even withdraw an LSC is critical since the question of what governmental measures or inputs draw FDI is complicated and non-binary. Indeed, depending on how other factors impacting the investment landscape has changed, substantially the same LSC may enjoy varying degrees of success over its lifetime. Rather than looking to its overall FDI levels—which do not necessarily correspond to the FDI levels attributable to the LSC—a host state can gather and act on significantly more reliable data regarding those investments generated under a Contractual LSC through the associated administrative approval system.

It is true that a host state could conceivably put in place a similar administrative system for Standard LSCs, and further that the increased stabilizing effect of Contractual LSCs would expose the state to greater liability risks. However, the enhanced stability provided by Contractual LSCs is precisely what would draw the investor, and thus necessary if the LSC is to serve a useful function for the host state. Otherwise, regardless of whether the LSC had a role in inducing the investor to invest, the investor may rely *ex post facto* and disingenuously on LSCs in subsequent disputes with host states to prop up their investment claims, leaving the host state to bear the cost but not reap the benefit of an LSC in a lopsided bargain. Additionally, given the pitfalls of privately-negotiated traditional contractual stabilization clauses, and the uncertainty of

161 *See supra* note Part 4.2.1–4.2.3 and accompanying text.

the renegotiation clauses' ability to achieve contractual stability and flexibility, the present study seeks alternative mechanisms to rebalance the interests and rights between the state and foreign investors. The study advocates that as it performs an important and public signaling role and presents investors with a more transparent and reliable process to access fortified contractual stability and flexibility guarantees, Contractual LSC would seem to be more appropriate instead of the traditional CSCs and renegotiation clauses. But a caveat must be made here: The Contractual LSC, in most cases, is limited to certain sectors. Therefore, in the occasional high-value contract outside the prescribed sectors for the LSC, it could possibly work in tandem with a traditional CSC or renegotiation clauses.

## 4.4 Conclusion

In its attempt to find a well-developed mechanism as a suitable alternative for achieving contractual stability and flexibility, this study pays special attention to the issue of LSCs. In so doing, it argues for a radical reorientation of LSCs. To get there, one must look beyond questions of their validity, and also ask if they are meeting their purpose for all stakeholders. For the investor, the LSC should ideally stabilize the investment against adverse changes to the governing legal regime, particularly in an economically and politically volatile environment. For the host state, the LSC should attract and increase FDI. Yet, the latter proposition is nowhere as finely examined as the former. Further exacerbating the problem, the unilateral nature of the Standard LSC also makes it difficult for the host state to track and monitor those foreign investments that it is obligated to stabilize. The government is as such unable to evaluate with confidence the utility of the Standard LSC and make the necessary adjustments in real time. What this has meant is that many existing Standard LSCs may be one-sided bargains that potentially obligate states to pay the high price of stabilizing foreign investments without any indication that the investor had relied on the LSC when first establishing the investment.

While it is true that not every Standard LSC may ultimately be enforced, the resulting uncertainty could nonetheless chill state regulatory behavior. Or else states carry on and out their subsequent legislative agenda on pain of incurring liability in arbitral cases brought and decided against them.

In contrast to the Standard LSC, the Contractual LSC is forward-looking by virtue of the attendant governmental approval mechanism, which allows the host state to monitor those investments it must stabilize under the LSC and thus the flexibility to make nimble adjustments going forward or even terminate the legislation as it sees fit. The approval mechanism also gives the host state the enhanced ability to anticipate, and therefore, avoid any violation of the stability guarantees.

Additionally, the previous analysis of the caselaw suggests that the stability contracts generated under Contractual LSCs are more enforceable than either Standard LSCs or standalone stability contracts, bolstering further the likelihood that Contractual LSCs will prove more adept than Standard LSCs in influencing FDI inflows. Conversely, investors will benefit from the more robust stability contracts generated under Contractual LSCs as well as the transparency afforded by the legislation relative to private contracting with the government. This study sees Contractual LSCs as key to restoring equilibrium between investors and host states in the context of legislative stability guarantees. Additionally, the study argues that traditional CSCs are highly speculative in terms of their validity and effectiveness, and renegotiation clauses' ability to achieve contractual stability and predictability is uncertain at best; therefore, Contractual LSCs would seem to be more effective than traditional CSCs, and certainly more so than renegotiation clauses. However, given the nature of Contractual LSCs, as it is limited to specific sectors, they could work in tandem with a traditional CSC or renegotiation clauses or a combination thereof if the state contract is outside the prescribed sectors for the LSC.

CHAPTER 5

# Legal Stability Guarantees in International Investment Agreements

## 5.1 Introduction

As outlined in the previous chapters, developing countries and emerging market economies are often vulnerable to political risks that hamper FDI inflow.[1] A 2013 World Bank Group survey confirms that the host state's breach of contract and adverse regulatory changes represent the most pressing political risks.[2] In mitigating such political risks, many developing countries and economies in transition concluded International Investment Agreements (IIAs) to provide international protection standards to foreign investors and their investments in these countries' territories.[3] Essentially, IIAs are investment agreements made between two countries (*e.g.,* Bilateral Investment Treaties, hereinafter "BITs") or multiple countries (*e.g.,* Multilateral Investment Treaties, hereinafter "MITs") to promote, encourage, and protect the private mutual investment. The IIAs also can be found in an FTA, which often includes an investment chapter that provides protection standards to foreign investment between the contracting states.[4] Practically, as was discussed in the previous chapters, there are other mechanisms that foreign investors can, and should, use to mitigate the host state's political risks, such as contractual stabilization clauses, legislative stabilization clauses, and government-sponsored insurance programs.[5] However, the presence of IIA, concluded between the host state

---

1 CAMERON (2010), at 146.

2 The World Bank, World Investment Trends and Corporate Perspectives: *The Political Risk Insurance Industry, Breach of Contract*, at 19 (2013) *available at* https://www.miga.org/sites/default/files/archive/Documents/WIPR13.pdf.

3 *Id; See also* DOLZER & SCHREUER (2012), at 22 (noting that "[t]hus, the purpose of investment treaties is to address the typical risks of a long-term investment project, and thereby to provide stability and predictability in the sense of an investment-friendly climate").

4 CAMERON (2010), at 146 (noting that unlike the BIT and MIT, FTA focuses on a broad economic subject matter than investment, but it is also an agreement that concluded between or among the countries).

5 Comeaux & Kinsella (1994), at 5–6.

 | DOI:10.1163/9789004692756_006

and foreign investor's home state, is a signal to foreign investors that a host state is obligated under international law to honor its obligations.[6]

The key feature of such IIAs is that they contain provisions that aim to give stability to the investment legal framework by imposing restrictions on the host state's regulatory power and restraining the host state's interference with the rights of foreign investors.[7] Guarantees of legal stability within IIAs can be provided explicitly through the express stabilization clause (IIA SC) or implicitly through the fair and equitable treatment standard (FET) and the meaning of legitimate expectations. It requires that "state authorities respect the legitimate expectations of individuals created through statements of policy or intention as part of their general duty of fairness, particularly when directed at a particular individual or entity."[8] In the context of international investment law practice, the notion of legitimate expectations is consistently acknowledged as the "dominant element of FET" standard[9] that arbitral tribunals can rely on to determine whether the host state breached the FET standard.

While there were a significant number of IIAs old generation particularly Italy's BITs contained the express SCs, such clauses have attracted limited scholarly scrutiny. This chapter provides a conceptual and legal analysis of the distinctive stability guarantees contained in the IIAs for promotion and

---

6 *Id.* (noting that "[w]hen a host state violates the rights guaranteed to the investor by the treaty, that state has not only violated norms of customary international law (such as the requirement to expropriate only for a public purpose, in a nondiscriminatory fashion, and upon the payment of prompt, adequate, and effective compensation6), but has also breached a treaty with the investor's home state.").

7 RANJAN (2019), at 1.

8 *See* James Crawford, *Treaty and Contract in Investment Arbitration*, 24 (3) Arb Intl 351, 371 (2008); *See also* Potesta (2013), at 93.

9 Among the arbitral awards to discuss and examine this, *see, e.g.*, Saluka Partial Award (2006), 302; *Técnicas Medioambientales Tecmed, S.A. v. The United Mexican States*, ICSID Case No. ARB (AF)/00/2, Award, 154 (May. 29, 2003); *CMS Gas Transmission Company v Argentine Republic*, ICSID Case No. ARB/01/08, Award, 279 (May. 12, 2005); *Sempra Energy International v Argentine Republic*, ICSID Case No. ARB/02/16, Award, 298 (Sep. 28, 2007); *Electrabel S.A. v Republic of Hungary*, ICSID Case No. ARB/07/19, Decision on Jurisdiction, Applicable Law and Liability, 7.74; *See also* Gian Maria Farnelli, *Recent Trends in Investment Arbitration Concerning Legitimate Expectations: An Analysis of Recent Renewable Energies Investment Case Law*, 23 Int'l Community. L. Rev. 27,30(2021). Among the scholars, see, e.g., Stephen Fietta, *The Legitimate Expectations Principle under Article 1105 NAFTA – International Thunderbird Gaming Corporation v. the United Mexican States*, 7 J. WORLD INVESTMENT & TRADE 423,425 (2006) (noting that ""legitimate expectations" principle ... forming a discrete part of the fair and equitable standard"); Potesta (2013), at 100. (noting that "protection of legitimate expectations rapidly came to be considered as the 'dominant element' or as 'one of the major components' of the fair and equitable treatment standard.").

protection of foreign investment projects. It aims to appraise and investigate the issue of the IIA SC and its value in achieving stability and predictability of contractual regime. The study, also, aims to provide a conceptual and legal analysis of the legal stability provided to foreign investors through FET clause and whether such clause can provide a legal stability equale to SCs in state contracts. While there were a few early arbitral awards that interpreted the FET clause as it imposes legal stability obligation (akin to CSCs),[10] the majority of tribunals attempt to avoid an overbroad reading of the FET clause by reference to the investor's legitimate expectations and have strived to specify elements that delimit the scope of such expectations. This dominant opinion appears to be a more nuanced approach as the foreign investor's legitimate expectations must be based on reality, experience, and context.[11] Such later approach by the majority seems to have recognized the need to balance the interestes and rights between the host state and foreign investors. However, one can still find recent arbitral awards still fail to set out the precise role of legal stability under the FET standard, which thus may raise fears that the FET clause may indeed interpret as imposing a legal stability in a strict sense.[12] This chapter argues that the purpose of the FET clause should not be understood to extend to strict stability. Otherwise, the existence of the long-standing CSCs would be redundant.

## 5.2 International Investment Agreements' Stabilization Clauses (IIA SC)

Generally, IIAs mainly aim at mitigating political risk and at strengthening the "reliability of the respective investment climates."[13] Almost all BITs contain provisions to protect foreign investment during the lifetime of the BITs and even for a specific period after the BIT has expired or been canceled. However, in exceptional cases, the stability provisions can exist expressly in IIAs.[14] The stabilization clauses aim to freeze the host state's law applicable to the

10 Federico Ortino, The Origin and Evolution of Investment Treaty Standards 19 (2019).

11 UNCTAD, Fair and Equitable Treatment, Series on Issues in International Investment Agreements II, at 67 (2012) [hereinafter, UNCTAD 2012].

12 Ortino, *supra* note 10, at 33.

13 August Reinisch & Christoph Schreuer, International Protection of Investments: The substantive Standards 461 (2020).

14 Gjuzi(2018), at 36; *See* Ortino, *supra* note 10, at 14.

investment project when the contract was signed. In a manner similar to the known categorization of contractual stabilization clauses (CSCs), Professor Tarcisio Gazzini has referred to such treaty clauses as "freezing clauses."[15]

The IIAs' stabilization clauses (IIA SCs) have attracted limited scholarly scrutiny. In addition to Professor Gazzini's[16] and Professor Federico Ortino's note,[17] the only references to such clauses are found in the 1988 report of the United Nations Center on Transnational Corporations (UNCTC) on Bilateral Investment Treaties[18] and in the 1998 report of the United Nations Conference on Trade and Development (UNCTAD), Bilateral Investment Treaties in the Mid-1990s.[19]

At that juncture, it was surprising to find that a significant number of Italy's BITs contained the express SCs. A notable example here can be found in the Italy-Mozambique BIT of 1998, in which Article 12.3 provides:

> whenever, after the date when the investment has been made, a modification should take place in law, regulations, acts, or measures of economic policies governing directly or indirectly the investment, the same treatment shall apply upon request of the investor that was applicable to it at the moment when the investment was agreed upon to be carried out.[20]

Similar clauses are also contained in Italy's BITs with Jordan (1996), Angola (1997), Armenia (1998), Azerbaijan (1997, terminated), Bosnia (2000), Cameroon (1999), Kazakhstan (1994), Macedonia (1997), Moldova (1997), Tanzania (2001), Uganda (1997, terminated) and Uzbekistan (1997).[21]

In particular, Article 12(3) of Italy-Mozambique BIT, articulated above, seems sufficiently clear as it grants the foreign investor of the other contracting party the right not to be subject to any changes of the host state's regulatory

---

15 Tarcisio Gazzini, *Beware of Freezing Clauses in International Investment Clauses*, 191 Colombia FDI Perspective, 1 (2017) *available at* https://academiccommons.colombia.edu/doi/10.7916/D85T3WHG.

16 Professor Tarcisio Gazzini is an international law professor at the University of Padua https://research-portal.uea.ac.uk/en/persons/tarcisio-gazzini.

17 Professor Federico Ortino is an international economic law professor at the King's College London, United Kingdom. https://www.kcl.ac.uk/people/federico-ortino.

18 UNCTC, *Bilateral Investment Treaties*, ST, CTC,65 (1988), *available at* https://digitallibrary.un.org/record/38784?ln=en.

19 UNCTAD, *Bilateral Investment Treaties in the Mid-1990s* (United Nations 1998) *available at* https://digitallibrary.un.org/record/264901?ln=en. [hereinafter, UNCTAD 1998].

20 Agreement for the Promotion and Reciprocal Protection of Investments, It-Mozam., art 12. 3, Dec. 14, 1998, *available at* https://rb.gy/rasovd.

21 ORTINO, *supra* note 10, at 15. n 50; *see also infra*-Appendix, pt. II.

framework that adversely affect its interest. As Professor Gazzini aptly summarized, such a clause "provides all investors of the other contracting party a total exemption from unfavorable laws, regulations, acts, or measures of economic policies adopted by host countries [...], it neutralizes the exercise of subsequent regulatory powers to the extent that such exercise is directly or indirectly detrimental to covered investors."[22]

Unsurprisingly, and analogous to CSCs, there are variations in drafting IIA SCs. While Article 12(3) of the 1998 Italy-Mozambique BIT, articulated above, provides a general IIA's SC, some IIA SCs are limited and aim to freeze the host state's laws concerning specific rules, such as the rules concerning on the transfer of capital, profits, and other payments related to the investment.[23] A remarkable example of such a limited IIA SCs can be found in Article 2 of the 1965 Belgium-Morocco BIT[24] (now terminated), which provided:

> Each Contracting Party undertakes to authorize, in conformity with the regulations promulgated in pursuance of the legislation in force in its territory at the time each investment is made or of any more favourable legislation that may be enacted, in the future or of rules agreed upon between the two Parties, the transfer:
> – Of net profits, interests, dividends and royalties due to nationals or corporations of the other Party;
> – Of the proceeds of the complete or partial liquidation of investments and reinvestments approved by the country in which they are made.[25]

The scope of IIA SCs may be even narrower and may apply only to the balance of payments exception to the free transfer of capital obligation.[26] For example, Article 6 of the 1981 UK-Paraguay BIT provides:

> Each Contracting Party shall in respect of investments guarantee to nationals or companies of the other Contracting Party the unrestricted transfer to the country where they reside of their investments and returns, subject to the right of each Contracting Party in exceptional balance of

22 Gazzini, *supra* note 15, at 1.

23 ORTINO, *supra* note 10, at 16.

24 Convention Concerning the Encouragement of Capital Investment and the Protection of Property (With Exchange Letters), Belg.-Morocco., Apr. 28, 1965, *available at* https://investmentpolicy.unctad.org/international-investment-agreements.

25 *Id.* Art. 2.

26 ORTINO, *supra* note 10, at 16.

> payments difficulties and for a limited period to exercise equitable and in good faith powers conferred by its laws existing when this Agreement enters into force.[27]

Furthermore, IIA SCs may apply to both contracting states, or they may be included in the IIA at the insistence of the capital-exporting party to be applied unilaterally to the capital-importing party only.[28] The 1974 agreement between France and Yugoslavia BIT is remarkable here, as Article 4 thereof provides that if new, less favorable legislation should be introduced, investments will continue to be governed by the law in force when they were admitted: However, the reference seems to have been made only to the '*législation yougoslave*'

> French nationals, natural or legal persons having a direct or indirect involvement in such investments in Yugoslavia cannot be deprived of all or part of their rights as for public purposes only in cases and in accordance with the procedures laid down in the laws of Yugoslavia and subject to the payment of just compensation, fixed at the latest by the time of dispossession[29]

In that regard, a close reading of the texts, as mentioned above, of IIA SCs indicates that the treaty drafters adopted a traditional stabilization clause (freezing clauses) that precludes the host state from applying any subsequent changes of its laws to the investment contracts. Despite that, an explicit stabilization clause is rarely included in the IIAs, and given the apparent absence of any arbitral decisions examining such IIA SCs, the express existence of SCs in IIAs provides a host state with strong incentive to respect its commitments under international law and its agreement with foreign investors. Conceptually, the explicit stabilization clause in IIAs is a clear indication of the willingness of the host state to keep intact the stability and predictability of its investment legal system. From foreign investor's perspective, the existence of an IIA SC would afford a very high level of protection against the host state's political risk. When the host state breaches the rights guaranteed to the investor under the treaty clause, the host state not only breaches the norms of customary international law (such as the requirement to expropriate only for a public

---

27 Agreement for the Promotion and Protection of Investments, Para-U.K., art. 6, Jun. 4, 1981.

28 ORTINO, *supra* note 10, at 17; Gazzini, *supra* note 15, at 1.

29 Convention on the Protection of Investments, Fr-Yugoslavia., art. 4, Mar. 28, 1974. () [Unofficial translation] *available at* https://rb.gy/yckz6w [https://perma.cc/FG4Y-MGY4].

purpose, in a nondiscriminatory fashion, and upon the payment of prompt, adequate, and effective compensation), it also violates a treaty with the investor's home country.[30]

The inserting of SCs in IIAs raises some serious consequences than traditional CSCs, as elaborated below:

First, while the IIA SCs apply to all current and future foreign investors protected by the treaty investment, making those investors immune to any subsequent regulatory framework changes,the traditional CSCs apply only to a specific foreign investor who is a party with the host state in the state contract.[31]

Second, inclusion in IIAs of the freezing SCs may lead the foreign investors of other countries with an investment treaty with the host state to invoke the most-favored-nation clause (MFN) to benefit from the IIA SCs which sequentially could amplify the effect of IIA SCs exponentially.[32] Third, as far as the author is aware, IIA SCs have yet to be tested in arbitral tribunals. Several questions remain open to the interpretation, content, and scope of IIA SCs. Finally, like traditional CSCs, it seems apparent that the primary purpose of including the freezing SCs in the IIAs is to create a conduciveness investment climate and attract FDI inflows into the contracting states. However, one may reasonably ask whether IIA SCs in practice facilitate FDI and thus are constructive for contracting states. Given the apparent lack of awareness of the IIA SCs in the legal literature and within the arbitral practice, no evidence conclusively establishes that IIA SCs entice FDI. Yet, this question will remain open, at least for now, because its answer is beyond the scope of this chapter and the book.

For the reasons previously explained, one may argue that IIA SCs can turn investment treaties into "treacherous legal products," and concerned governments "should have a clear and compelling interest in neutralizing them."[33] On the other, one might see IIA SCs as one of the main catalysts for foreign investors to invest in a contracting host state with large-scale volatility.

Indeed, IIA SCs can be categorized as provisions guaranteeing regulatory stability in the strict sense, since their key feature is to protect foreign investors against subsequent unilateral changes of the host state's regulatory framework applicable to the investment project. However, this thesis argues that the inclusion in IIAs of freezing SCs might seem undue restriction is placed on the regulatory powers of the host state. Expecting the potential investor to rely exclusively on IIA SCs is unrealistic when the investor often has access to CSCs,

30 Comeaux & Kinsella (1994), at 6.
31 Gazzini, *supra* note 15, at 2.
32 *Id.*
33 *Id.*

whereby specific commitments are given to particular investors. Therefore, if the IIA SC doesn't in fact increase the appetite of investors to invest in the host state, it represents a poor proposition for the host state since the state remains liable for any subsequent regulations the government passes that violate the stability guarantees in the IIAs. Therefore, this thesis concludes that adequate protection of regulatory powers to recalibrating the balance of interests and rights between the state and foreign investors might be achieved either by progressively replacing IIA SC with Contractual LSC, or by adopting modern stabilization clauses which are acombination of traditional SCs and renegotiation clauses.

## 5.3 Legal Stability under Fair and Equitable Treatment Standard (FET)

According to United Nations Conference on Trade and Development (UNCTAD), 95 % of IIAs contain provisions that require the host state to provide FET to investors and their investment from the other contracting party.[34] The FET clause has been present in BITs since World War II, but investment tribunals have only started applying it to a wide range of situations since the year 2000, after it had remained largely unused for many years. One could say that the clause had been a "sleeping beauty" until then.[35] Nevertheless, the FET standard has a widespread presence in current investment arbitration, and it is the most litigated standard in investor-state dispute settlement, accounting for 83% of such claims.[36] Frequently, the FET standard is combined with the full protection and security (FPS) standard.[37]

A typical example of the traditional FET standard can be found in the BIT between the United States and Argentina in Article II (2), which provides that "[i]nvestment shall at all times be accorded fair and equitable treatment."[38]

Another example can be found in the BIT between the United Kingdom and the Soviet Union in Article 2 (2), which provides that "[i]nvestment of [the]

34 Nathalie Bernasconi et el, *Investment Negotiation at the WTO and the IIA regime: Anticipating Unintended Interactions*, 11 AN ONLINE J. INV L& POL'Y. 4, at 6 (2020).

35 Moshe Hirsch, Between Fair and Equitable Treatment and Stabilization Clause: Stable Legal Environment and Regulatory Change in International Investment Law, 12 J. WORLD INVESTMENT & TRADE 783, 789 (2011).

36 Bernasconi et el, *supra* note 34.

37 REINISCH & SCHREUER, *supra* note 13, at 250.

38 The reciprocal encouragement and protection of investment, US.-Arg., art. II, 2, Nov. 14, 1991, U.S.T.

investors of each contracting party shall at all times be accorded fair and equitable treatment."[39]

Many Multilateral Investment Treaties (MITS) also contain FET provisions. A notable example here can be found in the Energy Charter Treaty of 1994, Article 10 (1) which provides:

> Each Contracting Party shall, in accordance with the provisions of this treaty, encourage and create stable, equitable, favorable and transparent conditions for Investors of other Contracting Parties to make Investments in its Area. Such conditions shall include a commitment to accord at all times to Investments of Investors of other Contracting Parties fair and equitable treatment. Such Investments shall also enjoy the most constant protection, and security and no Contracting Party shall in any way impair by unreasonable or discriminatory measures their management, maintenance, use, enjoyment, or disposal. In no case shall such Investments be accorded treatment less favorable than that required by international law, including treaty obligations. Each Contracting Party shall observe any obligations it has entered into with an Investor or an Investment of an Investor of any other Contracting Party.[40]

Similarly, the, Article 1105(1) of the North American Free Trade Agreement (NAFTA) provides that "each party shall accord to investments of investors of another Party treatment in accordance with international law, including fair and equitable treatment and full protection and security."[41] NAFTA has been superseded by the U.S-Mexico and Canada Agreement (USMCA),[42] which also contains an FET clause providing that "[e]ach Party shall accord to covered investments treatment in accordance with customary international law, including fair and equitable treatment and full protection and security."[43]

---

39 The Promotion and Reciprocal Protection of Investments, U.K.-U.S.S.R., GR. BRIT.T.S. No. 3 (1992). (Cm. 1791) https://investmentpolicy.unctad.org/international-investment-agreements/treaty-files/2235/download.

40 European Energy Charter Treaty art. 10, Dec 17, 1994, 34 I.L.M. 381, 389.

41 North American Free Trade Agreement, Can.-Mex.-U.S., Dec. 17, 1992, 32 I.L.M. 289.

42 In 2018, the United States, Mexico, and Canada renegotiated the 25-year-old NAFTA. As a result of these renegotiations, the parties agreed on new terms to formulate the U.S-Mexico-Canada Agreement (USMCA). The USMCA entered into force on July 1, 2020. Accordingly, NAFTA preferential treatment cannot be claimed on July 1, 2020, or afterward.

43 United States-Mexico-Canada Agreement (USMCA), Nov. 30, 2018, *available at* https://ustr.gov/trade-agreements/free-trade-agreements/united-states-mexico-canada-agreement. *See infra*-Appendix, Part III. B. and accompanying text.

Moreover, most investment chapters of the new post-2000 of FTAs, such as US FTAs and the EU FTAs, contain FET clauses.[44]

The FET provisions contained in the current IIAs take the form of one of two types. The first type ties the FET standard to the customary international minimum standard,[45] such as the standard mentioned in Article 1105 of the NAFTA and Article 14.6 of the USMCA articulated above. The standard provided in the USMCA is the same as that provided under NAFTA. But USMCA expressly states that the FET standard does not require treatment in addition to or beyond the minimum standard of treatment under customary international law.[46]

The second type is the *sui generis* or an independent standard, which refers to the general obligations of the host state and provide foreign investors with fair and equitable treatment without any reference to customary international law or a minimum standard of international law. When dealing with such provisions, the arbitral tribunal has discretion in determining how it should analyze them; it may or may not interpret them according to the minimum standard of international law.[47]

In terms of legal stability through IIAs, while the IIA SCs are a rare breed, the FET standard is a common feature of the modern IIAs. It is subject to variant interpretations of arbitral tribunals regarding its contribution in providing stability to the regulatory framework for the investment projects. Indeed, the stability of the host state's legal framework has been linked to the FET standard through the concept of foreign investors' legitimate expectations. The notion of legitimate expectations is present in the domestic public or administrative law in many jurisdictions.[48] It requires that "state authorities respect the legitimate expectations of individuals created through statements of policy or intention as part of their general duty of fairness, particularly when directed at a particular individual or entity."[49] Now, under international investment

---

44 Reinisch & Schreuer, *supra* note 13, at 259.

45 *See* Krista Nadakavukaren Schefer, International Investment Law: Text, Cases and Materials 377 (2nd ed. 2016).

46 *See* Niyati Ahuja, *USMCA: An Analysis of the Proposed ISDS Mechanism*, Kluwer Arbitration Blog (Nov 26. 2019), available at http://arbitrationblog.kluwerarbitration.com/2019/11/26/usmca-an-analysis-of-the-proposed-isds-mechanism/.

47 Schefer, *supra* note 45, at 377–378.

48 Cameron (2010), at 170.

49 Crawford, *supra* note 8, *at* 371; *See also* Potesta (2013), at 93 (noting that several domestic legal systems protect legitimate expectations, which are intended as "the entitlement of an individual to legal protection from harm caused by a public authority resulting from a previous publicly stated position, whether that be in the form of a formal decision or in the form of a representation.")[Quoting Chester Brown, The Protection of

treaties, it is well established that disappointed expectations by a host state can, in some circumstances, trigger an investment dispute.[50]

In the context of international investment law practice, the notion of legitimate expectations is consistently acknowledged as the "dominant element of FET" standard[51] that the arbitral tribunal can rely on to determine whether the host state breached the FET standard. In his separate opinion in *Thunderbird Gaming v. Mexico*, Prof. Thomas Wälde[52] pointed out that "[t]he wide acceptance of the "legitimate expectations" principle, therefore, supports the concept that it is indeed part of "fair and equitable treatment" as owed by governments to foreign investors under modern investment treaties and Art. 1105 of the NAFTA."[53]

Therefore, protecting foreign investors' legitimate expectations is the "primary objective of the FET standard."[54] In *Biwater v. Tanzania*, the tribunal stated unequivocally that:

> [T]he purpose of the fair and equitable treatment standard is to provide to international investments treatment that does not affect the basic expectations that were taken into account by the foreign investor to make the investment, as long as these expectations are reasonable and legitimate and have been relied upon by the investor to make the investment.[55]

---

Legitimate Expectations as a "General Principle of Law": Some Preliminary Thoughts' 6(1) Transnational Dispute Management 2 (2009)].

50 *Id*; *See also* CAMERON (2010), at 171.

51 *See supra* note 9.

52 Professor Thomas W. Wälde was "a specialist in international investment, economic, oil, gas, energy and mineral law, with a particular focus on arbitration in these fields. Former Interregional Adviser on Petroleum, Mineral & Investment Law with the United Nations and Executive Director of the Dundee University Centre for Energy, Petroleum and Mineral Law & Policy." https://www.transnational-dispute-management.com/about-author-a-z-profile.asp?key=6.

53 International Thunderbird Gaming Corporation v. The United Mexican States, UNCITRAL, separate opinion, para 30 (Dec. 1, 2005). [hereinafter Thunderbird Gaming v. Mexico, separate opinion].

54 50 YULIA LEVASHOVA, THE RIGHT OF STATES TO REGULATE IN INTERNATIONAL INVESTMENT LAW: THE SEARCH FOR BALANCE BETWEEN PUBLIC INTEREST AND FAIR AND EQUITABLE TREATMENT 113 (2019).

55 Biwater Gauff LTD v. United Republic of Tanzania, ICSID Case No. ARB/05/22, Award, 602 (Jul. 24, 2008). To the same effect, *see* Sociedad General de Aguas de Barcelona, S.A. and Vivendi Universal, S.A. v. Argentina Republic, ICSID Case No. ARB/03/19, Decision on Liability, 222 (the tribunal held that " In an effort to develop an operational method for determining the existence or nonexistence of fair and equitable treatment, arbitral tribunals have increasingly taken into account the legitimate expectations that a host country

The main objective of this section is to investigate whether and to what extent the arbitral tribunal has interpreted the FET standard as a guarantee of legal stability. In other words, do the FET standard protects against the host state's regulatory changes?

Accordingly, this study puts forwards all arguments articulated in this regard. In practice, arbitral tribunals have been sharply divided over the above question, and two schools of thought have emerged over it. While the first school of thought interprets the FET standard as granting a foreign project legal stability strict sense of the regulatory framework. The second school rejects such a broad interpretation of the FET-standard and has tried to subject the nation of legitimate expectations to qualifying requirements, denying any link between the FET standard and the legal stability guarantee in the strict sense.

### 5.3.1 *FET Standard Includes a Guarantee of Legal Stability (Pro-investor Approach)*

The early decisions of arbitral tribunals, particularly between 2003 and 2006, have adopted a so-called "pro-investor" approach and interpreted the FET clause as it guarantees legal stability in the traditional sense. To reach this conclusion, these investment tribunals relied mainly on three principles: First, that the preamble of the applicable investment treaty that links stability and FET; second, that a need exists to protect foreign investors' legitimate expectations; and/or third, that the conclusion is established by arbitral precedent.[56]

The classic statement of this permissive approach is found in the 2003 award of *Tecmed v. Mexico*, in which ICSID held that the FET standard contained in Article 4(1) of the Mexico-Spain BIT

> [R]equires the Contracting Parties to provide to international investments treatment that does not affect the basic expectations that were taken into account by the foreign investor to make the investment. The foreign investor expects the host State to act in a consistent manner, free from ambiguity and totally transparently in its relations with the foreign investor.[57]

has created in the investor and the extent to which conduct by the host government subsequent to the investment has frustrated those expectations.").

56 ORTINO, *supra* note 10, at 20.

57 Técnicas Medioambientales Tecmed, S.A. v. The United Mexican States, ICSID Case No. ARB (AF)/00/2, Award, 154 (May 29, 2003).

Some cases have followed Tecmed's approach. The tribunal in the *CMS v. Argentina* case shed light on the concept of investment stability under the FET. For its interpretation of the FET provision, the *CMS* tribunal specifically relied on the preamble of the applicable BIT (US-Argentina BIT) and stated:

> The Treaty Preamble makes it clear, however, that one principal protection envisaged is that fair and equitable treatment is desirable to maintain a stable framework for investments and maximum effective use of economic resources. There can be no doubt, therefore, that a stable legal and business environment is an essential element of fair and equitable treatment.[58]

The tribunal asserted that the FET is "inseparable from stability and predictability."[59] Likewise, in *Enron v. Argentina*, the tribunal relied on the preamble of the applicable BIT (US-Argentina BIT) to conclude that "a key element of fair and equitable treatment is the requirement of a 'stable framework for the investment' … Indeed, this interpretation has been considered 'an emerging standard of fair and equitable treatment in international law'."[60]

In *Occidential v. Ecuador*, the tribunal stated unequivocally that "the stability of the legal and business framework is … an essential element of fair and equitable treatment."[61] The tribunal in *LG&E v. Argentina* also aligned itself with the preceding arbitral views. It held that "the stability of the legal and business framework in the state party is an essential element in the standard of what is fair and equitable treatment."[62]

Similarly, the ICSID tribunal in *PSEG v. Turkey* emphasized the link between the FET provision and the stability of the legal framework, stating:

> The aggregate of the situations explained raise the question of the need to ensure a stable and predictable business environment for investors to operate in, as required not only by the Treaty but also by the Turkish Constitution as noted above. This is what the United States Technical Memorandum on the BIT had very much in mind when it referred to fair

58 CMS Gas Transmision Company v. Argentina, ICSID Case No. ARB/01/8, Award, 274 (May 12, 2005).

59 *Id.* 276.

60 Enron v. Argentina, ICSID Case No. ARB/01/3, Award, 260 (May 22, 2007).

61 Occidential Exploration and Production Company v. Ecuador, LCIA Case No. UN 3467, Award, 183 (July 1, 2004).

62 LG&E v. Argentina, ICSID Case No. ARB/02/1, Decision on Liability, 125 (2006).

> and equitable treatment as a standard "that can be invoked in arbitration to protect investments against possible vagaries of the host-Party's national laws and their administration."[63]

### Analysis of the Pro-investor Approach

After closely analyzing the above tribunal's reasoning it appears that adopting the pro-investor approach may lead to the conclusion that the FET provision is equivalent to the traditional CSCs. As a result, if regulatory changes by the host state diminish the investor's interests, the state may be liable to pay compensation. This would make inserting an SC in the state contract redundant. Moreover, interpreting the FET provision as imposes a legal stability obligation upon the host state based solely on the IIA's preamble would go against the intentions of the IIA's drafters. The purpose of IIAs is not solely to protect foreign investments, but rather to do so in a manner that is compatible with the host state's public policy objectives. Additionally, the IIA's preamble is only meant to offer interpretative guidance to decision-makers and does not impose any binding substantive obligations upon the host state.[64] Therefore, its practical impact in recognizing the legal framework's stability should be somewhat limited.

Furthermore, this approach appears to be unconvincing. It impedes the host state's prerogative to exercise its sovereign power while ignoring that foreign investors should legitimately expect the host state's regulations to change over time. In a study published in 2012, UNCTAD concluded that the pro-investor approach is unjustified as it undermines the host state's right to regulate; as put by UNCTAD :

> In these cases, tribunals have gone so far as to suggest that any adverse change in the business or legal framework of the host country may give rise to a breach of the FET standard in that the investor's legitimate expectations of predictability and stability are thereby undermined. This approach is unjustified, as it would potentially prevent the host State from introducing any legitimate regulatory change, let alone from undertaking a regulatory reformthat may be called for. It ignores the fact that

---

63 PSEG Global, Inc., The North American Coal Corporation, and Konya Ingin Electrik Üretim ve Ticaret Limited Sirketi v. Republic of Turkey, ICSID Case No. ARB/02/5, Award, 253 (Jan. 19, 2007).

64 Giannakopoulos, Charalampos, *The Right to Regulate in International Investment Law and the Law of State Responsibility: A Hohfeldian Approach, in* PERMUTATIONS OF RESPONSIBILITY IN INTERNATIONAL LAW 148, 157 (May 3, 2017).

> investors should legitimately expect regulations to change over time as an aspect of the normal operation of legal and policy processes of the economy they operate in.[65]

The pro-investor approach has been subjected too much criticism within doctrinal discussions that has unleashed a torrent of commentary. As examples, Professor Zachary Douglas aptly describes the Tecmed standard as "actually not a standard at all; it is rather a description of perfect public regulation in a perfect world, to which all states should aspire, but very few (if any) will ever attain."[66]

While Professor M. Sornarajah notes that "[t]he breadth of the rule in some awards is staggering and could not have been agreed to by the states concluding the treaties."[67] And professor Michele Potesta also criticizes the pro-investor approach stating that "first generation awards display an almost complete lack of analysis as to reasons for including the protection of legitimate expectations as a sub-element, or indeed the 'dominant' sub-element, of fair and equitable treatment."[68]

Because the pro-investor approach would stand in stark contrast to the host state's right to regulate, this has led some arbitral tribunals to opine that further qualifying elements to the principle of foreign investors' legitimate expectations are required.[69]

### 5.3.2 *Rejectionist Approach against Linking the FET Clause and Legal Stability in the Strict Sense (Reasonableness Approach)*

Most arbitral tribunals have rejected the pro-investor approach interpreting the FET clause to protect the foreign investor's general expectation of stability. The UNCITRAL tribunal in *Saluka v. the Czech Republic* was one of the first tribunals to reject interpreting the FET clause as imposing a legal stability obligation in its strict sense.[70] According to the *Saluka* tribunal, a strict reading of the FET provisions in the Czech Republic-Netherlands BIT "would impose

65 UNCTAD (2012), *supra* note 11, at 69.

66 Zachary Douglas, *Nothing if not critical for investment treaty arbitration: Occidental, Eureko and Methanex*. 22 Arb. Int'l 27, 28 (2006).

67 SORNARAJAH (2010), at 355.

68 Potesta (2013), at 121.

69 *See e.g.,* Infracapital F1 S. à r.l. and Infracapital Solar B.V. Kingdom of Spain, ICSID Case No. ARB/16/18, decision on jurisdiction, liability and directions on quantum (Sept. 13, 2021); Parkerings Compagniet A.S. v. Lithuania., ICSID No. ARB/05/8, Award (Sept. 11, 2007) [hereinafter Parkerings Award].

70 Saluka Partial Award (2006).

upon host States' obligations which would be inappropriate and unrealistic."[71] And, to be protected, foreign investors' legitimate expectations "must rise to the level of legitimacy and reasonableness *in light of the circumstances*."[72] In the view of the *Saluka* tribunal, "[n]o investor may reasonably expect that the circumstances prevailing at the time the investment is made remain totally unchanged."[73] The tribunal emphasized that "the host State's legitimate right subsequently to regulate domestic matters in the public interest must be taken into consideration as well."[74]

Also, the ICSID tribunal in *Continental v. Argentina*[75] opposed interpreting the FET provision as imposing a legal stability obligation upon the host state by relying on the preamble of the applicable BIT (US-Argentina BIT) that links FET with the legal framework stability. As the Continental tribunal explains:

> Stability of the legal framework for investments is mentioned in the Preamble of the BIT. It is not a legal obligation in itself for the Contracting Parties, nor can it be properly defined as an object of the Treaty. It is rather a precondition for one of the two basic objects of the Treaty, namely the promotion of the investment flow, rather than being related to its other objective, that of granting protection for investments on a reciprocal basis. Stability of the legal framework is undoubtedly conducive to attracting foreign investments ... On the other hand, it would be unconscionable for a country to promise not to change its legislation as time and needs change, or even more to tie its hands by such a kind of stipulation in case a crisis of any type or origin arose. Such an implication as to stability in the BIT's Preamble would be contrary to an effective interpretation of the Treaty; reliance on such an implication by a foreign investor would be misplaced and, indeed, unreasonable.[76]

There are several awards subsequent to the above arbitral decisions that avoid an overbroad reading of the FET standard by reference to foreign investors' legitimate expectations. For example, the ICSID tribunal in *Parkerings v. Lithuania* stressed:

71 *Id.* 304.
72 *Id.*
73 *Id.* 305.
74 *Id.*
75 Continental Casulty v. Argentina, ICSID Case No. ARB/07/27, Award (Sep. 5, 2008).
76 *Id.* 258.

> It is each State's undeniable right and privilege to exercise its sovereign legislative power. A State has the right to enact, modify or cancel a law at its own discretion. Save for the existence of an agreement, in the form of a *stabilisation* clause or otherwise, there is nothing objectionable about the amendment brought to the regulatory framework existing at the time an investor made its investment. As a matter of fact, any businessman or investor knows that laws will evolve over time.[77]

Likewise, the ICSID tribunal in *EDF v. Romania* aptly stated:

> The idea that legitimate expectations, and therefore FET, imply the stability of the legal and business framework, may not be correct if stated in an overly broad and unqualified formulation. The FET might then mean the virtual freezing of the legal regulation of economic activities, in contrast with the State's normal regulatory power and the evolutionary character of economic life. Except where specific promises or representations are made by the State to the investor, the latter may not rely on a bilateral investment treaty as a kind of insurance policy against the risk of any changes in the host State's legal and economic framework. Such expectation would be neither legitimate nor reasonable.[78]

The EDF tribunal concluded that the FET provision is not equivalent to stabilization clauses granted explicitly to foreign investors.[79]

Like the EDF tribunal, several tribunals that have adopted a rejectionist approach to linking the FET standard and legal stability in a strict sense have also identified several key requirement elements under FET. However, this requirement does not in themselves guarantee stability, as foreign investors' expectations are protected only if these are legitimate and reasonable under the circumstances.[80] Such elements are as follows: (a) specific representations; (b) presumption of awareness of the general regulatory environment, and (c) balancing of investor's expectations against legitimate regulatory action.[81]

The first factor to which arbitral tribunals refer to determine a foreign investor's legitimate expectations is the existence of specific commitments of legal stability undertaken by the host state and relied upon by the foreign investor.

77 Parkerings Award (2007), *supra* note 69, 332.

78 EDF (Services) Limited v. Romania, ICSID Case No. ARB/05/13, Award, 217 (Oct. 8, 2009).

79 *Id.* 218.

80 ORTINO, *supra* note 10, at 29.

81 UNCTAD (2012), *supra* note 11, at 68.

For example, the ICSID tribunal in *Total v. Argentina* rejected to read the FET clause as it implies legal stability guarantees for the foreign investor unless the host state makes a specific stabilization commitment. In the tribunal's words:

> In the absence of some "promise" by the host State or a specific provision in the bilateral investment treaty itself, the legal regime in force in the host country at the time of making the investment is not automatically subject to a "guarantee" of stability merely because the host country entered into a bilateral investment treaty with the country of the foreign investor. The expectation of the investor is undoubtedly "legitimate", and hence subject to protection under the fair and equitable treatment clause, if the host State has explicitly assumed a specific legal obligation for the future, such as by contracts, concessions or stabilisation clauses on which the investor is therefore entitled to rely as a matter of law.[82]

The tribunal in *White Industries v. India* concluded that legitimate expectations are based only on specific representations made to the foreign investor by the host state, as the tribunal held that:

The tribunal agrees with [the host state] that the alleged representations suffer from vagueness and generality. Consequently, they cannot give rise to reasonable, legitimate expectations that are amenable to protection under the fair and equitable treatment standard.[83] Similarly, in *El Paso Energy International Co v. Argentine,* the tribunal emphasized the significance of having specific commitments to create a foreign investor's legitimate expectations. In the words of the tribunal:

> A reasonable general regulation can be considered a violation of the FET standard if it violates a specific commitment towards the investor. The Tribunal considers that a special commitment by the State towards an investor provides the latter with a certain protection against changes in the legislation, but it needs to discuss more thoroughly the concept of "specific commitments." In the Tribunal's view, no general definition of what constitutes a specific commitment can be given, as all depends on the circumstances. However, it seems that two types of commitments

82 Total S.A. v. The Argentine Republic, ICSID Case No. ARB/04/01, Decision on Liability, 117 (Dec. 27, 2010).

83 White Industries v. India, UNCITRAL, Final Award, 10.3.17 (Nov. 30, 2011).

> might be considered "specific": those specific as to their addressee and those specific regarding their object and purpose.[84]
>
> First, in order to prevent a change in regulations being applied to an investor or certain behaviour of the State, there can indeed exist *specific commitments directly made to the investor*—for example in a contract or in a letter of intent, or even through a specific promise in a person-to-person business meeting—and not simply general statements in treaties or legislation which, because of their nature of general regulations, can evolve. The important aspect of the commitment is not so much that it is legally binding—which usually gives rise to some sort of responsibility if it is violated without a need to refer to FET—but that it contains a specific commitment directly made to the investor, on which the latter has relied.[85]
>
> Second, a commitment can be considered specific if its *precise object was to give a real guarantee of stability to the investor*. Usually, general texts cannot contain such commitments, as there is no guarantee that they will not be modified in due course. However, a reiteration of the same type of commitment in different types of general statements could, considering the circumstances, amount to a specific behaviour of the State, the object and purpose of which is to give the investor a guarantee on which it can justifiably rely.[86]

The tribunal in *Parkerings v. Lithuania* ably addresses contractual expectations and the absence of a host state's specific representation, such as stabilization clauses.[87] The tribunal observed that the breach of the FET standard occurs when the foreign investor is deprived of its legitimate expectations that the host state's legal and business framework will remain stable and unchanged.[88] To determine what the legitimate expectation of an investor, the *Parkerings* tribunal set out four criteria as elaborated below:

1. The host state provides an explicit promise or guarantees to a foreign investor that the legal framework will remain stable and unchanged;
2. The host state provides implied assurances or representations to a foreign investor, which are taken into consideration when deciding to invest in this host state.

84 El Paso Energy Award (2011), 375.
85 *Id.* 376.
86 *Id.* 377.
87 Parkerings Award (2007), *supra* note 69, 321–346.
88 *Id.* 330; *see also*, CAMERON (2010), at 214.

3 The host state makes no assurance or representations to the foreign investor; but the circumstances surrounding the conclusion of the investment contract are crucial to determining the legitimacy of the investor's expectations;
4 The conduct of the host state at the time of the investment.[89]

The *Parkerings* tribunal held that the Lithuanian government did not provide any explicit or implicit guarantees that the legal framework applicable to the investment project would remain stable and unchanged during the life of the investment contract.[90] As a result, the claim of FET alleged by the foreign investor had to fail.[91] However, the tribunal acknowledged that if the investment contract had contained stabilization clauses, the outcome would have been completely different, and the foreign investor's claim of FET would have prevailed. As shown from the tribunal words:

> By deciding to invest notwithstanding this possible instability, the claimant took the business risk to be faced with changes of laws possibly or even likely to be detrimental to its investment. The claimant could (and with hindsight should) have sought to protect its legitimate expectations by introducing into the investment agreement a stabilization clause or some other provision protecting it against unexpected and unwelcome changes.[92]

As articulated above, the tribunals' practice shows that the foreign investor's legitimate expectations of legal framework stability during the investment project's lifespan are not protected under the FET provision unless the host state has made specific stability guarantees.

The second factor that arbitral tribunals often refer to when evaluating the foreign investor's legitimate expectation under the FET clause is a presumption of awareness of the general regulatory environment. Several tribunals have emphasized that investors have a duty to conduct due diligence to claim protection of their legitimate expectations. For instance, in *Masdar v. Spain*, the tribunal concluded "the investor must demonstrate that it has exercised appropriate due diligence and that it has familiarized itself with the existing

89 Parkerings Award (2007), *supra* note 69, 331; CAMERON (2010), at 214.
90 *Id.* 334.
91 *Id.* 338.
92 *Id.* 336.

laws."[93] Similarly, in *Charanne v. Spain*, the tribunal held that "in order to exercise the right of legitimate expectations, the claimants should have made a diligent analysis of the legal framework for the investment."[94] The tribunal in *Parkerings v. Lithuania* noted that "[t]he investor will have a right of protection of its legitimate expectations provided it exercised due diligence and that its legitimate expectations were reasonable in light of the circumstances."[95] The tribunal in *Frontier Petroleum Services v. the Check Republic* explained:

> Tribunals have stated consistently that protected expectations must rest on the conditions as they exist at the time of the investment. They have pointed out that a foreign investor has to make its business decisions and shape its expectations on the basis of the law and the factual situation prevailing in the country as it stands at the time of the investment.[96]

In *Mamidoil v. Albania*, the tribunal underlined the importance of the investor's conduct and concluded:

> The investor is entitled to rely on the stability and transparency of the legal framework. However, the obligation of the state does not dispense the obligation of the investor to evaluate the circumstances. Reliance has at its prerequisite diligent inquiry and information. The investor has to understand the content and the context of the law and the administrative practice. Put differently, the standard is addressed to both the state and the investor. Fairness and equitableness cannot be established adequately without an adequate and balanced appraisal of both parties' conduct.[97]

Last, to evaluate the legitimacy of the foreign investor's expectations, other arbitral tribunals refer to the balancing act that considers the interest of both parties in the state contract (the foreign investor's legitimate expectations along with the host state's right to regulate). These arbitral tribunals suggest that the FET clause does not preclude the host state from exercising its regulatory power in the public interest, even if such acts badly hurt the investment project.[98]

93 Masdar Award (2018), *supra* note 41, 494.
94 Charanne Construction v. Spain, SCC Case No. 062/2012, Award, 505 (Jan. 21, 2016).
95 Parkerings Award (2007), *supra* note 69, 333.
96 Frontier Petroleum Services v. the Check Republic., PCA, Award, 287 (Nov. 12,2010).
97 Mamidoil Award (2015), 634.
98 UNCTAD (2012), *supra* note 11, at 73.

The foundations for this balancing approach were first found in the *Saluka v. Czech* case in which the tribunal aptly analyzed the balancing process involved in a claim based on the breach of legitimate expectations, stating:

> [Legitimate] expectations, in order for them to be protected, must rise to the level of legitimacy and reasonableness *in light of the circumstances.* No investor may reasonably expect that the circumstances prevailing at the time the investment is made remain totally unchanged. In order to determine whether frustration of the foreign investor's expectations was justified and reasonable, the host State's legitimate right subsequently to regulate domestic matters in the public interest must be taken into consideration as well [...] The determination of a breach of Article 3.1 by the Czech Republic therefore requires a weighing of the Claimant's legitimate and reasonable expectations on the one hand and the Respondent's legitimate regulatory interests on the other [...] A foreign investor protected by the Treaty may in any case properly expect that the Czech Republic implements its policies *bona fide* by conduct that is, as far as it affects the investors' investment, reasonably justifiable by public policies and that such conduct does not manifestly violate the requirements of consistency, transparency, even-handedness and nondiscrimination [...] Finally, it transpires from arbitral practice that, according to the "fair and equitable treatment" standard, the host State must never disregard the principles of procedural propriety and due process41 and must grant the investor freedom from coercion or harassment by its own regulatory authorities.[99]

The tribunal in *Joseph C. Lemire v. Ukraine* recognized unequivocally the right of the host state to regulate in the interest of its citizen, even if the regulatory changes badly hurt the foreign investor's interests. According to the *Joseph* tribunal

> The object and purpose of the Treaty is not to protect foreign investments per se, but as an aid to the development of the domestic economy. And local development requires that the preferential treatment of foreigners be balanced against the legitimate right of Ukraine to pass legislation and

99 Saluka Partial Award(2006), 304–308.

> adopt measures for the protection of what as a sovereign it perceives to be its public interest.[100]

Legal scholars also support the above arbitral practice regarding the host state's right to regulate and change its legislation in the absence of a specific stability commitment undertaken by the host state, but which was nonetheless relied upon by the foreign investor. As professors Andrew Newcombe and Lluís Paradell point out:

> *Legitimate expectations as a result of investor reliance on state conduct.* Legitimate expectations may arise as a result of specific state conduct directed at the investor upon which the investor relies. Any form of state conduct can, in principle, give rise to legitimate expectations. Typically, the conduct giving rise to the legitimate expectations will be in the form of oral or written representations, undertakings or commitments, various types of administrative acts such as licenses or permits or providing an official opinion or view.[101]

Professor Kenneth J. Vandevelde has noted that while arbitral tribunals have interpreted the FET standard as providing a form of security to the investment project in which the host state is required to act in a consistent way, these tribunals clearly emphasized that the FET standard does not impose a general obligation on the host state to always act consistently over time. Generally, "host states have discretion to change policies. A violation occurs, however, where the host state has promised to act in a certain way or has offered assurance to the investor (or investment) on which it has reasonably relied."[102]

In the same vein, the majority of the ICSID tribunal in *Infracapital v. Spain*,[103] in a recent decision on jurisdiction and liability, laid out a five-point test for legitimate expectations:

100 Joseph Charles Lemire v. Ukraine, ICSID Case No. ARB/06/18, Decision on Jurisdiction and Liability, 273 (Jan. 14, 2010).

101 ANDREW NEWCOMBE & LLUÍS PARADELL, LAW AND PRACTICE OF INVESTMENT TREATIES: STANDARDS OF TREATMENT (2009).

102 Kenneth J. Vandevelde, *A Unified Theory of Fair and Equitable Treatment*, 43 N.Y.U. J. INT'L L. & POL. 43, 66 (2010).

103 Infracapital F1 S. à r.l. and Infracapital Solar B.V. Kingdom of Spain, ICSID Case No. ARB/16/18, decision on jurisdiction, liability, and directions on quantum (Sept. 13, 2021).

> First, for an assurance or representation giving rise to legitimate expectations, the commitment must be grounded in the law [...] Second, the specific commitment must be made by a competent authority [...] Third, the assurance or representation must be clear and specific in order to generate an objective expectation and not a subjective perception of the content and scope of a purported legal commitment applicable to a plurality of people [...] Fourth, to assess the reasonableness of an expectation, the circumstances surrounding the making of the investment must be taken into account [...] Finally, and in any event, for the expectation to rise to the level of reasonable and legitimate, the State's policy interests must also be taken into account.

#### 5.3.2.1 Analysis of the Reasonableness Approach

Indeed, the above approach which rejects the overbroad reading of the FET standard as granting legal stability in its strict sense, by setting down factors that delimit the scope of the foreign investor's legitimate expectations, appears to be "a more sensible approach."[104] This is because evaluating the foreign investor's legitimate expectations must consider all circumstances, not only the facts surrounding the investment but also the "political, socioeconomic, cultural and historical conditions prevailing in the host state."[105] Moreover, these expectations must arise from the specific representations or commitments undertaken by the host state to the foreign investor, on which the foreign investor has relied.[106]

However, conditioning the legal stability obligation under the FET standard on the existence of specific stabilization guarantees may raise two fundamental issues. First, one may reasonably argue that the FET and umbrella clause appear to be similar in this regard. As reflected in both its language and history, the purpose of the umbrella clause is to convert any independent obligations the host state has assumed concerning the investor and investment—including in particular contractual obligations arising from investment agreements between the investor and the host state—into international obligations under the relevant treaty.[107] Therefore, while a CSC is likely to find protection through

104 UNCTAD (2012), *supra* note 11, at 67.

105 Duke Energy Electroquil Partners and Electroquil S.A. v. Republic of Ecuador, ICSID Case No. ARB/04/19, Award, 340 (Aug. 18, 2008).

106 *Id.* 340.

107 Wong (2006), at 143 ("Its purpose is to create an inter-state obligation to observe investment agreements that investors may enforce when the BIT confers a direct right of recourse to arbitration. More specifically, the history of the umbrella clause makes clear

the guarantee of contractual stability embedded in the umbrella clause, the same stabilization clause will be protected under the FET provision (understood to include stability conditioned on the existence of specific stabilization commitments) only within the strict ambit of the notion of legitimate expectations, which need to consider the host state's right to regulate.[108]

The second issue is whether, in the absence of a CSC, the stability provisions contained in the host state's general legislation satisfy reasonable and legitimate expectations of foreign investors that the host state's legal framework will remain unmodified. In other words, whether the stability provisions contained in the host state's national law will be protected under the FET (understood to include a soft stability obligation). The threshold issue that an arbitral tribunal faces in claiming legitimate expectations, which is based on the general legislative and regulatory framework, is a generality characteristic of such a regulatory framework, not a commitment specifically directed to the relevant investor.

It may be sufficient to note that arbitral tribunals and legal scholars have remained sharply divided over the above question and follow one of two schools of thought in this vein. In essence, *the first school* considers that the host state commitments must be specific to create legitimate expectations for foreign investors.[109] *The second school* argues that such obligations need only be expressed as a general statement in its laws.[110]

In sum, the majority of arbitral tribunals appear to have embraced the approach that interprets the FET provision to include a soft stability obligation rather than a strict stability obligation approach. However, a close reading of recent arbitral awards reveals that such a soft stability approach has not indeed consolidated. Several tribunals still failed to clearly determine

---

that it was designed to allow for any breach of a relevant investment contract to be resolved under the treaty in an international forum."). *See also* Sinclair (2004), at 413–18.

108 ORTINO, *supra* note 10, at 33.

109 For example, White Industries v. India, UNCITRAL, Final Award, 10.3.17 (Nov. 30,2011); El Paso Energy Award (2011), 375; Continental Award, 261; Mamidoil Award (2015), 642; Charanne Construction v. Spain, SCC Case No. 062/2012, Award, 493 (Jan. 21, 2016).

110 Masdar Award (2018), *supra* note 41, 490–510; Suez, Sociedad General de Aguas de Barcelona, S.A. and Vivendi Universal, S.A. v. Argentine Republic, ICSID Case No. ARB/03/19, Decision on Liability, 222 (July 30, 2010) [hereinafter Suez Decision on Liability]; Charanne Award, dissenting opinion, 5 (Jan. 21, 2016); Enron v. Argentina, ICSID Case No. ARB/01/3, Award, 264–26622 (May 22, 2007); *LG&E v. Argentina*, ICSID Case No. ARB/02/1, Award, 130, 131 (July 25, 2007) [hereinafter LG&E Award]; Novenergia II – Energy & Environment (SCA) (Grand Duchy of Luxembourg), SICAR v. Spain, SCC Case No. 2015/063, Award, 650 (Feb. 15, 2018); Electrabel S.A. v. Hungary, ICSID Case No. ARB/07/19, Award, 7.78 (Nov. 25, 2015).

the precise ambit of, and relationship between, the obligation to provide a stable regulatory framework and the obligation to protect the investor's legitimate expectations .[111] For example, to claim a breach of the FET clause for regulatory change, foreign investors often basetheir claim on two separate grounds, namely, violation of foreign investor's legitimate expectations (including the expectation that the legal framework would remain unmodified during the lifespan of investment project); and breach of the obligation to provide a stable regulatory framework. However, several arbitral tribunals fail to address the precise ambit and relationship between these two above obligations (obligation to provide a stable legal framework and obligation to protect the investor's legitimate expectations).[112] For example, in *Philip Morris v. Uruguay*, although the investor put forward the above two separate grounds to claim breach of the FET provision, the tribunal failed to clarify the relationship between two allegedly distinct claims and decided that "these two additional grounds of the Claimants' claim of breach of the FET standard [would]be considered in the same context due to their interrelation."[113] In *Antaris v. The Czech Republic*,[114] the tribunal, after setting out several propositions concerning the FET clause,[115] viewed it unnecessary to decide "the precise

111 ORTINO, *supra* note 10, at 33.

112 *Id.* at 33–34.

113 Philip Morris v. Uruguay, ICSID Case No. ARB/10/7, Award, 421 (July 8, 2016).

114 *Antaris Solar GmbH and Dr Michael Göde v Czech Republic,* PCA Case No 2014-01, Award (May 2, 2018).

115 After recognition of the existence of a vast arbitral practice interpreting and applying the FET standard, the Antaris tribunal laid out several propositions stemming from such practice, which are as follows: "(1) There will be a breach of the FET standard where legal and business stability or the legal framework has been altered in such a way as to frustrate legitimate and reasonable expectations or guarantees of stability. (2) A claim based on legitimate expectation must proceed from an identification of the origin of the expectation alleged, so that its scope can be formulated with precision. (3) A claimant must establish that (a) clear and explicit (or implicit) representations were made by or attributable to the state in order to induce the investment, (b) such representations were reasonably relied upon by the Claimants, and (c) these representations were subsequently repudiated by the state. (4) An expectation may arise from what are construed as specific guarantees in legislation. (5) A specific representation may make a difference to the assessment of the investor's knowledge and of the reasonableness and legitimacy of its expectation but is not indispensable to establish a claim based on legitimate expectation which is advanced under the FET standard. (6) Provisions of general legislation applicable to a plurality of persons or a category of persons, do not create legitimate expectations that there will be no change in the law; and given the State's regulatory powers, in order to rely on legitimate expectations the investor should inquire in advance regarding the prospects of a change in the regulatory framework in light of the then prevailing or reasonably

ambit of, and the relationship between, the propositions between, [those] propositions."[116]

## 5.4 Recent Treaty Practice

The legal stability provisions contained in the IIAs have increasingly dwindled in recent years. First, the IIA SCs are rare, except for Italian BITs. Some examples of IIA SCs are found in the old generation IIAs that have been terminated following renegotiation. The SCs were omitted in the new renegotiated IIAs.[117] Second, some recent IIAs excluded, either implicitly or explicitly, the broad interpretation of the FET standard as a guarantee of legal stability in the traditional sense.

A notable example of an implicit exclusion of the FET's link with the regulatory stability in its traditional sense can be found in the Australia-Uruguay BIT concluded on 5 April 2019. As the BIT's preamble recognized the rights of the

to be expected changes in the economic and social conditions of the host State. (7) An expectation may be engendered by changes to general legislation, but, at least in the absence of a stabilization clause, they are not prevented by the fair and equitable treatment standard if they do not exceed the exercise of the host State's normal regulatory power in the pursuance of a public interest and do not modify the regulatory framework relied upon by the investor at the time of its investment outside the acceptable margin of change. (8) The requirements of legitimate expectations and legal stability as manifestations of the FET standard do not affect the State's rights to exercise its sovereign authority to legislate and to adapt its legal system to changing circumstances. (9) The host State is not required to elevate the interests of the investor above all other considerations, and the application of the FET standard allows for a balancing or weighing exercise by the State and the determination of a breach of the FET standard must be made in the light of the high measure of deference which international law generally extends to the right of national authorities to regulate matters within their own borders. (10) Except where specific promises or representations are made by the State to the investor, the latter may not rely on an investment treaty as a kind of insurance policy against the risk of any changes in the host State's legal and economic framework. Such expectation would be neither legitimate nor reasonable. (11) Protection from arbitrary or unreasonable behaviour is subsumed under the FET standard. (12) It will also fall within the obligation not to impair investments by "unreasonable ... measures" (Article 10(1), ECT) or "arbitrary ... measures (Article 2(2), Czech Republic/Germany BIT)." (13) The investor is entitled to expect that the State will not act in a way which is manifestly inconsistent or unreasonable (i.e. unrelated to some rational policy). *Id.* 360".

116 *Id.* 363; ORTINO, *supra* note 10, at 37–38.

117 ORTINO, *supra* note 10, at 45.

governments "to regulate and resolving to preserve the flexibility of the Parties to set legislative and regulatory priorities, safeguard the public welfare."[118]

It bears mention that by inclusion in IIA's preamble of the state's right to regulate, contracting states send a clear message to international arbitrators that the primary goal of the IIA is not only investment protection, but rather that achieving investment policy objectives ought to be in a manner that is compatible with other public policy objectives.[119]

Indeed, adopting a broad interpretation of the FET standard as it guarantees legal stability in its strict sense would stand in stark contrast to an interpretation based on the general rule of interpretation enshrined in Article 31(1) of the Vienna Convention on the Law of Treaties (VCLT), that, in addition to the 'text,' rely on the 'context' and 'object and purpose' of the treaty.[120]

A notable example of the IIAs that contained express exclusions of regulatory stability in its strict sense can be found in the Colombia-France BIT, signed on 10 July 2014,[121] in which Article 4.1 thereof provides that " It is understood that the obligation to ensure fair and equitable treatment of investors and their investments does not include a legal stabilization clause and does not prevent each of the Contracting Parties to adapt its legislation in accordance with the provisions of this paragraph."[122] "*Se entiende que la obligacion de otorgar un trato justo y equitativo, no incluye una clausula de estabilizacion juridical ni impide a una Parte Contratante adaptar su legislacion de conformidad con los terminus de este paragrafo.*"[123]

---

118 Australia-Uruguay BIT (Apr. 5, 2019), *available at* https://investmentpolicy.unctad.org/international-investment-agreements/treaties/bilateral-investment-treaties/4895/australia---uruguay-bit-2019.

119 Charalampos, *supra* note 64, at 157.

120 *Id.* at 157, (noting that, the usefulness of the preamble is two-fold in light of this rule. First, it forms part of a treaty's context which the VCLT makes relevant for purposes of interpretation. 31 Second, a treaty's preamble is the place where adjudicators would often search for the treaty's object and purpose. 32 The object and purpose of a treaty is often used to pinpoint the ordinary meaning that should be given to the terms of the treaty in instances of textual ambiguity or normative disagreement.), available at SSRN: https://ssrn.com/abstract=2962686; ORTINO, *supra* note 10, at 45.

121 Agreement for the reciprocal promotion and protection of investments, Colombia-Fra., July 10, 2014, *available at* https://investmentpolicy.unctad.org/international-investment-agreements/treaties/tips/3488/colombia---france-bit-2014-.

122 *Id.* Art. 4.1 (b) [Unofficial translation].

123 *Id.* Art. 4. 1(b) [Original text].

Also, another example of an express exclusion of regulatory stability in its strict sense can be found in Canada–EU CETA[124] concluded on 30 October 2016, in which Article 8.1 stipulates that:

> 1. For the purpose of this Chapter, the Parties reaffirm their right to regulate within their territories to achieve legitimate policy objectives, such as the protection of public health, safety, the environment or public morals, social or consumer protection or the promotion and protection of cultural diversity.
> 2. For greater certainty, the mere fact that a Party regulates, including through a modification to its laws, in a manner which negatively affects an investment or interferes with an investor's expectations, including its expectations of profits, does not amount to a breach of an obligation under this Section.[125]

While the CETA drafters in paragraph 1 reaffirm the right to the contracting states to regulate to achieve their legitimate policy objectives, paragraph 2 clearly and explicitly states that host state's regulation which negatively affects an investment project or interferes with an investor's expectations does not tantamount to a breach of an obligation under this section.

## 5.5 Conclusion

The substantive provisions contained in the IIAs establish the backbone of modern international investment law. Several of these provisions have significant implications for the stability of the host state's regulatory framework. Such legal stability protection is imposed in the IIAs explicitly through the express stabilization clauses, or implicitely through FET clause. Plainly, for the investor, the IIA SC aims to stabilize the investment against adverse changes to the governing legal regime, particularly in an economically and politically volatile environment. Equally obvious, for the host state the IIA SC is a treaty mechanism aims to influence FDI inflows. Despite the claimed-trumpeted feature of the IIA SC as it purported to freeze the host state's legal framework in force when the investment was made, its validity and effectiveness-by analogy with traditional CSCs-are still highly speculative. Also, no empirical evidence shows that IIAs, in fact, stimulate greater foreign investment flows. A 2020

124 Canada-EU (CETA), *available at* https://ec.europa.eu/trade/policy/in-focus/ceta/ceta-chapter-by-chapter/.

125 *Id.* Art. 8.1.

meta-analysis of 74 empirical studies found that the effect of IIAs on FDI is "so small as to be considered zero."[126] Furthermore, there is no clear evidence that IIAs have had any significant effect on foreign investors' decisions regarding whether to invest in particular host state.[127] The study contend that host state should broadly assess the costs and benefits of IIA SC, and rethink the role of such clause as mechanism for attracting FDI inflows. This means looking more closely at the objectives of this clause, and how it may better align with the flexibility and stability of the contracual regime, as well as at alternative modes of stability mechanism such as Contractual LSCs that might better serve identified objectives.

Moreover, the purpose of the FET clause should not be understood as equivalent to or near equivalent to the CSCs. Otherwise, the existence of CSCs would be redundant. The new generation of IIAs clearly and precisely determines their content (specifying what the FET includes) and its scope (specifying what the FET does not include). Some recently concluded IIAs contained an exclusive list of the specific obligations of the contracting states under the FET clause.[128] The CETA is a paradigmatic example in that it combines an exclusive list with reaffirming the contracting states' right to regulate to achieve their legitimate policy objectives.[129]

---

126 Primer on International Investment Treaties and Investor-State Dispute Settlement, Colombia Center on Sustainable Investment (Jan 2022) https://ccsi.colombia.edu/content/primer-international-investment-treaties-and-investor-state-dispute-settlement.

127 Lise Johnson et al., *Briefing Note: Aligning International Investment Agreements with the Sustainable Development Goals*, COLOMBIA CENTER ON SUSTAINABLE INVESTMENT STAFF PUBLICATIONS, 3 (Nov 2020). https://scholarship.law.colombia.edu/sustainable_investment_staffpubs/187?utm_source=scholarship.law.colombia.edu%2Fsustainable_investment_staffpubs%2F187&utm_medium=PDF&utm_campaign=PDFCoverPages.

128 Charalampos, *supra* note 64, at 165–166.

129 CETA. Art. 8.9–8.10.

CHAPTER 6

# Summary and Final Conclusions

This concluding chapter summarizes the main findings of the study on the stability guarantees contained in state contracts, national laws, and IIAs, as well as renegotiation clauses in international investment law. The Traditional Contractual Stabilization Clauses (CSCs) are frequently employed by investors as a mechanism to attain regulatory stability; however, their validity and efficacy have encountered scruitny and skepticism in recent years. The traditional CSCs were found to be of limited efficacy in striking the right balance between the interests of investors and the host state. While traditional CSCs may mitigate the host state's political risk, they deny the flexibility of the long-term investment contract. In contrast, renegotiation clauses aim to provide stability and flexibility by bringing the contractual parties together to establish a new balance between them. While renegotiation clauses may seem like a viable alternative to traditional CSCs, their ability to provide contractual stability and predictability is greatly limited and constrained. Additionally, the lack of empirical data makes it difficult to determine their effectiveness. This uncertainty raises questions as to whether renegotiation clauses are truly more appropriate than traditional CSCs or if they would unnecessarily prolong disputes, resulting in additional expenses. Furthermore, parties always have the incentive to settle disputes amicably, and even in a traditional CSCs setting, nothing prevents them from renegotiating and coming to a different agreement. Therefore, it is unclear whether renegotiation clauses truly add value to investment contracts.

Therefore, the study proposes Contractual Legislative Stabilization Clauses (Contractual LSCs) as an adequate legal mechanism for recalibrating the balance of interests and rights between the host state and foreign investors. These LSCs would provide both stability and flexibility while addressing the concerns of the host state in a way that traditional CSCs and renegotiation clauses cannot. To further elaborate on the advantages of Contracual LSCs, the study proposes a new taxonomy of LSCs that divides them into three fundamental categories: Aspirational LSCs, Standard LSCs, and Contractual LSCs. Host states are advised to avoid Aspirational LSCs, which provide no stability guarantee or minimal purpose. Standard LSCs are stock LSCs that saddle host states with stability obligations without any demonstrated impact on foreign direct investment (FDI) inflows. Instead, host states should adopt Contractual LSCs, which grant investors stability guarantees through contracts approved

 | DOI:10.1163/9789004692756_007

by the government, often conditional on meeting particular investment profile criteria. Contractual LSCs enable host state to better target investment project and manage their stability obligations, allowing them to confidently assess the true benefit of such LSCs and respond accordingly. Additionally, Contractual LSCs signal to investors a more transparent and reliable process to access enhanced stability guarantees by way of stabilization contracts generated under the legislation. As such, host states are better positioned to evaluate the utility and value of the LSC and make appropriate adjustments. While the study advocates that Contractual LSCs would be more effective in achieving contractual stability and flexibility than traditional CSCs or renegotiation clauses, it acknowledges that Contractual LSCs are limited to certain sectors. Therefore, in contracts outside the scope of LSC, they could possibly work in tendem with a traditional CSCs and renegotiation clauses or a combination thereof.

In addition, the study addresses the issue of stability guarantees contained in the IIAs, such as express stabilization clauses and the Fair and Equitable Treatment (FET) clause. These provisions offer additional protections for foreign investors but may also limit the host state's regulatory space. The study examines the relationship between these provisions and CSCs/LSCs and their implications for regulatory stability. The study argues that the stability guarantees contained in IIAs are essential in attracting foreign investment. However, traditional stabilization clauses may exempt foreign investors from complying with human rights law, and environmental, labor, or social laws. In addition, the FET standard is a much poorer substitute as it does not provide legal stability equal to CSCs unless there is an express SC in the IIAs.

In Conclusion, The analysis highlights the importance of stability guarantees in international investment law and provides a comprehensive assessment of the different forms of such guarantees available to foreign investors. The findings suggest that there is no one-size-fits-all approach to achieving regulatory stability and that the most effective mechanisms will depend on the specific context and needs of each case. The study recommends that foreign investors and host states carefully consider the different types of stability guarantees available and choose the most appropriate one for their situation based on a thorough analysis of the legal framework, practice, and empirical evidence. Overall, the goal of this study is to contribute to more nuanced and informed debates on stability guarantees in international investment law and to promote greater legal certainty and predictability in the complex world of international investment.

# Table of Cases

## International Arbitrations

### *ICSID*

AES Summit Generation Limited & AES-Tisza Erömü Kft v. Hung., ICSID Case No. ARB/07/22, Award (Sept. 23, 2010)

AES Corporation and TAU Power B.V. v. Kazakhstan, ICSID Case No. ARB/10/16, Award (Nov. 1, 2013)

Aguaytia Energy, LLC v Republic of Peru, ICSID Case No ARB/06/13, Award (Dec. 11, 2008)

Asian Agricultural Products Ltd (AAPL) v. Republic of Sri Lanka, ICSID Case No ARB/87/3, Final Award (Jun. 27, 1990)

Azurix Corp. v. The Argentine Republic, ICSID Case No. ARB/01/12, Award (July 14, 2006)

Biwater Gauff LTD v. United Republic of Tanzania, ICSID Case No. ARB/05/22, Award (Jul. 24, 2008)

Burlington Resources Inc. v. Republic of Ecuador, ICSID Case No. ARB/08/5, Decision on Liability (Dec. 14, 2012)

Burlington Resources Inc. v. Republic of Ecuador, ICSID Case No. ARB/08/5, Decision on jurisdiction, 53 (June 2, 2010)

CMS Gas Transmission Co. v. Republic of Argentina, ICSID Case No. ARB/01/8, Decision of the Tribunal on Objections to Jurisdiction (July 17, 2003)

Continental Casualty v. Argentina, ICSID Case No. ARB/07/27, Award (Sep. 5, 2008)

Crystallex International Corporation v. Bolivarian Republic of Venezuela, ICSID Case No. ARB(AF)/11/2, Award (Apr. 4, 2016)

Duke Energy International Peru Investment No.1 Ltd v. Republic of Peru, ICSID Case No. ARB/03/28. Decision on Jurisdiction (Feb. 1, 2006)

EDF (Services) Limited v. Romania, ICSID Case No. ARB/05/13, Award (Oct.8, 2009).

Eiser Infrastructure Limited and Energy Solar Luxembourg S.A R.I. v. Spain, ICSID Case No. ARB/13/36, Award (May 4, 2017)

El Paso Energy International Co v. Argentina, ICSID Case No. Arb/03/15, Award (Oct. 31, 2011)

El Paso Energy International Co v. Argentina, ICSID Case No. Arb/03/15, Decision on Jurisdiction (Apr. 27, 2006)

Electrabel S.A. v Republic of Hungary, ICSID Case No. ARB/07/19, Decision on Jurisdiction, Applicable Law and Liability

Electrabel S.A. v. Hungary, ICSID Case No. ARB/07/19, Award (Nov. 25, 2015)

Enron v. Argentina, ICSID Case No. ARB/01/3, Award (May 22, 2007)

Ioan Micula v. Romania, ICSID Case No. ARB/05/20, Award (Dec. 11, 2013)

Ioannis Kardassopoulos v. Republic of Georgia, ICSID Case NoNos. ARB/05/18, and ARB/07/15, Award (Mar. 3, 2010)

Joseph Charles Lemire v. Ukraine, ICSID Case No. ARB/06/18, Decision on Jurisdiction and Liability (Jan. 14, 2010)

*LG&E v. Argentina*, ICSID Case No. ARB/02/1, Award (July 25, 2007)

*LG&E v. Argentina*, ICSID Case No. ARB/02/1, Decision on Liability (2006)

Mamidoil Jetoil Greek Petroleum Petroleum Products Société S.A. v. Republic of Albania, ICSID Case No. ARB/11/24, Award (Mar. 30, 2015)

Maritime International Nominees Establishment (MINE) v. Republic of Guinea. ICSID Case No. ARB/84/4, Decision partially annulling the award, (Dec. 22, 1989)

Marvin Feldman v. Mexico, ICSID Case No. ARB(AF)/99/1, Award (Dec. 16, 2002)

Masdar Solar & Wind Cooperatief U.A. v. Spain, ICSID Case No. ARB/14/1, Award (May 16, 2018)

Noble Ventures v. Romania, ICSID Case No. ARB/01/11, Award (Oct. 12, 2005)

Parkerings Compagniet A.S. v. Lithuania., ICSID No. ARB/05/8, Award (Sept. 11, 2007)

Philip Morris v. Uruguay, ICSID Case No. ARB/10/7, Award (July 8, 2016)

PSEG Global, Inc., The North American Coal Corporation, and Konya Ingin Electrik Üretim ve Ticaret Limited Sirketi v. Republic of Turkey, ICSID Case No. ARB/02/5, Award (Jan. 19, 2007)

RREEF Infrastructure (G.P.) Limited and RREEF Pan-European Infrastructure Two Lux S.à r.l. v. Republic of Spain, ICSID Case No. ARB/13/30, Decision on Responsibility and on the Principles of Quantum (Nov. 30, 2018)

Rumeli Telekom AS& Telsim Mobil Telekomunikasyon Hizmetleri AS v. Kazakhstan, ICSID Case No ARB/05/16, Award (July 29, 2008)

Sempra Energy International v Argentine Republic, ICSID Case No. ARB/02/16, Award (Sep. 28, 2007)

SGS Société Générale de Surveillance S.A. v. Philippines, ICSID Case No. ARB/02/6, Decision on Jurisdiction (Jan. 29, 2004)

SGS Société Générale de Surveillance S.A.v. Pakistan, ICSID Case No ARB/01/13, Decision on Jurisdiction (Aug. 6, 2003)

Sociedad General de Aguas de Barcelona, S.A. and Vivendi Universal, S.A. v. Argentina Republic, ICSID Case No. ARB/03/19, Decision on Liability (Jul. 30, 2010)

Société d'Exploitation des Mines d'Or de Sadiola S. A. v. Republic of Mali, 10, 114, ICSID Case No. ARB/01/5, Award (Feb. 25, 2003)

Stadtwerke München GmbH, RWE Innogy GmbH and Others v. Spain, ICSID Case No. ARB/15/1, Award (Dec. 2, 2019)

Suez, Sociedad General de Aguas de Barcelona S.A., and Vivendi Universal S.A. v. The Argentine Republic, ICSID Case No. ARB/03/19, Decision on Liability (July 30, 2010)

Técnicas Medioambientales Tecmed, S.A. v. The United Mexican States, ICSID Case No. ARB (AF)/00/2, Award (May 29, 2003)
Total S.A. v. Argentina, ICSID Case No. ARB/04/01, Decision on Liability (Dec. 27, 2010)
Wena Hotels Ltd. v. Arab Republic of Egypt, ICSID Case No. ARB/98/4, Award (Dec. 8, 2000)

### *NON-ICSID*

Greentech Energy Systems A/S, NovEnergia II Energy & Environment (SCA) SICAR, and NovEnergia II Italian Portfolio SA v. Italy, SCC Arbitration V (2015/095), Final Award (Dec. 23, 2018)
Charanne B.V. and Construction Investments S.A.R.L. v. Kingdom of Spain, SCC Case No. 062/2012, Award, 478–9, 487 (Jan. 21, 2016)
Saluka Invs. BV (Neth.) v. Czech Republic, UNCITRAL, Partial Award 305–06 (Mar. 17, 2006)
Methanex Corp. v. United States, UNCITRAL, Final Award, pt. IV, ch. D, P 7 (Aug. 3, 2005)
Novenergia II—Energy & Environment (SCA) (Grand Duchy of Luxembourg), SICAR v. Spain, SCC Case No. 2015/063, Final Award (Feb. 15, 2018)
Petroleum Servs. Ltd. v. Czech Republic, UNCITRAL, Final Award 285 (Nov. 12, 2010).
EnCana CorporationCorp. v. Republic of Ecuador, Case No. UN3481, Award, 45 I.L.M. 895 (London Ct. Arb. 2006)
Petroleum Servs. Ltd. v. Czech Republic, UNCITRAL, Final Award 285 (Nov. 12, 2010)
Liberian E. Timber Corp. (LETCO) v. Republic of Liberia, 26 I.L.M. 647 (1987)
AGIP Co. v. Popular Republic of the Congo, 21 I.L.M. 726 (1982)
Kuwait v. American Indep. Oil Co. (AMINOIL), 21 I.L.M. 976 (1982)
Libyan Am. Oil Co. (LIAMCO) v. Libyan Arab Republic, 20 I.L.M. 1 (1981)
Texaco Overseas Petroleum Co./California Asiatic Oil Co. v. Libyan Arab Republic, 17 I.L.M. 3, 55 (1977)
Mobil Oil Iran Inc. v. Government of the Islamic Republic of Iran, Award No. 311–74/76/81/150–3, 16 Iran-U.S. Cl. Trib. Rep.
North Sea Continental Shelf (Federal Republic of Germany v. Denmark), ICJ rep 1969,4,47 et seq.

### *National Courts*

Al-Mahkama al-Idariyah al-Ulya [Supreme Administrative Court], Case No 5546, Session of 27 Feb. 2010, year 55 (Egypt).
Amphitrite v. The King (1921) 3 KB 500. All ER Rep 542.
Arie Reich, *Israel's Foreign Investment Protection Regime in View of Developments in Its Energy Sector*. EUI WORKING PAPERS 2017/02, at 14, *available at* http://cadmus.eui.eu/handle/1814/45005.

Court of Appeals of Paris Decision in Arab Republic of Egypt v. Southern Pacific Properties, Ltd. et al. (Appellate Review of Arbitral Awards between States and Private Parties, 23 I.L.M. 1048 (1984)).
GabCikovo-Nagymaros Project (Hungary/Slovakia), Judgment, ICJ Reports (1997).
Mahkama al-Qada al-Idari [Administrative Court], Case No 33418, Session of 18 Nov. 2008, year 62 (Egypt).
Niger Delta Development Commission v. Nigeria Liquefied Natural Gas Company Limited, Suit Number FHC/PH/CS/313/2005, unreported Judgment, 11 July 2007.
Niger Delta Development Commission v. Nigeria Liquefied Natural Gas Company Limited, Suit Number CA/PH/520/2007, 2 Dec 2010.
The Movement for Quality Government in Israel v. Prime Minister (2016) (Isr.) HCJ 4374/15.

## Table of Legislation and Regulations

### Albania

Mining Law of Albania (Law No. 7796 of 1994)

### Madagascar

Investment Law (Law No. 2007-036 of 2008)

### Papua New Guinea

Resource Contracts Fiscal Stabilization Act (Act No. 33 of 2000)

### Armenia

The law of foreign investment (Law No. AL-115 of 1994)

### Azerbaijan

Law on Investment Activity (Law No. 952 of 1995)
Law on the Protection of Foreign Investments (Law No. 57 of 1992)

### Benin

Code of Investments (Law No 90-002 of 1990)

### Bosnia and Herzegovina

Law on the Policy of Foreign Direct Investment (No. 17/98)

### Cuba

Foreign Investment Act (Law No. 118 of 2014)

## Egypt

Law No.131 of 1948 (Civil Code), Al-Waqa'i'a al-Masriya, vol. 108 bis (a), 29 July 1984.

## Georgia

Law on the investment activity promotion and guarantees. (Law No. 473–10 of 1996)

## Guinea-Bissau

Investment Code, (Law no. 3/2011)

## German

Bürgerliches Gesetzbuch[BGB] [Civil Code],§ 313

## France

Ordonnance n° 2016–131 du 10 février 2016 portant réforme du droit des contrats, du régime général et de la preuve des obligations [Law 2016–131 of Feb 10,2016 on the Law of Contract, The General Regime of Obligations, and Proof of Obligations].

## Kazakhstan

Law on Investments (Law No. 373-II of 2003, amended 2014)

## Kyrgyzstan

Law on Investments (2003)

## Kosovo

Law on Foreign Investment (Law No. 04/L-220 of 2014)

## Mali

Investment Code (Law No. 016-2012)

## Nigeria

Liquefied Natural Gas Act (Law No 39/1990)

## Russian Federation

Federal Law on Foreign Investments (Law No. N 160-FZ of 1999)

## Tajikistan

The Law of the Republic of Tajikistan on Investments (2007)

## Turkmenistan

Law on Investment Activities (1992)

### Ukraine

The Law on the Regime of Foreign Investments (1996, as amended)

### Uzbekistan

Law on investments and investment activity (2019)

### Viet Nam

Law on Investment (Law No. 67/2014/QH13)

### Panama

Investment Stability Law (Law No. 54 of 1998)

### Bolivia

Hydrocarbons Law (Law No. 3058 of 2005)

### Chile

Establishes the Framework for Foreign Direct Investment in Chile and Creates the Respective Institutionality (Law No. 20,848 of 2015)

Foreign Investment Statute (Decree Law 600)

### Colombia

Legal Stability Contracts Law (Law No. 963 of 2005)

### Cameroon

Investment Incentive Law (Law N° 2013/004 of 2013)

### Mongolia

Law on Investment (2013)

### Peru

Foreign Investment Promotion Law (Legislative Decree 662 of 1991)

Organic Law for Hydrocarbons (Law No 26221)

### Timor-Leste

Tax Stability Act (Law No. 4/2003)

# Table of International Investment Agreements and Other International Instruments/Documents

Albania–Greece bilateral investment treaty (BIT) (1991)
Algeria–Italy BIT (1993)
Argentina–France BIT (1991)
Argentina–Germany BIT (1991)
Argentina–Mexico BIT (1996)
Argentina–Spain BIT (1991)
Argentina–United Kingdom BIT (1990)
Argentina–United States BIT (1991)
Australia–Poland BIT (1991)
Australia-Uruguay BIT (2019)
Austria–Croatia BIT (1997)
Belgium/Luxembourg Economic Union–Tajikistan BIT (2009)
BLEU–Egypt BIT (1999)
Canada–Czech Republic BIT (1990)
China–Switzerland BIT (2009)
Colombia–Switzerland BIT (2006)
Comprehensive Economic and Trade Agreement (CETA)
Concession Agreement for Petroleum Exploration and Exploitation between the Arab Republic of Egypt and the Egyptian General Petroleum Corporation xix, https://www.lawinsider.com/contracts/gtIJf5OkGGR.
Croatia–Ukraine BIT (1997)
Czech Republic–Netherlands BIT (1991)
Czech Republic–United States BIT (1991)
Denmark Model BIT (2000)
Ecuador–United States BIT (1993)
Egypt–Italy BIT (1989)
Energy Charter Treaty (1994)
France-Yugoslavia BIT of 1974
France–Hong Kong BIT (1995)
France–Moldova BIT (1997)
GA Resolution 1803 (XVII), para 4 (Dec. 14, 1962) *available at* https://www.un.org/ga/search/view_doc.asp?symbol=A/RES/1803%28XVII%29.
German Model BIT (2004)
German Model BIT (2008)

Germany–Ghana BIT (1995)
Germany–Pakistan BIT (1959)
Germany–Singapore BIT (1973)
Greek Model BIT (2001)
India Model BIT (2015)
Italy–Armenia BIT (1998)
Italy–Azerbaijan BIT (1997)
Italy–Cameron BIT (1999)
Italy–Kazakhstan BIT (1994)
Italy–Moldova BIT (1997)
Italy–Tanzania BIT (2001)
Italy–Uzbekistan BIT (1997)
Italy–Angola BIT (1997)
Italy–Mozambique BIT (1998)
Italy–Uganda BIT (1997)
Lithuania–Norway BIT (1992)
Mexico–Spain BIT (2006)
Netherlands–Serbia BIT (2002)
Netherlands–Poland BIT (1992)
Netherlands–Venezuela BIT (1991)
North American Free Trade Agreement (NAFTA) (1992)
Oman–U.S. FTA (2006)
Pakistan–Italy BIT (1997)
Pakistan–Switzerland BIT (1995)
Pakistan–Turkey BIT (2012)
Philippines–Switzerland BIT (1997)
Romania–Sweden BIT (2002)
Romania–United States BIT (1992)
Sri Lanka–United Kingdom BIT (1980)
Tanzania–United Kingdom BIT (1994)
The ASEAN–Australia–New Zealand Free Trade Area (2009)
The Belgium-Morocco BIT (1965)
Treaty of Friendship Commerce and Navigation (FCN) between the United States and Italy (1948)
Turkey–United States BIT (1985)
UK–Paraguay BIT (1981)
United States–Mexico–Canada Agreement (USMCA) (2018)
United States–Zaire BIT (1984)
United States Model BIT (2004) Declaratory Statement of Petroleum Policy in Member Countries, Res. No. XVI. 90 of the Sixteenth OPEC Conference, 7 I.L.M. (1968)

# Appendix

## Part. 1

### A *Traditional Renegotiation Clauses*

*The AMINOIL Clause* (the Supplementary Agreement of July 29, 1961, to the concession agreement between the state of Kuwait and the "American Independent Oil Company" (AMINOIL) of June 28, 1948.)

Article. 9

If, as a result of changes in the terms of concessions now in existence or as a result of the terms of concessions granted hereafter, an increase in benefits to Governments in the Middle East should come generally to be received by them, the Company shall consult with the Ruler whether in the light of all relevant circumstances, including the conditions in which operations are carried out, and taking into account all payments made, any alterations in the terms of the agreements between the Ruler and the Company would be equitable to the parties.

Retrieved from: Kuwait v. American Indep. Oil Co. (AMINOIL), 21 I.L.M. 976, at 18 (1982).

*The Ok Tedi Clause* (The OK Tedi Papua New Guinea Concession Agreement of 1976)

*Clause 42*

The parties may from time to time by agreement in writing add to, substitute for, cancel or vary all or any of the provisions of this Agreement.

Retrieved from: <http://www.paclii.org/pg/legis/consol_act/mtaa1976218/

*The Ghana/Shell Clause* (The Petroleum Production Agreement between the Government of Ghana and Shell Exploration and Production Company of Ghana Ltd., of 1974)

Article. 47(b)

It is hereby agreed that if during the term of this Agreement there should occur such changes in the financial and economic circumstances relating to the petroleum industry, operating conditions in Ghana and marketing conditions generally as to materially affect the fundamental economic and financial basis of this Agreement, then the provisions of this Agreement may be reviewed or renegotiated with a view to making such adjustments and modifications as may be reasonable having regard to the Operator's capital employed and the risks incurred by him always provided that no such adjustments or modifications shall be made within 5 years after the commencement of production of petroleum in commercial quantities from the production area and that they shall have no retroactive effect.

 | DOI:10.1163/9789004692756_008

TABLE 3 Illustrative cases of changes in relationships, including renegotiation in the petroleum sector

| Country | Transnational corporation | Year | Result |
|---|---|---|---|
| Algeria | Getty Oil | 1968 | 51% Sonatrach-Participation |
| Algeria | CFP/ERAP | 1971 | 51% Sonatrach-Participation (1971: Petroleum majority Code: State participation obligatory, state company Sonatrach as holder of concession/ licenses). |
| Algeria | ERAP | 1975 | 100% state ownership, severing of relations. |
| Algeria | CFP | 1975 | 51% state participation, renewed. |
| Colombia | | 1975 | Contract until 1980 Concessions cancelled, Renegotiation into association and service contracts. |
| Ecuador | Texaco-Gulf (et al.) | 1973/ 74 | 25% participation by CEPE (state company) |
| Ecuador | Texaco-Gulf | 1977 | 100% state ownership |
| Indonesia | | 1974<br>1976 | Excess-profits tax for contractors of PERTAMINA (by statute and renegotiation).<br>New agreement: share of net operating income, 85% for the government and 15% for the foreign firms |
| Iran | 'Consortium' (Gulf, Mobil, Exxon, Texaco, BP, ARCO, CPF, Standard Oil of Calif. Et al.) | 1973 | Consortium agreement of 1954 abrogated: Full management and control taken over by NICC Sales and Purchase Agreement with Consortium (5 years). |
| Kuwait | Kuwait Oil Company | 1972 | 25% of state participation |
| Kuwait | Kuwait Oil Company | 1974 | 60% of state participation |
| Kuwait | Kuwait Oil Company | 1976 | 100% state ownership (retroactive from 1975) |

TABLE 3 Illustrative cases of changes in relationships, including renegotiation in the petroleum sector (*cont.*)

| Country | Transnational corporation | Year | Result |
|---|---|---|---|
| Kuwait | BP/Gulf | 1975 | Supply contract (5 years) for transnational corporation. 100 % state ownership |
| Libyan Arab Jamahiriya | Exxon et al. | 1973/74<br>1977 | 51% participation<br>100% state ownership |
| Nigeria | Shell/BP | 1973 | Participation schedule: 35% to 51% in 1981 |
| Qatar | QGPC, OPC et al. | 1974 | 60% state participation |
| Qatar | QGPC, OPC et al. | 1976 | 100% state ownership; service contract for transnational corporations. |
| Saudi Arabia | ARAMCO | 1976 | 60% participation: long-term supply, technical assistance contract. |
| Saudi Arabia | ARAMCO | 1976 | 100% state ownership; maintain ARAMCO as operating entity (service contract). |
| United Arab Emirates | Abu Dhabi Oil Company | 1974 | 60% state participation |
| United Arab Emirates | Abu Dhabi Oil Company | 1976 | 100% state ownership of all gas, both associated and non-associated, formalized by decree. |
| Venezuela | | 1975 | Takeover of oil companies, replacement by oil sales agreements (2 years, renewable), technical assistance agreements (3 years). |

SOURCE: UNITED NATIONS CENTRE ON TRANSNATIONAL CORPORATIONS, BASED ON NATIONAL SOURCES. [CITED IN ASANTE (1979), AT 422–423]

TABLE 4 Change in fiscal terms 2002–2008

| Country | Year | Regime type | Fiscal change | Application |
|---|---|---|---|---|
| Algeria | 2006 | PSC | Exceptional Profits Tax Introduced | All PSCs with profit-sharing linked only to production levels |
| Argentina | 2002 | Concession | Crude oil duty introduced | All fields/ companies |
| Argentina | 2004 | Concession | Crude oil export duty rate increased, and gas export duty introduced. | All fields/ companies |
| Argentina | 2006 | Concession | Gas export duty rate increased | All fields/ companies |
| Australia | 2008 | Concession | Condensate liable to excise tax | NWS gas project; onshore fields |
| Bolivia | 2005 | Concession | Royalty rates increased | All PSCs |
| Bolivia | 2006–07 | Concession | Contracts overhauled | All PSCs |
| Canada (Alberta) | 2007 | Concession | Increased royalty rate | All fields/ companies |
| Canada (Newfoundland) | 2007 | Concession | Increased royalty rate | Specific new field |
| China | 2006 | PSC | Special Profits Tax Introduced | All PSCs |
| Ecuador | 2006 | PSC | Increased State Participation | All PSCs |
| Ecuador | 2007 | PSC | Participation share increased | All PSCs |
| India | 2006 | Concession | Increased cess payments | All fields/ companies |

TABLE 4 Change in fiscal terms 2002–2008 (*cont.*)

| Country | Year | Regime type | Fiscal change | Application |
|---|---|---|---|---|
| Italy | 2008 | Concession | Increased tax rate | All fields/ companies |
| Kazakhstan | 2008 | PSC | Law passed to allow retroactive changes to PSCs | All PSCs |
| Nigeria | 2008 | PSC | 1993 PSC terms under review | 1993 PSC (deepwater) contract areas |
| Papua New Guinea | 2008 | Concession | Additional Profits Tax re-introduced | PNG LNG project |
| Russia | 2002 | Concession | Royalty / tax terms | All fields/ companies |
| Russia | 2003 | Concession | MET (Royalty) and export duty rates increased | All fields/ companies |
| United Kingdom | 2005 | Concession | Supplementary Charge increased | All fields/ companies |
| United States (Alaska) | 2005 | Concession | Production tax rules changed | Prudhoe Bay satellite fields |
| United States (Alaska) | 2006 | Concession | Production tax replaced with Profit Tax (PPT) | All fields/ companies |
| United States (Alaska) | 2007 | Concession | PPT rates increased | All fields/ companies |
| Venezuela | 2002–06 | PSC (E&P) | Contracts converted to 'empresas mixtas' concessions | All fields/ companies |

TABLE 4 Change in fiscal terms 2002–2008 (*cont.*)

| Country | Year | Regime type | Fiscal change | Application |
|---|---|---|---|---|
| Venezuela | 2002–06 | Service Contract (Marginal Fields) | Contracts converted to 'empresas mixtas' concessions | All fields/ companies |
| Venezuela | 2002–07 | Concession (Heavy Oil) | Contracts converted to 'empresas mixtas' concessions | All fields/ companies |
| Venezuela | 2008 | Concession | Additional Profits Tax introduced | All fields/ companies |
| Vietnam | 2008 | PSCS | Export duty rate increased (twice) | All post 1993 PSCS |

SOURCE: PETER D CAMERON, INTERNATIONAL ENERGY INVESTMENT LAW, THE PURSUIT OF STABILITY 10–11 (2010)

Cited in <Asante (1979), at 417.

*The Lasmo Clause* (Lasmo Group Production Sharing Contract of August 19, 1992, between the "Vietnam National Oil and Gas Corporation of the Socialist Republic of Vietnam, Lasmo Vietnam Ltd. & C. Itoh Energy Development Co., Ltd for Offshore Block 04–2").

Article. 17.8 Introduction of New Laws and Regulations

If after the Effective Date, new law(s) and/or regulation(s) are introduced in Vietnam adversely affecting CONTRACTOR'S interest, or any amendments to existing laws and/or regulations are made then the Parties shall meet and consult each other and shall make the necessary changes to this Agreement to ensure that CONTRACTOR is restored to the same economic conditions which would have prevailed if the new law and/or regulation or amendment had not been introduced.

Cited in < Klaus Peter Berger, *Renegotiation and Adaption of International Investment Contracts: The Role of Contract Drafters and Arbitrators*, 36 VAND. J. TRANSNAT'L L. 1347, 1359–60 (2003)

*The Qatar Clause* (the Model Exploration and Production Sharing Agreement of the Sheikdom of Qatar of 1994)

Art. 34.12 Equilibrium of the Agreement

Whereas the financial position of the Contractor has been based, under the Agreement, on the laws and regulations in force at the Effective Date, it is agreed that, if any future law, decree or regulation affects Contractor's financial position, and in particular if the customs duties exceed … percent during the term of the Agreement, both Parties shall enter into negotiations, in good faith, in order to reach an equitable solution that maintains the economic equilibrium of this Agreement. Failing to reach agreement on such equitable solution, the matter may be referred by either Party to arbitration pursuant to Article 31.

Cited in> Klaus Peter Berger, *Renegotiation and Adaption of International Investment Contracts: The Role of Contract Drafters and Arbitrators*, 36 VAND. J. TRANSNAT'L L. 1347, 13560 (2003).

*The 1974 Supplemental LAMCO Iron Ore Agreement in Liberia*

In case of profound change in the circumstances existing at December 31, 1973, the parties, at the request of any one of them, will consult together for the purpose of considering such changes in or clarifications of this Mining Concession Agreement as the parties deem to be appropriate.

Supplemental agreement to the 1960 "LAMCO" Iron-Ore Agreement between the Republic of Liberia, the Liberian American-Swedish Minerals Co. and Liberia Bethlehem Iron Mines Co. of 1974 (paragraph 24).

The 1977 Contract of Work between the Government of the Republic of Indonesia and P.T.RIO Tinto Indonesia

*Clause 23C*

At any time during the terms of this Agreement the Government and the Company may consult with each other to determine whether in the light of all relevant circumstances the financial or other provisions of this Agreement operates *equitably and without major detriment to the interests of either party*. Such circumstances shall include the conditions under which the mineral production is carried out such as the size, location, and overburden of mineral deposits, the quality of the mineral, the market conditions for the mineral, the prevailing purchasing power of money and the terms and conditions prevailing for comparable mineral ventures. In reaching agreement on any revision of this Agreement pursuant to this Article, both parties shall ensure that no revision of this Agreement shall prejudice the Company's ability to retain financial credibility abroad and to raise finance by borrowing internationally in a manner and on terms normal to the mining industry.

Cited in Wolfgang Peter, Arbitration and Renegotiation of International Investment Agreements 245 (1995).

## Part II

Unless otherwise indicated, the LSCs are accessible at UNCTAD, Investment Laws Navigator, at https://investmentpolicy.unctad.org/investment-laws Also, due to space constraints, Aspirational and Standard LSCs have been substantially edited.

### 1 *Aspirational LSCs*

ALBANIA: Mining Law of Albania (Law No. 7796 of 1994)

*Article 100:* When the minister deems that the activity … is mainly oriented to the export of minerals … to the mining permit possessor and his shareholders … shall be granted … k) The guarantee that the … Amendments in this legislation, including … new laws shall not be applicable. …
https://www.lexadin.nl/wlg/legis/nofr/eur/lxwealb.htm#Mining%20Law.

Madagascar: Investment Law (Law No. 2007-036 of 2008)

Article 6. Stability: The state uses its best endeavours to set up and maintain a favourable climate for investment by establishing a simple, fair and growth-conducive tax system for investors. …

Papua New Guinea: Resource Contracts Fiscal Stabilization Act (Act No. 33 of 2000).

Article 2. Fiscal Stability Guarantee: The State may … guarantee[] the fiscal stability of the project … in respect of: (i) applicable taxes, duties, fees. …
http://www.paclii.org/pg/legis/consol_act/rcfsa2000409.pdf

### 2 *Standard LSCs*

Armenia: The Law of Foreign Investment (Law No. AL-115 of 1994)

Article 7. Guarantee in the event of amendments to the legislation of the Republic of Armenia.

In the event of amendments to the foreign investment legislation of the Republic of Armenia, the legislation that was effective at the moment of implementation of investments shall be applied, upon the request of a foreign investor, during a five years period from that moment.

### Bosnia and Herzegovina: Law on the Policy of Foreign Direct Investment (No. 17/98)

Article 20: The rights and benefits of foreign investors granted, and obligations imposed, by this Law cannot be terminated or eliminated by the subsequently passed laws and regulations. If such subsequently passed laws and regulations shall have been more favourable to foreign investors, they shall have the right to choose under which regime the respective foreign investment will be governed.

### Cuba: Foreign Investment Act (Law No. 118 of 2014)

Article 3: The Cuban State shall see to it that the benefits granted to foreign investors and their investments are maintained throughout the entire period for which they were granted.

### Georgia: Law on the Investment Activity Promotion and Guarantees. (Law No. 473–10 of 1996)

Article 15. Guarantees during amendment of legislation.

1) A new legislative act which worsens investment conditions established under this law shall nor apply to the already realized investments within ten years from the date of its entry into force. In such a case an investor shall conduct his activities in accordance with legislation being in force before the new legislative act has been effected.
2) Later on, Articles 7, 8 and 16 shall not be subject to the legislation amendment.

### Guinea-Bissau: Investment Code, (Law no. 3/2011)

Article 22 (Stability): The rights and guarantees of investors under this Code shall remain valid and will be respected in the event of transfer of the investment in any form, provided that the conditions set forth herein for obtaining and enjoyment are present and remain stable.

### Kazakhstan: Law on Investments (Law No. 373-II of 2003, Amended 2014)

Article 4. Guarantee legal protection of investors in the territory of the Republic of Kazakhstan

3) The Republic of Kazakhstan guarantees the stability of the agreements concluded between the investors and the public authorities of the Republic of Kazakhstan … This warranty does not apply to … changes … [regarding] conditions of import, production, sales of excisable goods … [and] to ensure national and environmental security, health and morality.

Article 18.3. Guarantees for stability at change of the legislation of the Republic of Kazakhstan

Legal entities realizing priority investment projects are guaranteed stability at change of the tax legislation of the Republic of Kazakhstan according to the Code of the Republic of Kazakhstan "On taxes and other obligatory payments in the budget" (the Tax code); legislation of the Republic of Kazakhstan on population employment in the sphere of attraction of foreign labor. Application of a guarantee for stability of the legislation of the Republic of Kazakhstan is cancelled in case of early cancellation of the investment contract in the order established by this Law.

### Kyrgyzstan: Law on Investments (2003)

Article 2. Legislation of the Kyrgyz Republic on investments

2) If any amendments are made to the investment legislation of Kyrgyz Republic ... investors shall have the right to opt for more favourable conditions within ten years from the date of approval of such amendments.

### Nigeria: Liquefied Natural Gas Act (Law No 39/1990)

Schedule II. Section 9: Guarantees and assurances to Nigeria LNG limited and its shareholders

The federal government of Nigeria...in consideration of the investments which shall have to be made in order to prosecute the venture described in the shareholders' contract dated 19th May,1989 between the Nigerian National Petroleum Corporation, Shell Gas B.V., CLEAG Limited and Agip International B.V., as amended, from time to time ... hereby grants to the Company, its successors and to each of the shareholders from time to time(in their capacity as such), the guarantees, assurances and undertakings following hereunder...2. The venture shall be subject to the fiscal regime contained in the provisions of this Act. Such fiscal regime shall not be amended in any way, except with the prior written agreement of the Government, the Company and each of the Company's shareholders. 3... neither the Company nor its shareholders in their capacity as shareholders in the Company, shall in any way be subject to new laws, regulations, taxes, duties, imposts or charges of whatever nature which are not applicable generally to companies incorporated in Nigeria ... 6. ... the Government further agrees to ensure that the said guarantees, assurances and undertakings shall not be suspended, modified, or revoked during the life of the venture except with the mutual agreement of the Government and the shareholders of the Company.

https://www.nigerialng.com/the-company/Shared%20Documents/NLNG%20 ACT.pdf

### Viet Nam: Law on Investment (Law No. 67/2014/QH13)

Article 13. Assurance of business investment upon changes of laws

2) Where a new law that provides less favorable investment incentives that those currently enjoyed by investor is promulgated, investors shall keep enjoying the

current incentives for the remaining period of the incentive enjoyment of the project. 3) The regulations in Clause 2 of this Article do not apply if regulations of law are changed for reasons of national defense and security, social order and security, social ethics, public health, or environmental protection. ...

## 3 *Contractual* LSCs

### Azerbaijan: Law on Investment Activity (Law No. 952 of 1995)

Article 17. Provision of rights of investment activity subjects

State ensures stability of conditions for implementation of investment activity, protection of rights and legal interests of its subjects. Terms of the contract, concluded between the subjects of investment activity remain valid during the whole period of the given contract even at the establishment by the legislation conditions, complicating or contradicting the state of subjects, if they have not agreed about their amendments. State bodies and their executive officers cannot interfere with the affairs of subjects of investment activity.

### Bolivia: Hydrocarbons Law (Law No. 3058 of 2005)

Article 63 (Tax Stability Agreements for Promoting Industrialization)

The Ministry of State Assets (...) and the Ministry of Hydrocarbons, ..., may establish with the investors, ..., tax stability agreements of the tax regime in effect at the time of the establishment of the agreements, for a period of no more than ten (10) years without extension; these agreements shall be approved by he National Congress.

*See*, A. F. M. Maniruzzaman, *National Laws Providing for Stability of International Investment Contracts: A Comparative Perspective*, 8 J. World Investment & Trade 233, 235 (2007).

### Chile: Foreign Investment Statute (Decree Law 600)

Article 7. Holders of foreign investments made under the terms of this Decree Law are entitled to include in the respective contracts a clause to the effect that, for a ten year period from the initiation of the company's operations, they shall be subject to an effective overall tax rate of 42% on taxable income, in relation to those taxes established in the Income Tax Law in force at the time the contract is executed. The tax referred to in article 64 bis of the Income Tax Law will not be considered for the determination of the effective overall tax rate on taxable income. Even if the foreign investor has opted to request this invariability regime, he may waive this right, only once, and be subject to the application of common tax legislation, in which case he shall remain subject to the general taxation scheme with the same rights, options and obligations as national investors, consequently forfeiting the contractual invariability.

Article 8. Foreign investments and companies participating therein shall be subject to the general indirect taxation regime and to the customs regulations applicable to national investments.

Notwithstanding the above paragraph, holders of foreign investment transferred into the country under the terms of this Decree-Law shall be entitled to include a clause in their contracts stating that, for the term authorized to carry out the stipulated investment, the tax regime on sales and services and customs duties in force at the time of signing the contract, applicable to the import of machinery and equipment not manufactures in the country included in the list refereed to in paragraph 10 of letter, Article 12, of Decree Law N 825 of 1974, will remain invariable. The same invariability shall apply to the companies receiving foreign investments, in which foreign investors participate, for the amount associated to such investment.

## Colombia: Legal Stability Contracts Law (Law No. 963 of 2005)

*Article 1. Legal Stability Contracts.*

Legal stability contracts are established in order to promote new investments and expand existing ones in the national territory… . Through these contracts, the State guarantees the investors who sign them, that if during their validity any of the regulations that have been identified in the contracts as a determinant of the investment is modified in an adverse way, the investors will have the right to be continue to apply these rules to them for the duration of the respective contract.

*Article 2: National and Foreign Investors.*

National and foreign investors be they natural or legal persons, as well as consortia, who make new investments or expand existing ones in the national territory, for an amount equal to or greater than 150,000 UVT, may be party to the legal stability contracts.

https://www.global-regulation.com/translation/colombia/6404587/by-which-a-law-of-legal-stability-for-investors-is-established-in-colombia.html

## Cameroon: Investment Incentive Law (Law N° 2013/004 of 2013)

Section 31. (1) The State shall ensure that the incentives granted to investors are stable in accordance with this law, throughout the period provided for by the instrument or agreement granting such incentives. (2) To that end, a Joint Monitoring Committee placed under the authority of the Prime Minister shall be responsible for the stability of the said incentives, in conjunction with the Regulation and Competitiveness Council.

## Mongolia: Law on Investment (2013)

*Article 6. Common Legal Guarantee of Investment*

2) The State shall provide an investor with a guarantee of ensuring stability of the tax rate by a way of granting a stabilization certificate to the investor or by a way of concluding an investment agreement with the investor as specified in this Law.

*Article 16. Criteria and Duration for Issuing Stabilization Certificate*

1) A stabilization certificate shall be issued to the investor whose project to be carried out in Mongolia meets the following criteria: 1. the total investment amount specified in the business plan and feasibility analysis reached the amount specified in the Articles 16.2 and 16.3 of this Law; 2. to get done the environmental impact assessment if required by the law; 3. to create stable workplaces;4. to introduce high tech and technologies.

## Peru-Foreign Investment Promotion Law (Legislative Decree 662 of 1991)

Article 10.-The National Competent Agency, on behalf of the State, may conclude with foreign investors, before the investment is made and the corresponding registration, agreements to guarantee the following rights;

a. Stability of the tax regime in force at the moment of execution of such agreement. The guaranteed legal stability of the tax regime, means that the foreign investor, with regard to the income tax levied on the enterprise, so as to the withholding tax, shall not be levied at a rate higher than that stated in the agreement. If the income tax levied on the enterprise is increased, the percentage of the withholding tax applied to the foreign investor will be reduced allowing the investor to receive at least a proportion of profit equal to the guaranteed in the agreement. b. Stability of the legal regime of free availability of foreign currency and of the rights considered in articles 7 and 9 of this Legislative Decree. c. Stability of the right of non-discrimination covered in article 2 herein.

Article 11.-Only investors that undertake the commitment to fulfill the following, in a maximum term of two years from the execution of the agreement, may enjoy the regime referred to in the preceding article:

a. Invest through the national financial system, to the capital of an enterprise established or to be established under peruvian law, or in joint ventures for an amount over U.S.$ 2,000,000 ...; or
b. Invest through the national financial system, to the capital of an enterprise established or to be established under peruvian law, or in joint ventures for an amount over U.S.$ 500,000 ...; provided that:

i. The investment generates more than twenty permanent jobs; or
ii. The investment generates export proceeds exceeding U.S.$ 2,000,000 ... during a three year period from the date of execution of the agreement.

*See*, English Text of Legislative Decree No 622, Foreign Investment Promotion Law, Sep. 1991, 5 INTER-AM. LEGAL Materials 158 (1992).

Peru: Organic Law for Hydrocarbons (Law No 26221)

Article 63. The State guarantees the Contractors that the tax and exchange systems in force at the time the Contract is entered into, shall remain unchanged during the life thereof. ...

https://cutt.ly/TkVKIKH

Timor-Leste: Tax Stability Act (Law No. 4/2003)

*Section 2: Tax Stability Agreement*

1 With respect to any long-term projects ..., for the carrying on of petroleum activities in the Joint Petroleum Development Area, the Government is authorised to enter into agreements with contractors to ensure the tax stability of the project, with reference to the laws of the Republic in force on the date of signing of the agreement, in regard to:
(a) the taxes on petroleum activities carried on by the contractor in the Joint Petroleum Development Area, or on activities related thereto, under the terms of article 5(b) of the Timor Sea Treaty; and
(b) the rates of those taxes, the calculation of tax obligation and the manner in which payments and refunds shall be made.

2 Tax Stability Agreements may be entered into by the Prime Minister of the Republic or by the Designated Minister. Such Agreements may establish that disputes that are likely to arise out of their application be settled in a fashion deemed appropriate ..., and, to this effect, the law of the jurisdiction agreed upon by the parties shall apply.

https://www.mof.gov.tl/petroleum-development-of-timor-sea-tax-stability-act/?lang=en.

## Part III

Unless otherwise indicated, the IIAs texts are accessible at UNCTAD, International Investment Agreements Navigator, at https://investmentpolicy.unctad.org/international-investment-agreements

## A *International Investment Agreements' Stabilization Clause* (IIA's SC)

### The Italy–Mozambique BIT of 1998

Article 12.3. Whenever, after the date when the investment has been made, a modification should take place in law, regulations, acts, or measures of economic policies governing directly or indirectly the investment, the same treatment shall apply upon request of the investor that was applicable to it at the moment when the investment was agreed upon to be carried out.

https://rb.gy/rasovd

### The Belgium–Morocco BIT of 1965

Article 2. Each Contracting Party undertakes to authorize, in conformity with the regulations promulgated in pursuance of the legislation in force in its territory at the time each investment is made or of any more favourable legislation that may be enacted, in the future or of rules agreed upon between the two Parties, the transfer:

- Of net profits, interests, dividends and royalties due to nationals or corporations of the other Party;
- Of the proceeds of the complete or partial liquidation of investments and reinvestments approved by the country in which they are made.

### The UK–Paraguay BIT of 1981

*Article 6.* Each Contracting Party shall in respect of investments guarantee to nationals or companies of the other Contracting Party the unrestricted transfer to the country where they reside of their investments and returns, subject to the right of each Contracting Party in exceptional balance of payments difficulties and for a limited period to exercise equitable and in good faith powers conferred by its laws existing when this Agreement enters into force.

### France–Yugoslavia BIT of 1974

*Article 4.* French nationals, whether natural or legal persons will be entitled to investments as referred to in article 1 of this Convention as well as on the Exercise of the business and economic activities associated with such investments, the most favourable treatment accorded to nationals of any other third country by the Yugoslav legislation. in the event that it would be amended in a less favourable, such investments will be governed by the provisions in force on the date when they have been approved.

https://rb.gy/yckz6w

### Italy–Jordan BIT of 1996

*Article 11.3.* Whenever, after the date when the investment has been made, a modification should take place in laws, regulations, acts or measures of economic policies governing directly or indirectly the investment, the same treatment will apply upon request of the investor that was applicable to it at the moment when the investment had been carried out.

### Italy–Angola BIT of 1997

*Article.12.3. Qualora, successivarnente alla data in cui e stato effettuato l'investimento, essivarnente alla data in cui e stato effettuato l'investimento, Ie leggi, i regolamenti, Ie norme o i provvedimenti di politica economica che, direttamente o indirettamente, vigono sugli investimenti dovesser o; subire modifiche, verra applicato, su richiesta delı'investitore, il medesimo trattamento applicabile nel momento in cui e stato effettuato l'investimento.*

### Italy–Armenia of 1998

*Article 11.3.* Whenever. after the date when the investment has been made, any modification of protection conditions extended to investments should take place in the legislation of the Contracting Party on whose territory the investment has been carried out, the protection granted under previous legislation will not be affected.

### Italy–Azerbaijan of 1997

*Article 11.3.* Whenever, after the date when the investment has been ·made, any modification of protection conditions extended to investments should take place in the legislation of the Contracting Party on· whose territory the investment has been made, the protection granted under previous legislation will not be affected.

### Italy–Bosnia of 2000

*Article 12.3.* Whenever, after the date when the investment has been made, a modification should take place in laws, regulations, acts or measures of economic policies governing directly or indirectly the investment, the same treatment will apply upon request of the investor that was applicable to it at the moment when the investment had been started.

### Italy–Cameron of 1999

*Article 10.4. Se, successivamente alia data in cui l'investimemo e stato effeuuato. Ie leggi, i regolamenti, Ie norme o le misure di politica economica che sono in vigoro direttamente o indirettamente per gli investitori. devono essere oggetto di modificbe. sm. mcsso in opera io stesso trattamcnto applicabile di quello in vigore nel momento in cui l'investilnento e stato cffettuato.*

### Italy–Kazakhstan of 1994

*Article 12.3.* Whenever. after the date when the investment has been made, a modification should take place in laws, regulations, acts or measures of economic policies governing directly or indirectly the investment. the same treatment will apply upon request of the investor that was applicable to it at the moment when the investment has been carried out.

### Italy–Moldova of 1997

Article 11.3. Whenever, after the date when the investment has been made, any modification of protection conditions extended to investments should take place in the legislation of the Contracting Party on whose territory the investment has been carried out, the protection granted under previous legislation will not be affected.

### Italy–Tanzania of 2001

*Article 11.3.* Whenever after the date when the investment has been made, a modification should take place in laws, regulations, acts or measures of economic policies governing directly or indirectly the investment, the same treatment will apply upon request of the investor that was applicable to it at the moment when the investment had been carried out.

### Italy–Uganda of 1997

*Article 13.3 Qualora dopo la data in cui è stato effettuato un investimento venga introdotta una modifica nelle leggi, nei regolamenti, helle norme o nelle misure di politica economica che governano, direttamente o indirettamente, gli investimenti, verrà applicato, su richiesta dell'investitore, il medesimo trattamento applicabile nel momento in cui è stato effettuato l'investimento.*

### Italy–Uzbekistan of 1997

*Article 11.3.* Whenever, after the date when the investment has been made, any modification of protection conditions extended to investments should take place in the legislation of the Contracting Party on whose territory the investment has been carried out, the vested rights under national and international law, will not be affected.

## B *FET*

### Argentina–U.S. BIT (1991)

*Article II 2. (a).* Investments shall at all times be accorded fair and equitable treatment, shall enjoy full protection and security and shall in no case be accorded treatment less than required by international law.

### Argentina–France BIT (1991)

*Article 3.* Each of the Contracting Parties undertakes to grant, within its territory and its maritime area, fair and equitable treatment according to the principles of international law to investments made by investors of the other Party, and to do it in such a way that the exercise of the right thus recognized is not obstructed de jure or de facto.

### France–Hong Kong BIT (1995)

*Article 2(2).* Investments and returns of investors of each Contracting Party shall at all times be accorded fair and equitable treatment and shall enjoy full protection and security in the area of the other Contracting Party.

### Austria–Croatia BIT (1997)

*Article 2(1).* Each Contracting Party shall in its territory promote, as far as possible, investments of investors of the other Contracting Party, admit such investments in accordance with its legislation and in any case accord such investments fair and equitable treatment.

### Pakistan–Italy BIT (1997)

*Article 2(2)* Both Contracting Parties shall at all times ensure fair and equitable treatment of the investments of investors of the other Contracting Party.

### Oman–U.S. FTA (2006)

*Article 10.5 1.* Each Party shall accord to covered investments treatment in accordance with customary international law, including fair and equitable treatment and full protection and security. 2. For greater certainty, paragraph 1 prescribes the customary international law minimum standard of treatment of aliens as the minimum standard of treatment to be afforded to covered investors. The concepts of 'fair and equitable treatment' and 'full protection and security' do not require treatment in addition to or beyond that which is required by that standard, and do not create additional substantive rights.

### Belgium/Luxembourg Economic Union–Tajikistan BIT (2009)

*Article 3* All investments made by investors of one Contracting Party shall enjoy a fair and equitable treatment in the territory of the other Contracting Party.

### China–Switzerland BIT (2009)

*Article 4(1)* Investments and returns of investors of either Contracting Party shall at all times be accorded fair and equitable treatment and shall enjoy full protection and security in the territory of the other Contracting Party.

### Pakistan–Turkey BIT (2012)

*Article 3(2)* Investments of investors of each Contracting Party shall at all times be accorded treatment in accordance with international law minimum standard of treatment, including fair and equitable treatment and full protection and security in the territory of the other Contracting Party. Neither Contracting Party shall in any way impair the management, maintenance, use, operation, enjoyment, extension, sale, liquidation or disposal of such investments by unreasonable or discriminatory measures.

### Article 10(1) Energy Charter Treaty (1994)

Each Contracting Party shall, in accordance with the provisions of this Treaty, encourage and create stable, equitable, favourable and transparent conditions for Investors of other Contracting Parties to make Investments in its Area. Such conditions shall include a commitment to accord at all times to Investments of Investors of other Contracting Parties fair and equitable treatment. Such Investments shall also enjoy the most constant protection and security and no Contracting Party shall in any way impair by unreasonable or discriminatory measures their management, maintenance, use, enjoyment or disposal. In no case shall such Investments be accorded treatment less favourable than that required by international law, including treaty obligations.

https://www.ecolex.org/details/treaty/energy-charter-treaty-tre-001209/.

### The ASEAN–Australia–New Zealand Free Trade Area (2009)

*Article 6 Chapter 11.1.* Each Party shall accord to covered investments fair and equitable treatment and full protection and security. 2. For greater certainty: (a) fair and equitable treatment requires each Party not to deny justice in any legal or administrative proceedings; (b) full protection and security requires each Party to take such measures as may be reasonably necessary to ensure the protection and security of the covered investment; and (c) the concepts of 'fair and equitable treatment' and 'full protection and security' do not require treatment in addition to or beyond that which is required under customary international law, and do not create additional substantive rights. 3. A determination that there has been a breach of another provision of this Agreement, or of a separate international agreement, does not establish that there has been a breach of this Article.

https://rb.gy/1rpsjf

### Denmark Model BIT (2000)

*Article 3(1)* Each Contracting Party shall in its territory accord to investments made by investors of the other Contracting Party fair and equitable treatment which in no case shall be less favourable than that accorded to its own investors or to investors of any third state, whichever is the more favourable from the point of view of the investor.

### German Model BIT (2004)

Article 2(2) Each Contracting State shall in its territory in any case accord investments by investors of the other Contracting State fair and equitable treatment as well as full protection under the Treaty.

### U.S. Model BIT (2004)

*Article 5.* 1. Each Party shall accord to covered investments treatment in accordance with customary international law, including fair and equitable treatment and full protection and security. 2. For greater certainty, paragraph 1 prescribes the customary international law minimum standard of treatment of aliens as the minimum standard of treatment to be afforded to covered investments. The concepts of 'fair and equitable treatment' and 'full protection and security' do not require treatment in addition to or beyond that which is required by that standard, and do not create additional substantive rights. The obligation in paragraph 1 to provide: (a) 'fair and equitable treatment' includes the obligation not to deny justice in criminal, civil, or administrative adjudicatory proceedings in accordance with the principle of due process embodied in the principal legal systems of the world; and (b) 'full protection and security' requires each Party to provide the level of police protection required under customary international law. 3. A determination that there has been a breach of another provision of this Treaty, or of a separate international agreement, does not establish that there has been a breach of this Article.

https://ustr.gov/sites/default/files/U.S.%20model%20BIT.pdf

### India Model BIT (2015)

*Article 3(1).* No Party shall subject investments made by investors of the other Party to measures which constitute a violation of customary international law through: (i) Denial of justice in any judicial or administrative proceedings; or (ii) fundamental breach of due process; or (iii) targeted discrimination on manifestly unjustified grounds, such as gender, race or religious belief; or (iv) manifestly abusive treatment, such as coercion, duress and harassment.

https://dea.gov.in/sites/default/files/ModelBIT_Annex_0.pdf

### Comprehensive Economic and Trade Agreement (CETA) (2016)

*Article 8.10.* 1. Each Party shall accord in its territory to investors and to covered investments of the other Party fair and equitable treatment and full protection and security in accordance with paragraphs 2 through 7. 2. A Party breaches the obligation of fair and equitable treatment referenced in paragraph 1 if a measure or series of measures constitutes (a) denial of justice in criminal, civil or administrative proceedings; (b) fundamental breach of due process, including a fundamental breach of transparency, in judicial and administrative proceedings; (c) manifest arbitrariness;

(d) targeted discrimination on manifestly wrongful grounds, such as gender, race or religious belief; (e) abusive treatment of investors, such as coercion, duress and harassment; or (f) a breach of any further elements of the fair and equitable treatment obligation adopted by the Parties in accordance with paragraph 3 of this Article. 3. The Parties shall regularly, or upon request of a Party, review the content of the obligation to provide fair and equitable treatment. The Committee on Services and Investment, established under Article 26.2.1(b) (Specialised committees) may develop recommendations in this regard and submit them to the CETA Joint Committee for decision.

4. When applying the above fair and equitable treatment obligation, a Tribunal may take into account whether a Party made a specific representation to an investor to induce a covered investment, that created a legitimate expectation, and upon which the investor relied in deciding to make or maintain the covered investment, but that the Party subsequently frustrated.

https://ec.europa.eu/trade/policy/in-focus/ceta/ceta-chapter-by-chapter/

USMCA (2018)

Each Party shall accord to covered investments treatment in accordance with customary international law, including fair and equitable treatment and full protection and security. 2. For greater certainty, paragraph 1 prescribes the customary international law minimum standard of treatment of aliens as the standard of treatment to be afforded to covered investments. The concepts of "fair and equitable treatment" and "full protection and security" do not require treatment in addition to or beyond that which is required by that standard, and do not create additional substantive rights. The obligations in paragraph 1 to provide: (a) "fair and equitable treatment" includes the obligation not to deny justice in criminal, civil, or administrative adjudicatory proceedings in accordance with the principle of due process embodied in the principal legal systems of the world; and (b) "full protection and security" requires each Party to provide the level of police protection required under customary international law. 3. A determination that there has been a breach of another provision of this Agreement, or of a separate international agreement, does not establish that there has been a breach of this Article. 4. For greater certainty, the mere fact that a Party takes or fails to take an action that may be inconsistent with an investor's expectations does not constitute a breach of this Article, even if there is loss or damage to the covered investment as a result.

https://rb.gy/ruds5d

# Bibliography

## Books and Similar Publications


Bartels, M. Contractual Adaptation and Conflict Resolution: Based on Venture Contracts for mining Projects in Developing Countries (1985).

Bishop, Doak R. International Arbitration of Petroleum Disputes: The Development of a Lex Petrolea (2002).

Cameron, Peter D International Energy Investment Law: The Pursuit of Stability (2010) Oxford University Press.

Cameron, Peter D International Energy Investment Law: The Pursuit of Stability, Second edition, 2021, Oxford University Press.

Cohen-Jonathan, *Les concessions en droit international public*, These dactyls., (Paris 1966).

Constantine Partasides QC & Lucy Martinez, *Of Taxes and Stabilisation, in* The Guide to Energy Arbitrations 60 (J William Rowley QC 2d ed. 2019).

Declaratory Statement of Petroleum Policy in Member Countries, Res. No. XVI. 90 of the Sixteenth OPEC Conference, 7 I.L.M. 1183 (1968).

Dolzer, Rudolph Investment Contracts, in Principles of International Investment Law (3rd Edition, 2022).

Dolzer, Rudolph Petroleum Contracts and International Law (2018).

El-Haddad, Hafeza ala'koud almbrmah bin aldoul wala'shkhas ala'jn-biah, [The contracts between the states and foreign individuals] 391 (2007).

Erkan, Mustafa International Energy Investment Law, Stability through Contractual Clauses (2011).

Fair and Equitable Treatment, Series on Issues in International Investment Agreements (2012).

Faruque, Abdullah Al Stability in Petroleum Contracts: Rhetoric and Reality, (Lessons from the Experiences of Selected Developing Countries and Economies in Transition (1980–2002)) PhD thesis, University of Dundee, Scotland (2005) *available at* https://www.semanticscholar.org/paper/Stability-in-petroleum-contracts-%3A-rhetoric-and-%3A-Faruque/430301644df5ad9fc87baa60d31b74147aaa9014.

Foreign Direct Investment, net inflows (Bop, Current US$)-Colombia.

Foreign Direct Investment, net inflows (Bop, Current US$)-Kazakhstan.

Foreign Direct Investment, net inflows (Bop, Current US$)-Peru.

Foreign Direct Investment, net inflows (Bop, Current US$)-Zambia.

Foreign Direct Investment, net inflows (Bop, Current US$)-Chile.

Frank, Sotonye Stabilisation Clauses And Sustainable Development In Developing Countries. PhD thesis, University of Nottingham (2014), *available at* http://eprints.nottingham.ac.uk/14466/1/PhD_Thesis.pdf.

*Giannakopoulos, Charalampos, The Right to Regulate in International Investment Law and the Law of State Responsibility: A Hohfeldian Approach, in* Permutations of Responsibility in International Law (May 3, 2017).

Gjuzi, Jola Stailization Clauses in International Investment Law: A Sustainable Development Approach (2018).

Goode, Roy Commercial Law 136 (2004).

Horn, Norbert Adaptation and renegotiation of contracts in international trade and finance 9 (1985).

International Institute for the Unification of Private Law (unidroit), Principles of International Commercial Contracts (2016).

Investment Policy Hub, Kazakhstan.

Investment Policy Review: Colombia (2006).

Investment Policy Review: Peru 3 (2000).

Investment Policy Review: Zambia 3 (2006).

Kröll, S. *The Renegotiation and Adaptation of Investment Contracts, in* N. Horn, Arbitrating Foreign Investment Disputes (2004).

Levashova, 50 Yulia The Right of States to Regulate in International Investment Law: The Search for Balance Between Public Interest and Fair and Equitable Treatment (2019).

Mapping of iia clauses. Investment Policy Hub.

Matter of Westinghouse Elec. Corp., Etc., 517 F. Supp. 440 (e.d. Va. 1981).

McLachlan Campbell Et Al, International Investment Arbitration: Substantive Principles (2017).

Moses, Margaret L. The Principles and Practice of International Commercial Arbitration (3d ed. 2017).

Newcombe Andrew & Lluís Paradell, Law and Practice of Investment Treaties: Standards of Treatment (2009).

Omorogbe, Yinka The Oil and Gas Industry Exploration& Production Contracts (1997).

Org. for Econ. Co-operation and Dev. (oecd), Competitiveness and Private Sector Development: Kazakhstan (2010).

Org. for Econ. Co-operation and Dev. (oecd), Investment Policy Reviews: Peru 29 (2008).

Org. for Econ. Co-operation and Dev. (oecd), Investment Policy Reviews: Colombia (2012).

Org. for Econ. Co-operation and Dev. (OECD), Investment Policy Reviews: Kazakhstan (1998).

Ortino, Federico The Origin and Evolution of Investment Treaty Standards (2019).

Permanent Sovereignty over Natural Resources, 14 December 1962, UN Doc A/Res/5217.

Peter, Wolfgang Et Al., Arbitration and Renegotiation of International Investment Agreements (2d ed. 1995).

Radi, Yannick Rules and Practices of International Investment Law and Arbitration 119 (2020).

Ranjan, Prabhash India and Bilateral Investment Treaties: Refusal, Acceptance, Backlash 1 (2019).

Reinisch August & Christoph Schreuer, International Protection of Investments: The substantive Standards (2020).

Rep. of the Secretary-General—Report of the Group of Eminent Persons to Study the Impact of Multinational Corporations on Development and on International Relations, at 38, E_5500_Rev.1_ST_ESA_6-EN—(1974) *available at* https://digitallibrary.un.org/record/819904?ln=en.

Schefer, Krista Nadakavukaren International Investment Law: Text, Cases and Materials (2nd ed. 2016).

Schreuer Christoph H. Schreuer et al., The ICSID Convention: A Commentary (2d ed. 2009).

Sornarajah, M. The International Law on Foreign Investment (3rd ed, 2010).

Sornarajah, The Settlement of Foreign Investment Disputes 55 (2000).

Stoever, William Alfred Renegotiations in International Business Transactions: The Process of Dispute Resolution Between Multinational Investors and Host Societies, PhD thesis, New York University, Faculty of the Graduate School of Business Administration (1978).

Subedi, Surya P International Investment Law, Reconciling Policy and Principles (2008).

The World Bank, World Investment Trends and Corporate Perspectives: The Political Risk Insurance Industry, Breach of Contract (2013) *available at* https://www.miga.org/sites/default/files/archive/Documents/WIPR13.pdf.

UNCTAD, Best Practice in Investment for Development: How to Attract and Benefit from FDI in Mining: Lessons from Canada and Chile (2011).

UNCTAD, Bilateral Investment Treaties in the Mid-1990s (1998).

United Nations Center on Transnational Corporations (UNCTC) on Bilateral Investment Treatise (1988).

van Houtte, Hans *Changed Circumstances and Pacta Sunt Servanda. In* TRANSNATIONAL RULES IN INTERNATIONAL COMMERCIAL ARBITRATION, 105 (ICC Publ. Nr. 480,4), (Paris 1993), *available at* https://www.trans-lex.org/117300.

Weil, Prosper *Les clauses de stabilisation ou d'intangibilité insérées dans les accords de développement économique, in* MÉLANGES OFFERTS A CHARLES ROUSSEAU, LA COMMUNAUTÉ INTERNATIONALE, 301 (Charles Rousseau ed., 1974).

World Bank, Foreign Direct Investment, Net Inflows (Bop, Current US$)-Peru.

World Bank, What would it Take for Zambia's Copper Mining Industry to achieve its Potential? (2011).

World Investment Report 2020.

World Investment Report 3 (2017).

YANNACA-SMALL, KATIA *INTERPRETATION OF THE UMBRELLA CLAUSE IN INVESTMENT AGREEMENTS*, OECD WORKING PAPERS ON INTERNATIONAL INVESTMENT, 2006/03, OECD PUBLISHING, AT 22 (OCT.2006), *AVAILABLE AT* https://www.oecd.org/investment/internationalinvestmentagreements/WP-2006_3.pdf.

## Journal Articles and Papers

Adaralegbe, Bayo *Stabilizing Fiscal Regime in Long Term Contracts: Recent Development in Nigeria*, 3 J. World Energy L & Bus. 239 (2008).

Ahuja, Niyati *USMCA: An Analysis of the Proposed ISDS Mechanism*, KLUWER ARBITRATION BLOG (NOV 26. 2019), AVAILABLE AT http://arbitrationblog.kluwerarbitration.com/2019/11/26/usmca-an-analysis-of-the-proposed-isds-mechanism/.

Al Faruque, Abdullah *Renegotiation and Adaptation of Petroleum Contracts: The Quest for Equilibrium and Stability*, 9 J. WORLD INVESTMENT & TRADE 113 (2008).

Al Faruque, Abdullah *The Rationale and Instrumentalities for Stability in Long-Term State Contracts*, 7 J. WORLD INVESTMENT & TRADE 85 (2006).

Al Qurashi, Zeyad A. *Renegotiation of International Petroleum Agreements*, 22 J. Int'l Arb. 261 (2005).

Alexander, Frank *Comment on Articles on Stabilization by Piero Bernardini, Lorenzo Cotula and AFM Maniruzzaman.* 2 J. WORLD ENERGY L & BUS, 243 (Nov.1, 2009), *available at* https://doi-org.eres.qnl.qa/10.1093/jwelb/jwp015.

Asante, Samuel K.B. *Stability of Contractual Relations in the Transnational Investment Process*, 28 INT'L & COMP. L.Q. 401 (1979).

Bauxite Agreement between the Government of the Republic of Indonesia and the Investors for Asahan Hydroelectric and Aluminium Project, clause 26.4 (1975).

Bernardini, Piero *Stabilization and Adaptation in Oil and Gas Investments*, 1 J. World Energy & Bus.98 (2008).

Bernardini, Piero *The Renegotiation of Investment Contract*, 13 ICSID REV. FOREIGN. INV. J. 411 (1998).

Bernardini, *The Renegotiation of Investment Contract*, 13 ICSID REV. 411 (1998).

Bernasconi, Nathalie et el, *Investment Negotiation at the WTO and the IIA regime: Anticipating Unintended Interactions*, 11 AN ONLINE J. INV L& POL'Y. 4 (2020).

Boute, Anatole *The Quest For Regulatory Stability in the EU Energy Market: An Analysis Through the Prism of Legal Certainty*, 37(6) EUR. L. REV. 675 (2012).

Brown, Roland *The Relationship between the State and the Multinational Corporation in the Exploitation of Resources*, 33 INT'L & COMP. L. Q. 218, 224 (1984).

Bruno Oppetit, *L'adaptation des contrats internationaux aux changements de circonstances: La Clause de (Hardship)*, 101 Clunet, 794 (1974), *available at* https://www.trans-lex.org/127600.

Cameron, Peter D *Stability of Contract in the International Energy Industry*, 27 J. ENERGY & NAT. RESOURCES L. 305 (2009).

Cameron, Peter D *Stabilization in Investment Contracts and Changes of Rules in Host Countries: Tools for Oil& Gas Investors*, AIPN Research Paper Final Report (2006), *available at* https://www.international-arbitration-attorney.com/wp-content/uploads/arbitrationlaw4-Stabilisation-Paper.pdf.

Chatterjee, Syamal Kumar *The Stabilisation Clause Myth in Investment Agreements*, 5 J. INT'L ARB. 97 (1988).

Chavez Benjamin & Jaime Dupuy, *Inward FDI in Peru and its Policy Context*, COLUMBIA UNIVERSITY LIBRARIES (Aug. 2010), *available at* https://doi.org/10.7916/D8GB29WZ.

Comeaux Paul E. & N. Stephen Kinsella, *Reducing Political Risk in Developing Countries: Bilateral Investment Treaties, Stabilization Clauses, and MIGA & (and) OPIC Investment Insurance*, 15 N.Y.L. SCH. J. INT'L & COMP. L. 1 (1994).

Commission, Jeffery *The Full Protection and Security Standard in Practice*, KLUWER ARBITRATION BLOG (Apr.16, 2009) *available at* http://arbitrationblog.kluwerarbitration.com/2009/04/16/the-full-protection-and-security-standard-in-practice/.

Crawford, James *TREATY AND CONTRACT IN INVESTMENT ARBITRATION*, 24 (3) ARB INTL 351 (2008).

Curtis, Christopher T. *The Legal Security of Economic Development Agreements*, 29 HARV. INT'L. L. J. 317 (1988).

de Vries, Rachel Frid *Stability Shaken? Israeli High Court of Justice Strikes Down the Stabilization Clause in the Israeli Government's Gas Plan*, 18 J. WORLD INV. & TRADE 332 (2017).

Doudko, Alexei G. *Hardship in Contract: The Approach of the UNIDROIT Principles and Legal Developments in Russia*, 5 UNIF. L. REV. n.s. 483 (2000).

Douglas, Zachary *Nothing if not critical for investment treaty arbitration: Occidental, Eureko and Methanex*. 22 Arb. Int'l 27 (2006).

El Chiati, Ahmed Z. *Protection of Investment in the Context of Petroleum Agreement, in* 204 COLLECTED COURSES OF THE HAGUE ACADEMY OF INTERNATIONAL LAW 9, 110 (1987).

El-Koheri, Ahmed S. *The Particularity of the Conflict Avoiding Methods Pertaining to Petroleum Agreements*, 11 ICSID REVI. FOREIGN INV. L. J, 272 (1996).

El-Kosheri Ahmed S & Tarek F. Riad, *The Law Governing a New Generation of Petroleum Agreements: Changes in the Arbitration Process*. 1 ICSID REV. FOREIGN INV.L.J, 257 (1986).

Ernst & Young's Investor Opinion Survey, Kazakhstan Investment Attractiveness (2011), *available at* https://www.mpo.cz/assets/dokumenty/43916/49303/577174/prilohaoo1.pdf.

Faruque, Abdullah *Validity and Efficacy of Stabilization Clauses, Legal Protective v. Functional Value*, 23 J. INT'L. ARB. 317 (2006).

Flores, Michelle *A Practical Approach to Allocating Environmental Liability and Stabilizing Foreign Investment in the Energy Sectors of Developing Countries*, 12 COLO. J. INT'L ENVTL. L.& POL'Y, 141 (2001).

Foster Halabi, Sam *Efficient Contracting Between Foreign Investors and Host States: Evidence from Stabilization Clauses*, 31 NW. J. INT'L L. & BUS. 261 (2011).

Franck, Susan D. *Empirically Evaluating Claims About Investment Treaty Arbitration*, 86 N.C. L. REV. 1 (2007).

Frank, Sotonye *Stabilisation Clauses and Foreign Direct Investment: Presumptions versus Realities*, 16 J. WORLD.INV. & TRADE 88 (2015).

Gazzini, Tarcisio *Beware of Freezing Clauses in International Investment Clauses*, 191 COLOMBIA FDI PERSPECTIVE, 1 (2017).

Gotanda, John Y. *Renegotiation and Adaptation Clauses in Investment Contract, Revisited*, 36 VAND. J. TRANSNAT'L L. 1461 (2003).

Guasch J. Luis & Stephane Straub, *Renegotiation of Infrastructure Concessions: An Overview*, 77 Annals of Public and Cooperative Economics. 479 (2006).

Hepburn, Jarrod *Domestic Investment Statutes in International Law*, 112 AM. J. INT'L. L. 658 (2018).

Hirsch, Moshe *Between Fair and Equitable Treatment and Stabilization Clause: Stable Legal Environment and Regulatory Change in International Investment Law*, 12 J. WORLD INVESTMENT & TRADE (2011).

Horwitz, Morton J. *The Historical Foundations of Modern Contract Law*, 87 HARV. L. REV. 917 (1974).

Jennings, R. Y. *State Contracts in International Law*, 37 BRIT. Y. B. INT'L L. 156 *ET SEQ* (1961).

Jones, Tom *Ecuador Bids Goodbye to BITs*, Global Arb. Rev. (May 17, 2017), *available at* https://globalarbitrationreview.com/article/1141801/ecuador-bids-goodbye-to-bits.

Kakembo, Dennis *Stabilisation Clauses in International Petroleum Contracts: Illusion or Safeguard?* Deloitte & Touche 2 (April 2014). https://www2.deloitte.com/content/dam/Deloitte/ug/Documents/tax/tax_StabilisationClauses_2014.pdf.

Kemp, Karen *Applying the Hardship Clause*, 1 J. Energy &Nat. Resources L. 119 (1983).

Kessler, Friedrich *Contracts of Adhesion--Some Thoughts about Freedom of Contract*, 43 Colum. L. Rev. 629 (1943).

Kolo Abba & Thomas W. Walde, *Renegotiation and Contract Adaptation in International Investment Projects—Applicable Legal Principles and Industry Practices*, 1 J. World Investment 5 (2000).

Kroll, Stefan Michael *The Renegotiation and Adaptation of Investment Contracts*, *in* Arbitrating Foreign Investment Disputes: Procedural and Substantive Legal Aspects 425 (2004).

Kuznetsov, Andrey V. *The Limits of Contractual Stabilization Clauses for Protecting International Oil and Gas Investments Examined through the Prism of the Sakhalin-2 PSA: Mandatory Law, the Umbrella Clause, and the Fair and Equitable Treatment Standard*, 22 Willamette J. Int'l L. & Dis. Res. 223 (2014).

Laura Marceddu Maria & Pietro Ortolani, *What Is Wrong with Investment Arbitration? Evidence from A Set of Behavioural Experiments*, 31 Eur. J. Int'l L. 405 (2020).

Lazo, Rodrigo Polanco *Legal Framework of Foreign Investment in Chile*, 18 Law & Bus. Rev. Am. 203 (2012).

Letnar Černič, Jernej *Corporate Human Rights Obligations under Stabilization Clauses*, 11 German L.J. 210, 213 (2010).

Maniruzzaman, A.F.M. *Drafting Stabilisation Clauses in International Energy Contracts: Some Pitfalls for the Unwary*, 5 Oil Gas & Energy. L. 23 (2007).

Maniruzzaman, A.F.M. *National Laws Providing for Stability of International Investment Contracts: A Comparative Perspective*, 8 J. World Investment & Trade 233 (2007).

Maniruzzaman, A.F.M. *The pursuit of stability in international energy investment contracts: A critical appraisal of the emerging trends*, 1 J. World. Energy. L& Bus, 121 (2008).

Manne, Geoffrey *A Signaling Theory of Law* 1 (2012), *available at* https://papers.ssrn.com/sol3/papers.cfm?abstract_id=2180698.

Mineral Park Land Co. v. Howard, 172 Cal. 289, 156 P. 458 (1916).

Neuhaus, Joseph E *The enforceability of Legislative Stabilization Clauses*, *in* Practicing Virtue: Inside International Arbitration 318. n 4 (David D. Caron et al. eds., 2015).

Ng'ambi Sangwani Patrick & Prince Mwiinga, *Ownership of Large Scale Mining in Zambia and Stabilisation Clauses*, 47 ZAM. L.J. 35 (2016).

Nna Emeka, J. *Anchoring Stabilizing Clauses in International Petroleum Contracts*, 42 INT'L LAW. 1317 (2008).

Nwete, Bede *To what extent Extent Can Renegotiation Clauses Achieve Stability and Flexibility in Petroleum Development Contracts*, I.E.L.T.R. 56 (2006).

O'Connor Erin O'Hara & Susan D. Franck, *Foreign Investments and the Market for Law*, 2014 U. Ill. L. Rev. 1617 (2014).

Oshionebo, Evaristus *Stabilization Clauses in Natural Resource Extraction Contracts: Legal, Economic and Social Implications for Developing Countries*, 10 ASPER REV. INT'L BUS. & TRADE L. 1, 12 (2010).

Oyewunmi, Tade *Stabilization and Renegotiation Clauses in Production Sharing Contracts: Examining the Problems and Key Issues*, 9 OIL, GAS & ENERGY L. INTELLIGENCE 1,11 (2011) *Available at* https://www.ogel.org/article.asp?key=3184.

Paasivirta, Esa *Internationalization and Stabilization of Contracts Versus State Sovereignty*, 60 BRIT. Y.B. INT'L. L. 315 (1989).

Pereira, Alvaro *Legal Stability Contracts in Colombia: An Appropriate Incentive for Investments: Historical Causes and Impact Analysis of Law 963 of 2005*, 12 RICH. J. GLOBAL L. & BUS, 237 (2013).

Peter Berger, Klaus *Renegotiation and Adaption of International Investment Contracts: The Role of Contract Drafters and Arbitrators*, 36 VAND. J. TRANSNAT'L L. 1347 (2003).

Peter, Wolfgang *Arbitration and Renegotiation Clause*, 3 J. INT'L ARB. 29, 29 (1986).

Potesta, Michele *Legitimate Expectations in Investment Treaty Laws: Understanding the Roots and Limits of controversial Concept*, 28 ICSID REV.—FOREIGN INVESTMENT L. J. 88 (2013).

*Protection of Foreign Direct Investment in a New World Order: Vietnam--A Case Study*, 107 Harv. L. Rev. 1995 (1994).

Ryan, Christopher M. *Meeting Expectations: Assessing the Long-Term Legitimacy and Stability of International Investment Law*, 29 U. PA. J. INT'L L. 725 (2008).

Salacuse, Jeswald W. *After the contract, What? Negotiating to Work Successfully with a Foreign Partner*, 2 CANADIAN. INT'L.LAW, 195, 197 (1997).

Salacuse, Jeswald W. *Renegotiating International Project Agreements*, 24 FORDHAM INT'L L.J. 1319 (2001).

Salacuse, Jeswald W. Renogotiating *International Business Transactions: The Continuing Struggle of Life against Form*, 35 INT'L L. 1507 (2001).

Salacuse, Jeswald W. *Ten Ways that Culture Affects Negotiating Style: Some Survey Results*.14 Neg.J. 221 (1998).

Salih Mohsin Shareef & Akram Yamulki, *Stabilisation and Renegotiation Clauses in Iraqi Kurdistan Oil and Gas Contracts: A Comparative Study*, 100 J.L. POL'Y & GLOBALIZATION 101, 109 (2020).

Samples, Tim R *Winning and Losing in Investor-State Dispute Settlement*, 56 AM. BUS. L.J. 115 (2019).

Schill, Stephan *Enabling Private Ordering: Function, Scope and Effect of Umbrella Clauses in International Investment Treaties*, 18 MINN. J. INTL L. 1 (2009).

Schmitthoff, C.M. Hardship and Intervener Clauses, *J. Bus. L.* 82, 85 (1980).

Schreuer, Christoph Travelling the BIT Route: Of Waiting Period, Umbrella Clauses and Forks in the Road, 5 J. World Inv. & Trade 231 (2004).

Shearman & Sterling, *Force Majeure and Imprévision Under French Law* (Mar.26, 2020). *Available at* https://www.shearman.com/Perspectives/2020/03/Force-Majeure-and-Imprevision-under-French-Law-COVID-19.

Shemberg, Andrea *Stabilization Clauses and Human Rights*, INT'L FIN. CORP (2009), *available at* https://www.ifc.org/wps/wcm/connect/corp_ext_content/ifc_external_corporate_site/home.

Sinclair, Anthony C. *The Origins of the Umbrella Clause in the International Law of Investment Protection*, 20 ARB. INT'L 411 (2004).

Sornarajah, Muthucumaraswamy *Supremacy of the Renegotiation Clause in International Contracts*, 5 J.INT'L ARB. 97,110 (1988).

Tschanz, Pierre-Yves *The Contributions of the AMINOIL Award to the Law of State Contracts*, 18 INT'L L. 245 (1984).

Umirdinov, Alisher *The End of Hibernation of Stabilization Clause in Investment Arbitration: Reassessing Its Contribution to Sustainable Development*, 43 DENV. J. INT'L L. & POL'Y 455 (2015).

Umurzakov, Kubat *Investment Climate in Kazakhstan Country Report, United Nations Economic and Social Commission for Asia and the Pacific, Regional Round Table on Foreign Direct Investment for Central Asia*, 4 (Feb. 2003).

Vandevelde, Kenneth J. *A Unified Theory of Fair and Equitable Treatment*, 43 N.Y.U. J. INT'L L. & POL. 43, 66 (2010).

Verhoosel, Gaetan *Foreign Direct Investment and Legal Constraints on Domestic Environmental Policies: Striking A "Reasonable" Balance Between Stability and Change*, 29 LAW & POL'Y INT'L BUS. 451 (1998).

Vielleville, D E, B S Vasani, *Sovereignty over Natural Resources Versus Rights under Investment Contracts: Which One Prevails?* (2006) OIL, GAS & ENERGY L J (2006).

Waelde Thomas W. & George Ndi, *Stabilizing International Investment Commitments: International Law Versus Contract Interpretation*, 31 TEX. INT'L L. J. 215 (1996).

Wälde, Thomas W. *Renegotiating acquired rights in the oil and gas industries: Industry and political cycles meet the rule of law*, 1 J. WORLD ENERGY L. & BUS. 55 (2008).

Wälde, Thomas W. *The "Umbrella Clause" in Investment Arbitration: A Comment on Original Intentions and Recent Cases*, 6 J. WORLD INV. & TRADE (2005).

Wilhelm, Suzanne *Peru and the Myth of Independent Statehood*, 15 THIRD WORLD LEGAL STUD. 153, (1999).

Wong, Jarrod *Umbrella Clauses in Bilateral Investment Treaties: Of Breaches of Contract, Treat Violations, and the Divide between Developing and Developed Countries in Foreign Investment Disputes*, 14 GEO. Mason L. REV (2006).

Yackee, Jason Webb *Do Bilateral Investment Treaties Promote Foreign Direct Investment? Some Hints from Alternative Evidence*, 51 VA. J. INT'L L. 397 (2011).

# Index

www.ingramcontent.com/pod-product-compliance
Ingram Content Group UK Ltd.
Pitfield, Milton Keynes, MK11 3LW, UK
UKHW022209051026
15624UKWH00001B/77

9 789004 692749